Rethinking Work Experience

Andrew Miller

School Curriculum Industry Partnership

A.G. Watts

National Institute for Careers Education and Counselling

Ian Jamieson

University of Bath

 Falmer Press

(A member of the Taylor & Francis Group)
London • New York • Philadelphia

for the School Curriculum Industry Partnership

UK The Falmer Press, 4 John St, London WC1N 2ET

USA The Falmer Press, Taylor & Francis Inc., 1900 Frost Road, Suite 101, Bristol, PA 19007

© Andrew Miller, A.G. Watts and Ian Jamieson, 1991

First published 1991

British Library Cataloguing in Publication Data
Miller, Andy
    Rethinking work experience.
    1. Great Britain. Secondary schools. Students. Work experience
    I. Title II. Watts, A.G. (Anthony Gordon) *1942–* III. Jamieson,
    Ian *1944–* IV. School Curriculum Industry Partnership
    373.270941

    ISBN 1–85000–895–7
    ISBN 1–85000–896–5 pbk

Library of Congress Cataloging-in-Publication Data
Miller, Andrew, 1949–
    Rethinking work experience/Andrew Miller, A.G. Watts, Ian
Jamieson.
        p. cm.
    Includes bibliographical references and index.
    ISBN 1–85000–895–7: .—ISBN 1–85000–896–5 (pbk.):
        1. Education, Cooperative—Great Britain. 2. Education,
Cooperative—Great Britain—Case studies. 3. Education,
Cooperative—Great Britain—Curricula. I. Watts, A.G. (Anthony
Gordon) II. Jamieson, Ian. III. Title.
LB1029.C6M5 1991
370.19'31—dc20   90–26105
                                                              CIP

Set in 10/12 pt Bembo
by Graphicraft Typesetters Ltd, Hong Kong

Printed in Great Britain by Burgess Science Press, Basingstoke
on paper which has a specified pH value on final paper
manufacture of not less than 7.5 and is therefore 'acid free'.

Contents

Contents

Contents

List of Boxes

Preface

This book has been prepared for the School Curriculum Industry Partnership as part of its research programme. The research upon which the book is based began in 1987 when SCIP was a School Curriculum Development Committee project, and continued during 1988–89 when the National Curriculum Council was the host organization. Since September 1989 SCIP and its research programme have been under the auspices of the Centre for Education and Industry at the University of Warwick.

In addition to drawing on secondary source material, the research involved several other investigations. First, three research workshops were held: for work-experience organizers from across England and Wales; for employers in large national companies; and for small employers in one urban education authority. Second, case-study research was conducted in six contrasting local education authorities: Bradford, Coventry, Doncaster, Newham, Northumberland, and Sunderland. This involved interviews with central work-experience coordinators, with school-based link teachers, and with students who had recently returned from work experience. Third, guidelines and reports from many of the ninety SCIP local education authorities were examined. Finally, case-study material submitted by schools entering for the 1989 Rover Award for Quality in Work Experience was investigated.

The book is divided into three parts. We begin Part I (Chapters 1–4) by reviewing the development of work experience in the United Kingdom, considering the current policy framework, and posing some possible future scenarios. This is followed by an exploration of the concept and aims of work experience, and the introduction of a theoretical framework which is then used throughout the book as a point of reference. The context of work experience is investigated through overviews of work-experience developments in other countries, and of the history and current patterns of the world of work in the United Kingdom. In Part II (Chapters 5–8), some key organizational issues are explored through an overview of school-based

organization, and case-studies of three centralized work-experience structures. Two particular issues are given special attention: the current state of
the law relating to work experience; and the perspectives of employers.
Finally, in Part III (Chapters 9–14), a number of curricular issues are examined:
the integration of work experience into the school curriculum; progression
in work-experience programmes; the matching of students to placements;
teaching strategies; the assessment of student learning; and the evaluation of
work-experience schemes. We have tried to provide extensive cross-references
between the chapters, to help readers who want to begin reading the book in
different places.

The preparation of the book has been a close collaborative activity. We
have met regularly to brainstorm ideas and to discuss drafts. Each member of
the team took primary responsibility for particular chapters; all the chapters,
however, include ideas and suggestions from other members of the team.
Tony Watts was responsible for coordinating the editing process. Chapter 3
has already been published in the *British Journal of Education and Work*
(Volume 3 No. 1, 1989); parts of Chapter 2 were published in *SCIP News*
(No. 24, Summer 1989) and in *Education* (Volume 173 No. 25, 23 June 1989).

We would like to express our gratitude to all the teachers, work-
experience coordinators, local education authorities and employers who have
contributed information and ideas. In particular, we wish to thank Eunice
Roberts, SCIP Regional Coordinator for the North, for conducting much of
the case-study research; Anthony Johns from Garth High School in Merton
in for his contribution to Chapter 7; and Bob Newman of Project Trident for
supporting the project, particularly in its initial stages.

Andrew Miller
Tony Watts
Ian Jamieson

September 1990

Abbreviations

A-level	GCE Advanced level
AMMA	Assistant Masters and Mistresses Association
AS-level	GCE Advanced Supplementary level
BTEC	Business and Technician Education Council
CASCAID	Careers Advisory Service Computer Aid
CBI	Confederation of British Industry
CIPFA	Chartered Institute of Public Finance and Accountancy
CPVE	Certificate of Pre-Vocational Education
CRE	Commission for Racial Equality
CSE	Certificate of Secondary Education (now merged into the GCSE)
CSO	Central Statistical Office
DES	Department of Education and Science
DTI	Department of Trade and Industry
EBCE	experience-based career education (USA)
EcATT	Economic Awareness in Teacher Training
EITB	Engineering Industry Training Board
EOC	Equal Opportunities Commission
FE	further education
FEU	Further Education Unit
GCE	General Certificate of Education (at O-level, now merged into the GCSE)
GCSE	General Certificate of Secondary Education
GDP	gross domestic product
H&S	health and safety
HMI	Her Majesty's Inspectorate
INSET	in-service education and training
IPM	Institute of Personnel Management
JBPVE	Joint Board for Pre-Vocational Education
JIIG–CAL	Job Ideas and Information Generator; Computer Assisted Learning

LAPP	Lower Attaining Pupils' Programme
LEA	local education authority
LMS	Local Management of Schools
MSC	Manpower Services Commission (now the Training Agency)
NCC	National Curriculum Council
NROVA	National Record of Vocational Achievement
NUT	National Union of Teachers
NVQ	National Vocational Qualification
OPCS	Office of Population Censuses and Surveys
PAI	personal accident insurance
PRAO	practical working life orientation (Sweden)
PRYO	practical vocational orientation (Sweden)
PSE	personal and social education
SCDC	School Curriculum Development Committee
SCIP	School Curriculum Industry Partnership
TUC	Trades Union Congress
TVEI	Technical and Vocational Education Initiative
UBI	Understanding British Industry
YTS	Youth Training Scheme

Part I

Concept and Context

Chapter 1

History and Policy Context

Ian Jamieson and Andrew Miller

The marked growth of interest in work experience can be viewed as part of a wider movement to reintegrate education and work. If one takes a long enough historical perspective, it is possible to recall a period of time when work was fully integrated into the lives of individuals, particularly in the context of family life in the household. In the family, the distinctions which we currently draw between work, education and other aspects of social and economic life were largely absent: such functions were intimately and unthinkingly knitted together in household activities. Education consisted of families passing on the skills, knowledge and attitudes necessary for the household to exist as a functioning unit. It is customary to argue that industrialization changed all that and that the world of work gradually separated from the world of the household and became distinct from it. For its part, education became enshrined in formal schooling, and this too became separate both from the family *and* from the world of work.

This historical process is extensively described in Chapter 4 of this book and it forms an important backdrop to discussions about work experience, because there are distinct signs that the process of separation of education from the world of work (and indeed the more general fragmentation of society that occurred as a result of industrialization) might now have run its course. There is increasing concern to reintegrate various aspects of society — for example, the renewed interest in the concept of community in the context of health policy-making — and although part of this is driven by economic considerations, there is also a strong social thrust in such policy-making. These developments can be seen very clearly in education too. Recent legislation, for example, has given parents a much greater stake in the educational process, and representatives of the business community are now formally on the governing bodies of most maintained schools.

It can thus be argued that work experience is an attempt to reintegrate the world of work into schooling by transacting a period of education in a work-place under the joint supervision of the representatives of education and work. Its growth is an international phenomenon, as is demonstrated in Chapter 3.

Within a British context, the growth of work experience has occurred gradually over three decades, and indeed in this chapter will be analyzed in terms of these decades: 1963–72; 1973–82; and 1983–92. Each period begins with a significant development: 1963 saw the publication of the Newsom Report, the first major educational document to discuss the use of work experience in British schools; 1973 witnessed the passage of the Education (Work Experience) Act, which enabled schools and local education authorities to establish work-experience schemes; 1983 was the year in which the Technical and Vocational Education Initiative commenced—under the plan for its extension, this should lead by 1992 to work experience for all students reaching compulsory school-leaving age. In the discussion of each decade, we will outline the main national developments and explain how these affected work experience in schools. In addition, we will refer to evidence on the growing extent of work experience in schools in England and Wales. We will conclude the chapter with a discussion of a range of possible scenarios for work experience in the future, and an exploration of the possible impact of some of the longer-run changes that appear to be taking place both in education and in the world of work.

Beginnings: 1963–72

The report of the Newsom Committee (Central Advisory Council for Education, 1963) has been acknowledged as the first major educational report to make reference to work-experience programmes (Watts, 1983a). It focused on the education of students of average and below-average ability, noting examples of work-experience schemes in Sweden (see pp. 39–41) and some limited experiments in the United Kingdom. It argued that 'the school programme, in the last year especially, ought to be deliberately outgoing' (*ibid*, p. 72). But it fell short of endorsing the spread of school-based work-experience programmes, arguing that it was unlikely that they would be either 'practicable or even desirable for the large majority of boys and girls' (*ibid*, p. 76). The report ended with the tentative conclusion that 'experiments enabling some pupils over the age of fifteen to participate to a limited extent, under the auspices of the school, in the world of work in industry, commerce, or in other fields, should be carefully studied' (*ibid*, p. 79).

Although the case for a more outgoing curriculum in the final year of schooling suggests work experience as one possible solution, this was expressly ruled out by the Newsom Report. Opposition to the notion of school-based work experience came from the General Council of the Trades Union Congress, which felt that is was an inappropriate use of the limited time available for full-time schooling (TUC, 1974). In addition to these objections, there was considerable uncertainty as to the legality of work experience for younger students. In 1969 an Administrative Memorandum (12/69) issued by the Department of Education and Science advised LEAs to exclude students below the age limit of compulsory schooling from participating in work-experience schemes unless they could be sure that such programmes were within the law.

The prevailing uncertainty about the legal position was reflected in the decision in at least one area for an absolute prohibition on work experience for all students below the statutory leaving age (Institute of Careers Officers, 1974). Other LEAs, however, were prepared to allow work experience for such students. Even so, a survey by the Institute of Careers Officers in 1968/69 estimated that under 2 per cent of students reaching the school-leaving age had been on a work-experience placement (*ibid*). The turning point for work-experience development came in 1972 with the raising of the school-leaving age to 16. Many educationalists felt that, in order to cope with the many students who would formerly have left school for work at 15, the 'outgoing curriculum' recommended by the Newsom Report was now imperative.

Work Experience for Some: 1973–82

The issue of permissibility was resolved by the Education (Work Experience) Act 1973 which, subject to certain restrictions (see Chapter 7) allowed students to undertake work experience on employers' premises in the last year of compulsory schooling. Controversy over the 1973 Act concerning issues of safety, the artificial nature of the experience, and the fact that work experience would be used only for less-able students (TUC, 1973, pp. 162–3), contributed to the detailed guidance issued by the Department of Education and Science in Circular 7/74 (DES, 1974). Through this Circular, the government sought to dispel some of the criticisms of school-based work experience, which 'should have value for pupils of varying ability and aptitudes and should neither be designed as vocational training nor aimed at a limited range of ability' (para. 8).

The clarification of the law and the challenge of the raising of the school-leaving age stimulated an expansion in school-based work experience. A survey in 1975–76 based upon statistics supplied by Principal Careers Officers estimated that 7 per cent of school-leavers had engaged in some form of work experience (Walton, 1977). It found that 33 per cent of secondary schools and 27 per cent of special schools had implemented work-experience programmes, with an average number of thirty students per school participating. A DES secondary-school survey carried out during 1975–78 in a sample of 384 schools found that 37 per cent had work-experience schemes, but that only five were for all students (DES, 1979b).

Prime Minister James Callaghan's speech at Ruskin College, Oxford, in 1976 is widely regarded as a watershed in the development of schools–industry links in the United Kingdom (Jamieson, 1985). The Great Debate which followed focused attention on the weak relationship between the education system and the economy, and led to the establishment of numerous organizations and projects aiming to bridge the divide between education and the world of work. The so-called schools–industry movement has been described variously as a 'galaxy', an 'alphabet soup' and a 'mafia'. The link body most directly concerned with work experience, Project Trident, had established itself in the early 1970s in six LEAs, and the ferment engendered by the Ruskin speech stimulated the development of Trident-organized work-experience schemes in twenty-two further LEAs between 1975 and 1980 (Kerry, 1983). The growth of the schools–industry movement has been significant for the proliferation of work experience in that it has generated a lot of publicity promoting closer links with industry, and work experience has been widely seen as an important aspect of such links.

The final years of the decade 1973–82 were marked by rising unemployment, particularly youth unemployment. The government enacted various initiatives to alleviate this problem and to train young people for suitable jobs. Most of these initiatives were channelled through the Manpower Services Commission, which had been set up in 1973 to coordinate vocational training. The major successive schemes which were launched through the MSC — Work Experience on Employers' Premises (WEEP), the Youth Opportunities Programme (YOP) and the Youth Training Programme (YTP) — all made 'work experience' a central feature, though this differed from school-based work experience in a number of important respects: it was, for example, for much longer periods of time; the young people involved were regarded as work-based trainees rather than as education-based students; and they were paid an allowance (Watts, 1983b, pp. 183–4). Nonetheless, the origin of these schemes in attempts to alleviate youth unemployment, and the varied quality of the programmes, had three main effects on school-based work-experience programmes. Firstly, they caused some confusion in the minds of employers and trade unionists about the nature and purpose of work experience. Secondly, they did nothing to improve the image of work experience amongst teachers and students in schools. Thirdly, they reinforced the view that work experience was for the less able and for those who might have difficulty in obtaining employment.

Two attempts were made to confront some of these issues towards the end of the decade. The first was the announcement in 1981 of the New Training Initiative, which instituted national training objectives for the first time and attempted to make educational quality an important goal of the Youth Training Scheme. The second occurred in the following year, when — amid much controversy (Dale, 1985) — the government established new institutional arrangements for technical and vocational education for 14–18-year-olds: the Technical and Vocational Education Initiative.

Work Experience for All: 1983-92

The decade beginning in 1983 has witnessed many initiatives affecting work-experience development from three government departments: the Department of Employment, the Department of Education and Science, and the Department of Trade and Industry. These initiatives have increased the quantity of work experience, but they have also improved its quality in terms of its relationship to the curriculum (see Chapter 9). Central-government interest has been mirrored by the concern of LEAs to extend and improve practice through issuing guidelines, through coordinating and centralizing work-experience organization (see Chapter 6), and through promoting curriculum and professional development.

The *Department of Employment* through the MSC and subsequently the Training Commission/Training Agency has been the arm of central government most involved in direct work-related interventions in the education system. The most significant development for the spread of work experience was the Technical and Vocational Education Initiative which began in 1983 as a five-year pilot programme in fourteen LEAs. All proposals to join the scheme had to include at least one week of work experience for TVEI students in their final year of compulsory schooling. By 1988, all LEAs had joined TVEI, and forty-eight had begun the phase of extension to all secondary schools and colleges of further education. The contracts for both pilot and extension phases with the Training Agency (as it was renamed in 1988) made work experience mandatory. The implication of this was that by 1992 all students would be entitled to a period of work experience.

Meanwhile, the impact of TVEI and other programmes on participation in work experience was already evident. A survey by HMI based upon inspections in 371 secondary schools in England during 1982-86 estimated that 66 per cent of schools offered work experience for older students, although only in seventeen schools was work experience available for all students in their final year of compulsory schooling (HMI, 1988b). The DES survey of schools-industry links in Industry Year 1986 found that 90 per cent of secondary schools reported work experience for a proportion of their students during the year, and that 66 per cent of students during their last compulsory year were involved (DES, 1987). A similar survey carried out during 1988-89 found that the corresponding figures had increased marginally to 91 per cent of schools and 71 per cent of students, respectively (DES, 1990b).

Another policy intervention from the Department of Employment affecting work-experience provision was the Compacts initiative which was announced in 1988. This initiative was part of the government's Action for Cities programme, designed to ameliorate inner-city problems including high youth unemployment and low educational motivation and achievement. Funding for thirty Compacts was agreed during 1988, and all proposals included work experience as a key element. Generally, in the Compact 'agreement', employers offered work-experience places, schools agreed to arrange work experience, and students agreed to undertake satisfactory periods of work experience in return for a collective job-plus-training guarantee which was held out to all students successfully achieving their individual goals (Lawlor and McKay, 1989). By 1990, fifty Compacts were being funded, involving some 3,800 employers, 250 schools and 36,000 young people (Incomes Data Services, 1990).

A further development occurred in 1990 when the Secretary of State for Trade and Industry announced that from 1991 the Training Agency would assume responsibility from his department for the Partnership initiative, which aimed to provide funding to support the development of local Education–Business Partnerships. Such partnerships seem likely to lead to the institutionalization of links between employers and schools, including arrangements for work experience. The proposed hosts for many of the local partnerships are the Training and Enterprise Councils, which were proposed in a 1988 White Paper as employer-led bodies which would 'contribute to existing initiatives and encourage work experience and exposure to new opportunities' (Department of Employment, 1988, pp. 5–6).

While the Department of Employment and its agencies have had a major impact on the extent of work experience and upon the organizational framework within which work-experience schemes operate, the *Department of Education and Science* has initiated various curriculum reforms which have influenced the development of work-experience programmes.

In 1982, it instituted the Lower Attaining Pupils' Programme (LAPP), which — as with TVEI — included work experience as a mandatory element. Introduced for the 'bottom 40 per cent' of the ability-range, the programme covered over 100 schools in seventeen LEAs (HMI, 1986).

In 1984, the initiation of the records of achievement pilot projects encouraged the recording and accreditation of non-traditional forms of learning, including learning from work experience (see Chapter 13). A policy statement that by 1990 all 16-year-olds would have a record of achievement, although rescinded in 1989, promoted the assessment of learning from work experience, and encouraged Project Trident and other work-experience organizers, both LEA and school-based, to develop statements of achievement linked to work experience.

In 1985, the Certificate of Pre-Vocational Education was launched, offering a broad pre-vocational programme based on work-related education, including not less than fifteen days of work experience or simulated work experience. The CPVE not only offered some progression for students who had undertaken TVEI courses 14–16, but also gave a stimulus to the expansion of school-based work experience post-16.

In 1986, the General Certificate of Secondary Education replaced the previous O-level General Certificate of Education and the Certificate of Secondary Education as the major qualification at the end of compulsory schooling. A significant feature of the new arrangements was that at least 20 per cent of the marks in the new examination were to be based upon continuous assessment or project work. This enabled projects arising from work-experience placements to be submitted for GCSE assessment at once, adding to its legitimacy and status, as well as leading to greater linkages with the mainstream curriculum (see Chapter 10). The DES (1990b) survey of school/industry links conducted in 1988/89 found that in 44 per cent of secondary schools work experience had contributed to assessed GCSE course-work — mainly in English and Business Studies, though with more limited contributions in a wide range of other subjects.

It was, however, the 1988 Education Reform Act which contained the most profound implications for work experience. Although the Act stipulated a curriculum which would prepare pupils for 'the opportunities, responsibilities and experiences of adult life', it was not at all clear what this would mean for work experience. Indeed, the Secretary of State for Education and Science declared in May 1988, in a speech to an Institute of Personnel Management and Project Trident conference on work experience, that 'with the sharper focus on curricular objectives that the National Curriculum will bring about, I have to say that I doubt many schools will be able to devote much time to workplace activities unless they contribute explicitly to curriculum objectives'. In spite of this unpromising beginning, publications from the body established to implement and monitor the introduction of the new curriculum — the National Curriculum Council — have tended to view work experience as an important work-related activity that can contribute not only to the achievement of cross-curricular objectives (NCC, 1990a; 1990b; 1990c), but also to the delivery of the programmes of study and attainment targets of the core and foundation subjects.

In 1988, the DES issued revised guidance on work experience for both schools and employers (DES, 1988a; 1988b). This guidance was intended to replace the outdated Circular 7/74 in the light of curriculum and institutional developments since the earlier document was issued. It made clear the policy commitment of the government to extend work experience to all students reaching the end of compulsory schooling, and emphasized the role of the DES in ensuring the quality of the educational experience.

The year 1988 was also the one in which the *Department of Trade and Industry* launched the Enterprise and Education Initiative. There were two main prongs to the initiative: teacher placements and pupil work experience (DTI, 1988). The Teacher Placement Service was set up with Understanding British Industry (UBI) to help meet the DTI target of 10 per cent of teachers every year having direct experience of the world of business and enterprise. A total of 140 DTI Advisers were appointed to market the Education and Enterprise Initiative to local businesses in an attempt to increase the supply of work-experience placements. It was estimated that in order to achieve the government target of all 16-year-olds having two or more weeks' work experience by 1992, around 700,000 work placements needed to be found each year, or one work-experience student per thirty employees. The publicity attached to the Enterprise Initiative contributed to many leading companies pledging additional placements for students and teachers. The main focus of the DTI was thus on increasing the supply of available placements.

Scenarios for the Future

It is not possible to predict the future, even the near future. Looking back to the Newsom Report of 1963, who then would have predicted an era which might bring in work experience for all within thirty years? Predictions are even more difficult at the present time because of the great policy ferment that has been created in the late 1980s and early 1990s in education and training. This ferment has itself been created by a confluence of factors: industrial restructuring and problematic economic performance; technological change; social and demographic trends; concern about the performance of education and training systems; and political currents favouring market-based solutions to economic and social problems. All that it seems prudent to do, given this context, is to contruct some possible scenarios for the future of work experience in schools and colleges. We will outline four such scenarios: the *status quo* scenario; the *magnetization* scenario; the *experiential entitlement* scenario; and the *educational franchise* scenario.

The Status Quo Scenario

The first scenario takes as its starting point the National Curriculum as currently enacted and assumes that little will change. In the short run this appears to be a reasonably secure prediction, if only because there is a widespread view that the school system is suffering from 'innovation fatigue' (e.g. TVEI, GCSE and the National Curriculum) and that these initiatives need to settle into schools before any more changes are launched. Under such a view, work experience will survive and grow if, and only if, it is seen to be useful, even necessary, for the delivery of the National Curriculum.

In practice, there will tend to be a good deal of variation between schools. Some will undoubtedly continue their practice of using work experience to provide relevant course-work for GCSE, although many may find other features of the work-related curriculum, like work-based projects or mini-enterprises, at least as useful in this respect. Some schools will also take the view that the existence of Economic and Industrial Understanding and of Careers Education and Guidance as cross-curricular themes makes work experience highly desirable or even essential. Certainly the non-statutory guidance gives a strong lead in suggesting that work experience should feature in the delivery of these themes, and although the themes themselves are not compulsory in the same way that the core and foundation subjects are, they have been given a great deal of emphasis and publicity by government ministers and others.

We suspect that the major factors determining whether, under this scenario, a school would provide work experience for all its students would be:

- Whether the school already has a well-funded scheme for work experience for the vast majority of its students.
- The costs of running work experience under LMS.
- The attitude of the governing body to work experience: in particular, the role and interest of the business governor(s) in this area.
- The perceived opportunities for GCSE course-work through work experience, and the practice of the GCSE examination boards in setting examination questions with an 'industrial' orientation.

The Magnetization Scenario

Our second scenario suggests even greater diversity of practice by focusing on the shifting balance between LEA control of schools and the increasing autonomy of schools and colleges. Two changes made by the 1988 Education Reform Act have moved the balance of power away from LEAs towards individual institutions. One is Local Management of Schools, which has meant that the LEA now has markedly less control over school policies and activities — for example, it can no longer insist that each school undertakes work experience. The government intention behind this measure was clearly to remove the responsibility of delivering education from the LEAs to the schools, leaving the LEAs with a monitoring and quality-control function. The other significant change brought about by the Act is 'open enrolment': the provision which abolishes catchment areas and artificially low admission levels to schools.

The effect of these changes, other things being equal, is to make schools compete with one another for students. How are parents to choose? The government's preferred strategy has appeared to be centred around the concept of magnet schools, if not around the specific introduction of such schools. The idea of 'magnetization' is that each school will develop a distinctive character under the twin incentives of LMS and open enrolment so that parents will be able to make a genuine choice between styles of school. Such choices will be aided by a greater flow of information about schools through such provisions as the annual parents' meeting, fuller information in the school's prospectus, and the publication of examination results (as well as, probably, the test results from the National Curriculum when these become available).

How might these changes affect work experience? In this scenario, schools will strive to distinguish themselves one from another in order to attract a large and distinctive group of parents. Ultimately, their very survival will depend on their ability to attract a sufficient number of students. It is likely that most schools will choose to compete in the 'academic marketplace', attempting to attract parents by the demonstration of good academic results. These schools may well find that work experience is an unnecessary drain on their resources and makes no notable contribution to their academic results: indeed, some might view it as detracting from the academic image they seek.

Not all schools, however, will feel able to compete in this particular way. Those schools whose geographical location places them in a position where their 'local' students are drawn from largely working-class areas will find it difficult, no matter how good the quality of the teaching, to produce good results. Such schools — and possibly some others too — may well come to believe that the best way they can compete is by demonstrating their *vocational* credentials: that is, by showing parents that their curriculum is directly geared to the needs of employment. They could do this by building up very strong links with local employers, offering a range of vocationally oriented qualifications in addition to GCSE, and of course offering substantial periods of work experience. We already have a variant of such a scenario in City Technology Colleges, although their avowed aim is to cater for the entire ability-range. In this scenario, we are effectively talking about magnet schools whose attracting power is vocationally oriented education.

The Experiential Entitlement Scenario

The third scenario is an optimistic one and revolves around the idea of an experiential entitlement for all students. At the core of this entitlement is work experience — perhaps several placements in contrasting organizations. It is unlikely, however, that such an entitlement would be confined to work experience: it is more likely that it would be extended to other areas of the work-related curriculum and beyond, to include residential and community experience. Such an experiential entitlement could be strongly curriculum-related, in which case it would form part of the National Curriculum. This would probably require changes to the core and foundation National Curriculum subjects to make them more applied, at least at Key Stage 4 (14–16-year-olds).

There are two further alternatives within this particular scenario, both of which attract some credence from recent initiatives. The first is to pursue the notion of an experiential entitlement but not through the core and foundation subjects of the National Curriculum. This route could build on the present policy of guaranteeing work experience through some separate initiative like TVEI. TVEI, or something similar, and could be continued under the auspices of a local Training and Enterprise Council and/or through a local Education–

Business Partnership. It is feasible to think of these organizations having responsibility for the delivery and/or the monitoring of work experience provision in the 14–18 curriculum. This provision could be in addition to the National Curriculum, or it could be part of the relevant cross-curricular theme (Economic and Industrial Understanding and/or Careers Education and Guidance).

The other alternative is to leave work experience in its present *ad hoc* state in the 14–16 curriculum and to concentrate attention on making it part of an experiential entitlement within the post-16 curriculum. This would be consistent with the government's core skills initiative in the 16–19 curriculum (NCC, 1990d).

The Educational Franchise Scenario

The fourth scenario is the most radical and therefore the least likely, at least in the immediate future. It envisages radical changes both in the curriculum and in the organization of schooling. It might be heralded by the creation of a new ministry, the Department of Education and Training, which would merge the Department of Education and Science with parts, if not all, of the Department of Employment. This new ministry would oversee a breaking-down of the traditional barriers between academic and vocational curricula and a drawing together of the worlds of education and industry.

The most likely curricular change would be a wholesale 'practicalization of the intellectual', much along the lines proposed by the advocates of the British Baccalauréat (see Finegold *et al.*, 1990). Here academic subjects would be taught in ways which showed their connection to life outside school. Work placements would be central to the conception, and students would find themselves placed in a wide variety of establishments in the community. This itself would herald big changes in the organization of schooling. At its most radical, non-school institutions — e.g. museums, hospitals, commercial and industrial organizations — would be franchised both to deliver and to accredit part of the curriculum. By taking certain courses, young people would have an entitlement to certain work experience. Something similar to this model is currently being piloted in the shape of training vouchers for certain post-16 students, but the full scenario would see it extended to *all* students, perhaps from year 9 (14-year-olds).

Other Changes in Education and the World of Work

Each of these scenarios is possible in the medium-term future, although some are clearly more likely than others. There are other changes occurring as well which are more difficult to fit into any particular scenario but which may turn out to be very significant for work experience. Interestingly, these changes concern both halves of the work-experience equation — education and industry.

Within the education system, it looks as though new ideas about the learning process may be engineering a slow revolution in the organization of teaching and learning. There are many different strands here, most of them leading in the same direction. Perhaps of greatest importance is the rediscovery and development of the early work of Lewin (1951) by Kolb (1984) and the latter's elucidation of the theory of experiential learning (see pp. 22–3). This has provided for those working in education a sound and respectable theory of learning on which to hang developments in work experience. Helpfully, such models are not wholly alien to the industrial world where they have penetrated the spheres of both training and management development. The work of Schon (1983), and his ideas of 'reflection in action', are known by practitioners in both education and industry, whilst Revans (1971) with his concept of action learning has had a largely industrial audience. All of these theorists are providing a theoretical focus for the development of practices like work experience.

If writers like Kolb, Schon and Revans have provided theoretical insights into how to develop the learning gains from work experience, then other writers have provided an initial justification for the activity. Developments in cognitive psychology (see Sternberg and Wagner, 1986) have stressed the importance of *contexts* in learning and have thus given support to teachers, like those involved in work experience, who wish consciously to extend such contexts and to relate learning to them in direct and specific ways. The emphasis on context has also led to a broader view of skills and knowledge, encapsulated in the concept of competence. Such work has served to underline the narrow view of knowledge and skills which traditional schooling has fostered. Work experience has demonstrated both to young people and to teachers the wider range of abilities required outside the world of education. Handy (1989) has usefully encapsulated and popularized some of these ideas by referring to the 'seven different types of intelligence', only some of which are conventionally developed in schools.

This new accent on the variety of teaching and learning strategies has been given a considerable boost by TVEI. Although the main emphasis of TVEI is supposed to be on work-related learning, it is now a commonplace to argue that its core has been its impact on teaching and learning styles (Hopkins, 1990): in both respects, work experience is clearly a major focus. TVEI has also given a strong boost to student records of achievement and this too has significance for work experience because it provides a means through which the learning yields from work experience can be recorded and assessed (see Chapter 13). Such arrangements fit in with developments in industry. The new National Vocational Qualifications (NVQs) require the recording of work-based learning, and it is likely these will form part of a permanent portfolio of a person's work-based achievements in the form of the National Record of Vocational Achievement (NROVA). Eventually it seems possible that the education-based record of achievement will be integrated with the employment-based NROVA.

The NROVA and NVQ are both indications that industry is beginning to take learning at work much more seriously. As the pace of industrial and technological change quickens, so learning becomes of central importance to work organizations. Such developments should make work experience easier for industrial organizations to manage, encouraging them to develop more effective ways of using placements for learning purposes.

The development of separate institutions for schooling has been taken as one of the marks of industrialization: indeed, it is often argued that as industrialization develops, so the length of time that individuals spend in educational institutions grows, to cope with the increasing complexity of occupations. There are no signs that this process is reversing, but there are some indications that the nature of education might be changing. There is a widespread view that education has become too detached from the reality which it purports to serve and teach about, and there are clear signs of a process of reintegration. Work experience is one of the classic policy instruments helping to bring this about.

Chapter 2

The Concept of Work Experience

A.G. Watts

The aim of this chapter is to explore the concept of work experience. In doing so, we will look at narrow and broad definitions both of 'work' and of 'experience'. We will examine the various aims which are attached to work-experience schemes, and the extent to which they can be achieved through alternative kinds of experience both inside and outside the work-place. We will then look at some of the different forms which work experience may take in practice. Finally, we will explore the arguments for broadening the concept of 'work', and at their implications for work-experience programmes.

The Core Concept

'Work experience' is a paradoxical phrase, in that it is firmly distinguished from 'work', and is used to describe schemes in which only *part* of the full 'experience' of work is available. To be more specific, it is applied to schemes in which people experience work tasks in work environments, but without taking on the full identity of a worker (Watts, 1983a). The key distinction is that the role of students on a work-experience scheme is that not of *employee* but of *learner*. Accordingly, they are only attached to the work-place on a short-term basis, and are not normally paid by the 'employer' (apart perhaps from travelling expenses). On the other hand — a further paradox — it is arguable that the learning yield will be substantial and distinctive only if the experience gets as close as possible to that of being an employee. Many of the difficulties and confusions about work experience stem from this role tension.

Our concern in this book is with school-based work-experience programmes, under which school[1] students go out to work-places for periods of, usually, between one and three weeks (though there are other patterns too — see pp. 98–103). It is worth noting, however, that work experience also forms a part of many courses in further and higher education, including 'sandwich' courses in which the work placement may be much longer — sometimes up to a year.

In addition to these education-based examples, the term 'work experience' has confusingly also been applied to schemes like the Youth Training Scheme in which participants are work-based: here the work experience is central, and off-the-job education and training is cast in a supportive role. In school-based work-experience programmes, this relationship is reversed: such programmes are designed — in principle, anyway — to support activities within the school curriculum.

Aims and Curricular Frames

Work-experience schemes have a variety of aims: some declared, and some latent; some highly respectable, and some more dubious in character. We have analyzed the aims in a variety of documents at national, local and school level, and we believe that the great majority can be grouped under the ten categories shown in Box 2.1, which we have labelled enhancing, motivational, maturational, investigative, expansive, sampling, preparatory, anticipatory, placing, and custodial. We will look at each of these in turn.

The *enhancing* aim is concerned with enabling students to deepen their understanding of concepts learned in classroom settings, and to apply skills learned in such settings. This tends to be specific and planned, and to cover what Fuller (1987) refers to as 'coursework integration'. As the DES guidelines put it:

> Work-related activities offer valuable opportunities for project work which can enhance understanding of the subject(s) concerned (DES, 1988a).

The most effective examples tend to occur in particular departments like English, Mathematics, Social Studies, or Humanities, where the work experience has been used to conduct research into topics being covered within the classroom (see e.g. Fortune, Jamieson and Street, 1983; Holmes, Jamieson and Perry, 1983; see also Chapter 9). But surveys within TVEI, where one would expect this kind of integration to be more common than elsewhere, have suggested that it is rarely achieved to any significant extent (Barnes *et al.*, 1987; Saunders, 1987).

The *motivational* aim is concerned with making aspects of the school curriculum more meaningful and significant to students, so improving their levels of academic attainment. This is more general and unplanned than the enhancing aim, and views applicability as a means of increasing motivation for further learning. Here work experience is seen as:

> . . . an opportunity for them to relate prior learning to real world applications and begin to understand the need to take care of their own learning, that is, to learn how to learn (IPM, 1988).

Box 2.1   *Possible aims of work experience*

1. *Enhancing* — to enable students to deepen their understanding of concepts learned in classroom settings, and to apply skills learned in such settings.

2. *Motivational* — to make the school curriculum more meaningful and significant to students, so improving their levels of academic attainment.

3. *Maturational* — to facilitate students' personal and social development.

4. *Investigative* — to enable students to develop their knowledge and understanding of the world of work.

5. *Expansive* — to broaden the range of occupations that students are prepared to consider in terms of their personal career planning.

6. *Sampling* — to enable students to test their vocational preference before committing themselves to it.

7. *Preparatory* — to help students to acquire skills and knowledge related to a particular occupational area, which they will be able to apply if they wish to enter employment in that area.

8. *Anticipatory* — to enable student to experience some of the strains of work so that they will be able to manage the transition to work more comfortably.

9. *Placing* — to enable students to establish a relationship with a particular employer which may lead to the offer of a full-time job.

10. *Custodial* — to transfer some of the responsibility for particular students for a period.

Source: Adapted with modifications from Watts (1983a). The main changes are the splitting of the 'social-educational' aim into the maturational and investigative aims, the splitting of the 'vocational' aim into the expansive and sampling aims, and the addition of the enhancing and preparatory aims.

The argument is that once students have seen the general applicability of the knowledge and skills they are learning in school, they will be more motivated to acquire them. Even if this is not the case in terms of the 'use value' of the knowledge and skills themselves, it may be so in terms of the 'exchange value' of the examination qualifications to which they lead: the students may recognize more clearly the importance of such qualifications for entering particular occupations at particular levels of the labour market.

The *maturational* aim is concerned with facilitating students' personal and social development. Holmes, Jamieson and Perry (1983) point out that 'work experience ... provides a unique opportunity for young people both to test and assess their ownership of social skills and develop them further' (p. 16). AMMA develop the point:

> Working alongside adults as colleagues can contribute powerfully to young people's social development. Work experience gives students opportunities to develop self-confidence and social skills, to form relationships outside their peer group and to learn how to make their own decisions in an adult environment (AMMA, 1988).

Also, students can learn more about themselves and about their own strengths and weaknesses by experiencing how they cope with a new environment in which new and different demands are made of them.

The *investigative* aim is concerned with enabling students to develop their knowledge and understanding of the world of work. This covers such matters as:

> How different work places are organised, what the work processes are, what social relations at work are like, and what part trade unions play at the workplace (TUC, n.d.)

It may be seen mainly in localized terms:

> Promoting a knowledge of the industrial, commercial and public employers in the area and understanding of how they function (HMI, 1988a).

It may also be seen in much broader terms:

> To understand what is meant by 'work' is to understand the structure of society and why it is organised as it is, and how the economy operates (AMMA, 1988).

If it forms part of a course concerned with such world-of-work learning, this could be regarded as a particular application of the enhancing aim: even where it does not form part of such a course, however, work experience may be expected to deliver in these terms. Stronach (1984) notes that this concept of learning *about* work rather than learning *for* work opens the door to less normative and more genuinely educational approaches to work experience. Shilling (1987), too, demonstrates that work experience can provide a basis for critical explorations of labour relations and work-place practices rather than performing a purely adaptive role (for similar Australian evidence, see pp. 49–50). In practice, though, HMI (1990) report that 'rarely is work experience seen as an opportunity to explore a wider industrial and economic brief' and that 'despite the high quality of experiences many students gain little understanding of the structure and organization of business or of the nature of the local economy' (p. 20).

The *expansive* aim is concerned with broadening the range of occupations that students are prepared to consider in terms of their personal career planning. This embraces what Barnes *et al.* (1987) term 'work testing' — 'testing more than one of the work experiences on offer in order to identify the likes and dislikes associated with different kinds of work experience' (p. 115). In addition, it covers challenges to traditional sex-stereotyping of occupations:

> An important opportunity for girls to gain experience in work tradi-
> tionally reserved for men and for boys to be placed in traditionally
> female areas of employment (TUC, n.d.).

The need to take account of such equal-opportunities considerations is also
mentioned in the guidelines from government (DES, 1988a) and employer
organizations (IPM, 1988).

The *sampling* aim is concerned with enabling students to test their vocational preference before committing themselves to it. Official views here are
more ambivalent: though approved by HMI (1988a), it is not mentioned in
the DES (1988a) guidelines, and the TUC (n.d.) declare that work experience
'should not be used simply as job sampling'. But it is very common in
practice: Barnes *et al.* (1987) noted that 'virtually all the schools [in their
sample] appeared to have oriented placements towards pupils' preferred
vocational interest whenever this was possible' (p. 115). Indeed, Fuller (1987)
found that post-16 'there were extreme cases where we felt that [work-
experience programmes] were being used as a substitute for vocational counselling in institutions which appear to make rather perfunctory efforts in that
direction for their academic students' (p. 45).

The *preparatory* aim is concerned with helping students to acquire skills
and knowledge related to a particular occupational area, which they will be
able to apply if they should subsequently enter employment in that area. It
mainly occurs in relation to vocational courses post-16; even in pre-
vocational post-16 courses, notably CPVE, it is not very common (FEU,
1985, p. 119), and pre-16 it is very rare indeed. The TUC (n.d.) state firmly
that school-based work experience 'should not be part of any training for a
particular job', and the DES (1988a) agree that it 'must not be seen as a
preparation . . . for any particular job or career'.

The *anticipatory* aim is concerned with enabling students to experience
some of the strains of work so that they will be able to manage the transition
to work more comfortably. This includes such matters as:

> To understand the expectations that employers and adult workers
> will have of them, and how they themselves will fit into working
> patterns and working relations that are very different from those at
> school (TUC, n.d.).

The purpose here is clearly adaptive:

> Young people who have had the advantage of well managed work
> experience are likely to adapt more quickly to working life, YTS or
> apprenticeship (IPM, 1988).

Whereas the expansive and sampling aims were concerned with preparation
for *choices*, this aim is concerned with preparation for *transitions*.

The *placing* aim is concerned with enabling students to establish a relationship with a particular employer which may lead to the offer of a full-time job. As with the sampling and preparatory aims, this is regarded by the TUC as an abuse of the concept:

> Work experience should not be ... a means for employers to decide which young people they might like to employ (TUC, n.d.).

The DES concur:

> Must not be seen as a ... means of entry to any particular job or career (DES, 1988a).

Employers' bodies tend to take a more benign view:

> A potential means of finding a job ... seems to be a perfectly legitimate sub-aim (IPM, 1988).

AMMA attempts to steer a middle course:

> Work experience is neither a job sampling exercise for students, nor a recruitment drive for employers. Nonetheless, it would be naive to pretend that many students, teachers, parents and employers view work experience as anything other than a way for young people to find a job. Indeed, this is a perfectly legitimate aim — but only one of very many potential benefits (AMMA, 1988).

This indeed seems to represent what happened in practice: HMI (1983) in a survey of schools in Wales reported that 'few schools regarded actual entry into employment as a principal aim of work experience schemes but all saw this as a useful side-effect' (p. 3). The advent of Compacts has helped to make the placing aim more respectable (see p. 143).

Finally, the *custodial* aim is concerned with transferring some of the responsibility for particular pupils for a period. This is rarely defended as a principle, but Barnes *et al.* (1987) note that work experience in some instances represents 'a way of filling in the post-examination vacuum in a legitimate sort of way and, in some cases, a way of taming the more truculent pupils' (p. 117). In a survey of 227 area careers officers conducted in the mid-1970s, four quoted instances of school refusers who were persuaded to try work experience, and twenty-two mentioned that in their opinion schemes were being used 'to get rid of disruptive youngsters' (Walton, 1977, p. 9). This still happens, but is becoming less common as work experience is increasingly coming to be viewed as being appropriate for all students rather than only for a few.

Of these ten aims, seven provide a basis for a curricular frame for work

---

Box 2.2   Possible curricular frames for work experience

Curricular frame	Related aim(s)
A. Academic subject(s)	Enhancing
B. Personal and social education	Maturational
C. World-of-work learning	Investigative
D. Careers education	Expansive; sampling; anticipatory
E. Vocational course	Preparatory

---

experience (see Box 2.2). Thus the enhancing aim provides a basis for work experience to be incorporated within one or more *academic subjects*; the maturational aim for it to be incorporated within *personal and social education*; the investigative aim for it to be incorporated within *world-of-work learning*; the expansive, sampling and anticipatory aims for it to be incorporated within *careers education*; and the preparatory aim for it to be incorporated within a *vocational course*. We will examine these different frames and their implications in more detail in subsequent chapters.

For the present, two points are worth noting. The first is that the five frames occupy different points on what we might call the 'work-experience triangle': the relationship between the student, the world of work, and school subjects (Box 2.3). Thus a 'personal and social education' frame focuses on the effect of work experience on the personal development of the individual student; a 'world-of-work learning' frame is concerned with its effect on the student's understanding of the world of work; and an 'academic subject(s)' frame is concerned with its effect on the student's understanding of, and motivation for, his or her traditional school subjects. The other two frames are located along two of the sides of the triangle: a 'careers education' frame is concerned with the effect on the student's personal career planning in relation to the world of work; and a 'vocational course' frame with its effect on the student's capacity to relate what he or she is learning in school to the sector of the world of work with which it is linked.

The second point is that all five of these frames make it possible to incorporate work experience as part of the experiential learning cycle developed by Lewin (1951) and Kolb (1984). This views effective learning as occurring in a four-stage cycle of concrete experience, reflective observation, abstract conceptualization, and active experimentation (Box 2.4). Work experience can offer opportunities both for concrete experience and for active experimentation. But its learning potential will only be harnessed if it is integrated into a curriculum frame which also provides opportunities for reflective observation and abstract conceptualization, and for maintaining the momentum of the cycle. We will discuss this point in more detail in Chapter 12.

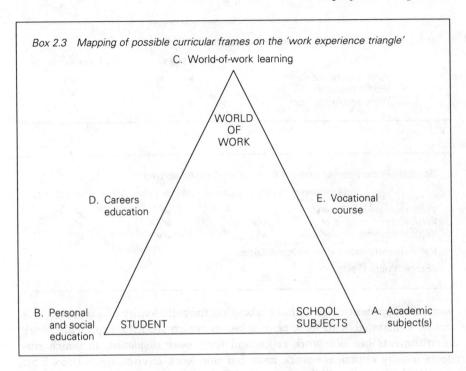

Box 2.3 *Mapping of possible curricular frames on the 'work experience triangle'*

C. World-of-work learning

WORLD
OF
WORK

D. Careers
education

E. Vocational
course

B. Personal
and social
education

STUDENT

SCHOOL
SUBJECTS

A. Academic
subject(s)

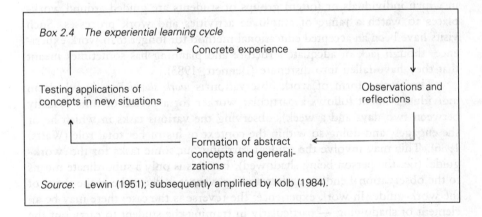

Box 2.4 *The experiential learning cycle*

Concrete experience

Testing applications of
concepts in new situations

Observations and
reflections

Formation of abstract
concepts and generali-
zations

Source: Lewin (1951); subsequently amplified by Kolb (1984).

Related Concepts

It is important to recognize that many of the aims attached to work-
experience schemes can also be achieved through other forms of experiential
learning about work. In seeking to clarify the concept of work experience, it
is helpful to relate it to some of these other forms. We earlier defined work
experience as describing schemes in which students experience work tasks in

---

Box 2.5   *Work experience and some related concepts*

	Work tasks	Work environments
Work experience	✔	✔
Work observation		✔
Work simulation	✔	

Box 2.6   *Primary foci of different forms of work-based learning*

	Work tasks	Work processes	Worker roles	Work environments
Work experience	✔✔	✔	✔	✔
Work visits	✔	✔✔	✔	✔
Work shadowing	✔	✔	✔✔	✔

✔✔ — primary focus; ✔ — additional focus.

Source: Watts (1986).

---

work environments, but without taking on the full identity of a worker. This can be contrasted with *work observation*, in which students experience work environments but not work tasks; and with *work simulation*, in which students usually experience work tasks but not work environments (Box 2.5).

Work observation takes two main different forms. The first is *work visits*, in which individuals or (often) groups of students are guided around workplaces to watch a range of employee activities and work processes. Such visits have been an accepted educational method for longer than work experience, though lack of adequate structure and planning has sometimes meant that they have fallen into disrepute (Bennett, 1983).

The second form of work observation is *work shadowing*, in which an individual student follows a particular worker for a period of time (usually between two days and a week), observing the various tasks in which he or she engages, and doing so within the context of his or her total role (Watts, 1986). This may involve the student carrying out some tasks for the 'work-guide' (i.e. the person being shadowed), but this is only a subordinate means to the observational end: to understanding what it is like to be in the shoes of the work-guide. In work experience, the reverse is the case: there may be an element of shadowing — particularly in training the student to carry out the tasks which he or she has been allocated — but this is merely a subordinate means to the task-performance end (*ibid*).

Thus not only are work observation and work shadowing different in their nature from work experience, but they also focus on different aspects of the work-place. Whereas work experience focuses primarily on work *tasks*, work visits focus primarily on work *processes*, and work shadowing on worker *roles* (Box 2.6). These foci are not of course mutually exclusive: a student on work experience may well also learn about work processes and worker roles. But because the *primary* focus is different, the nature of the learning yield is likely to vary in character.

Work simulations consist of operating representations of work tasks outside real work situations (Jamieson, Miller and Watts, 1988). They can take many different forms, including 'design and make' simulations, production simulations, mini-enterprises, work practice units, business games, and school work tasks. In many cases they may take place within schools, though various devices can be used — including the use of 'adults other than teachers' — to add an element of verisimilitude and to enable students to test the simulation against the reality it is purporting to represent. One of the distinctive virtues of work simulation as a form of work-related learning is that it is easier to organize and control for learning purposes: this makes it easier to secure effective integration into the curriculum (*ibid*).

All these different approaches have their own strengths and weaknesses. There has been a tendency to regard work observation and work simulation as flawed forms of work experience. We refute this view. Certainly the *direct* experience offered by work experience is qualitatively different from the *constructed* experience offered by work visits, the *vicarious* experience offered by work shadowing, and the *simulated* experience offered by work simulations. On the other hand, work observation and work shadowing have three distinct advantages over work experience.

The first is that they provide access to work situations and to occupations which do not lend themselves to work experience. Limitations are imposed on work experience by various considerations, notably that of skill requirement: only the simplest operations which can be learned quickly can be undertaken during a short period of work experience, and such experience tends therefore to be confined to unskilled or routine activities (Watts, 1983b). Work observation and work simulation are not subject to such restrictions. It is possible, for example, to observe or simulate highly skilled occupations like those of a doctor or senior manager, for which work experience is inconceivable.

The second is that work observation and work simulation tend to be more economical in terms of time. This may not always be the case: some mini-enterprises and work practice units, for example, may be very demanding in time terms. But it is often possible to mount effective simulations or visits or shadowing schemes within the space of a day or two. This makes them less vulnerable to the most common objection levelled at work-experience schemes: the amount of time they consume and the opportunity costs this involves in terms of classroom learning (see pp. 98–100 and 268).

The third advantage is that work observation and work simulation can be used with a much wider age-range. Work experience is limited by the Education (Work Experience) Act 1973 to students in or beyond the final twelve months of compulsory schooling — i.e. from the age of 15. Work

observation and work simulation, on the other hand, have been used extensively in the lower years of secondary schools and indeed in primary schools
(see Jamieson, Miller and Watts, 1988; Smith, 1988; Watts, 1986).

It is worth noting, however, that the aims of these different techniques
are very similar to those we outlined earlier in this chapter for work experience. There are a few exceptions. The *placing* and *custodial* aims apply to
work simulations marginally if at all. In addition, the primary foci of the
different techniques may imply particular strengths in relation to particular
aims: the focus of work shadowing on work roles, for example, may mean
that it is particularly appropriate for the *sampling* aim, whereas the focus of
work visits on work processes may make it particularly appropriate for the
investigative aim. But these are only differences of degree, and are likely to be
less influential than the particular characteristics of a particular scheme.

Forms of Work Experience

Our discussions so far have implied that work experience is a unitary concept. In practice, however, it can take a number of different forms. We
suggest that at least five such forms can be distinguished (Box 2.7). We will
look at each of these in turn.

The first is *doing an actual job*. This involves being given tasks which are
integral to the operations of the work organization, and which another
employee would normally have to carry out if the student were not there. As
Hodge (1987) points out, this allows the students to feel a sense of responsibility for the work undertaken, and to develop an impression of being part of
the organization. Since, however, there is little time for training, the tasks
tend — as we have seen — to be low-level and to involve little real responsibility: they typically include such activities as filing, checking, simple assembly work, and clerical routines.

The second is *providing an 'extra pair of hands'*. This is particularly risky
from the point of view of student learning and of student satisfaction,
because it tends to mean being given tasks which no one else wants to do,
and can also mean that there are times when the student is doing nothing.
HMI (1983) cites a couple of examples:

> A girl placed in a local primary school expressed resentment at being
> 'given the dirty jobs'. She was clearing up paint work which pupils
> had been allowed to leave in a mess but with the promise, which in
> the event was not fulfilled, that when this was completed she could
> help a pupil with her painting. She had spent her previous visits
> cleaning out cupboards (p. 15).

> A boy from a remedial class was attending for 2 or sometimes 3 days
> a week a garage mainly concerned with haulage.... He was given no

Box 2.7 Forms of work experience
1. Doing an actual job.
2. Providing an 'extra pair of hands'.
3. Helping someone in an actual job.
4. Rotating around different departments.
5. Carrying out specifically constructed tasks.

more than unskilled, routine tasks, such as sweeping the floor and
operating the push-button steam cleaners, and was occasionally
allowed to travel on a lorry. The proprietor was not prepared for
him to take any part in work like dismantling or reassembling; in
inclement weather he might spend the day sitting by the fire (p. 17).

Such 'dogsbody' work seems, however, to be mentioned only by a small
percentage of students (Sims, 1987, p. 102). More positively, this kind of
approach can involve being given a series of well-designed tasks which are
drawn from existing jobs but do not currently form a particular job: the
current trend towards flexible job structures based on multi-skilling makes
this easier to mount, and indeed pushes it closer towards our first form,
doing an actual job — with its attendant advantages.

The third is *helping someone in an actual job*. This incorporates an element
of work shadowing, and indeed may sometimes *become* work shadowing:

One interviewee was based with an optician for two weeks. His
employer introduced him to a wide range of activities opticians
are involved in, including clinic and hospital work, methods of lens
grinding and contact lens manufacture, and both prophylactic and
curative therapeutics. However, the student spent his entire time
watching, since there wasn't anything he could actually do (Fuller,
1987, p. 89).

In other cases, however, the student may genuinely act as a kind of assistant,
fully occupied in a series of work tasks. This has the merit of being likely to
ensure a high level of supervision.

The fourth is *rotating around different departments*. Fuller (1987), for
example, cites a case of a local authority environmental health department
where students spent each half-day with a specific supervisor on a specific
task (p. 109). Fuller regards this with approval. Hodge (1987), however,
points out that:

Pupils often enjoy the stimulation and variety of this sort of
approach, but during a two-week Work Experience placement, the

time available is arguably too short for any lasting impression to be gained and it can be confusing for the pupil. It can also give a false impression about the amount of variety available in a worker's life, since the pupil is unable to discover for himself that work can be both routine and boring at times (p. 10).

Such an approach incorporates elements of a work visit, and indeed this produces the countervailing advantage cited by Hodge:

The use of this approach by firms can also provide the analytical pupil with a useful overview of the structure and organisation of the company, leading to a fuller understanding of the concepts involved (p. 10).

The fifth is *carrying out specifically constructed tasks*. In this case tasks are thought up which, while of possible use to the work organization, are extraneous to its normal operations. Such 'work-based projects' were a familiar feature of the Youth Training Scheme (MSC, 1985). When developed for use in school-based work-experience schemes they may in some cases be designed by the employer; in other cases they may be designed jointly by the employer and the school, and may also involve some negotiation with the students themselves (see p. 211). Thus, for example an A-level course in Business Studies included a work-experience research project which was designed by the Business Studies tutor and an employer's representative and was designed to contribute to the company: the written report was presented to the GCE board, but in addition the student had to present a ten/fifteen minute talk to people at the firm as well as to the tutor (Fuller, 1987, pp. 56, 58–9, 93–4). In another example, Ursuline High School in Wimbledon set up a 'Taskweek' which involved year-10 students working in groups of four to six on specific tasks designed to be of value to an employer. They were given the format of the task by the employer, but were allowed to plan and organize the week. Examples of the tasks that emerged are shown in Box 2.8. In a sense, such practices are at the boundary of the concept of 'work experience'. The extent to which this term can properly be applied to them is related to the extent to which the student feels accountable to the employer. If such accountability is weak, then the student is in reality carrying out a school project which happens to be linked to a work-place; if it is strong, then the student can genuinely feel that he or she is carrying out a project for an employer, as a form of work experience. In such terms, its merit is that it leaves considerable scope for initiative and responsibility, and may provide opportunities for finding out a lot about the nature and structure of the work organization; its disadvantage is that the students may be given too little guidance and support, and may be left largely to their own devices, which may tend to make them feel extraneous to the work of the organization (Hodge, 1987).

Box 2.8 *Examples of tasks in the Ursuline High School 'Taskweek'*

Task employer	Title of task	Activities
Electricity Council	The functions and workings of the Electricity Council's staff training college at Horsley Towers.	To investigate the role of Horsley Towers in staff training and produce a video highlighting these activities.
SEGAS	Investigation of staff sports facilities.	Finding out: 1. what facilities are used and how often; 2. factors influencing their use; 3. whether job/status has any bearing on facilities used; 4. improvements/changes which could be made.
British Telecom	Safety campaign.	To look at existing health and safety material and identify areas where health and safety literature is needed. To design health and safety posters.
CAFOD (Catholic Association for Overseas Development)	Investigation into homelessness and child labour.	To interview young people on their views about the reasons why their peers feel the need to leave home. To investigate the extent of child labour in England.

Source: Barry (1985–86).

These five forms of work experience are not necessarily mutually exclusive, and it is possible to combine elements of two or more of them. For example, some element of rotating around different departments might be used in the early stages of a placement, as part of the induction process, before settling down to doing an actual job or helping someone in an actual job. Nonetheless, it is useful to tease out the pros and cons of each form, and indeed such an analysis might be useful in negotiating what form or forms a placement should take. In addition to the points already noted, it is worth pointing out that the later forms in the list leave the student in a 'student' role, whereas the earlier ones move them closer to an 'employee' role involving accountability and responsibility to the employer (rather than the school) for work undertaken. Linked with this, the later forms involve the student in a kind of voyeurism in relation to the work-place, whereas the earlier ones prefer immersion.[2] Both are 'real' but in different ways: immersion feels 'real' in experiential terms, whereas the voyeurism of rotation and of constructed tasks may feel forced and artificial; on the other hand, the latter may provide an experience which is more 'real' in cognitive terms (understanding how the organization as a whole is structured and operates).

Broadening the Concept of 'Work'

So far, we have been defining 'work' in conventional terms as referring to 'paid employment'. In recent years, however, some concern has been expressed about the need to broaden this definition. In part this has stemmed from high levels of youth unemployment, and the pressure this has posed to explore alternatives to paid employment (see Watts, 1983b; also, e.g. Smith and Storey, 1988). Stronach (1984) notes how high unemployment paradoxically led to the expansion of vocational preparation, and how 'the paradox was resolved by creating a comprehensive, if vague, definition of "work" as separate from employment and by positing the need for personal development' (p. 54). In part, too, the demand for a broader definition has been related to the linked but separable growth of interest in 'education for enterprise' (Gibb, 1987; Rees, 1988; Watts and Moran, 1984), and in encouraging students to consider the possibility of generating their own work through becoming self-employed or setting up a small business or cooperative.

The link between work experience and this wider concept of work has been established, for example, by HMI (1988):

> Preparation for working life presupposes that pupils will be encouraged to interpret the concept of work in relation to a series of definitions: these range from work seen as paid employment to work viewed as the tasks to which human creative energies can be focused. Work experience helps in this process (p. 14).

The CPVE 'notes of guidance', too, note that

> It is one of the main aims of CPVE to enable young people to familiarise themselves with a range of occupations including both those associated with paid employment and those associated with work at home or within the community from which no income is derived (JBPVE, 1985, p. 180).

The CPVE notes go on, however, to view work experience as providing a 'substantial opportunity to concentrate upon work which is associated with employment, often in a particular and limited form' (*ibid*, p. 180), In what senses could the concept of 'work' in work experience *per se* be defined more widely?

One possibility is to extend the concept to cover voluntary work of various kinds: in other words, to break down the barrier between work experience and community service. At one school in an area of high unemployment, for example, the concept of work experience was increasingly being integrated with that of community service, with 'work' being defined not just as employment but more broadly as 'corporate activity towards some end' (Watts, 1983b, p. 45). Again, a project in Renfrew was designed 'to analyse work and other community placements and relate them to pupil needs': it found that 'although pupils recognised the differences between community placements and work placements, they approached them in a similar manner' (Clarke, 1985). A further work-experience scheme with a strong community-service orientation is described in Box 9.12 (p. 167). In all such schemes, however, it is important that the differences between paid work and unpaid work are brought out very clearly, and placed in a political and economic framework which explores their implications for standards of living and for economic independence. There also may be difficulties about allocation of placements, particularly if only a single placement per student is possible: there is a danger that students allocated community rather than work placements may regard themselves as being labelled as unemployable.

A second possibility is to extend the concept of work experience to cover self-employment, and setting up small businesses and cooperatives. This could be done by looking for work-experience placements with sole traders, in cooperatives, etc. It could also be done by enlarging the definition of work experience to embrace mini-enterprises, in which typically a group of students sets up a company or cooperative, develops a product or service, and trades for a period, before winding up the business. We would regard this in strict terms as being a form of work simulation (see Jamieson, Miller and Watts, 1988, ch. 5). In some important senses, however, mini-enterprises are 'real': in particular, they involve real money. Carney and Turner (1987) have suggested a form of progression in which students move from (A) a traditional work-experience placement in a local company, through (B) forming work-experience project teams that undertake a task set by the teacher (in consultation with local employers) which enables them to examine various aspects of employment, to (C) designing an enterprise which provides goods and services to the community. This is shown diagrammatically in Box 2.9, which also shows what Carney and Turner term 'line X . . . Y', which shows how young people who participate in this range of activities can become increasingly involved in the design and management of their learning through work experience.

Harnessing Students' Existing Experience of Work

In considering such wider concepts of work, it is important to recognize the experiences of work which students may already have had both inside and, more particularly, outside school. Dewey (1963) pointed out how 'the principle of continuity of experience means that every experience both takes up

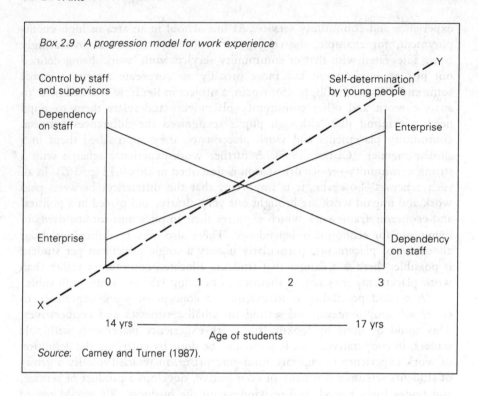

Box 2.9   A progression model for work experience

Source: Carney and Turner (1987).

something from those which have gone before and modifies in some way the quality of those which come after' (p. 35). If part of the function of work experience is to develop students' concepts of work, it is important that it should not be seen in a vacuum.

There is for example a considerable research literature on the ways in which children's *household work* is related to the development of helping behaviour, the growth of independence, and induction into work. As Good-now (1988) points out in a review of this literature, such work 'calls for effort, it is regarded by most other people as useful, and it usually involves relationships with other people, often in the form of proceeding toward their goals or requiring their cooperation in order to proceed towards one's own' (p. 7). Zelizer (1985) notes that two rationales or justifications tend to be put forward for children's household activities: parents' *need* for children's work; and the developmental value of tasks (their capacity to develop 'body, mind and character' [p. 98]). She also notes the evolution of a third rationale: an egalitarian ethos in which all family members share the chores. There is, however, clear evidence that the allocation of tasks to boys and to girls tends to reflect the domestic division of labour: girls tend to be more frequently involved in domestic chores than their male counterparts; and girls tend to be predominantly involved in tasks like washing and laundry work, cooking meals, cleaning about the house, looking after other children, and sewing or mending clothes, whereas boys tend to be involved in gardening, painting, fixing things and washing the car (see, e.g. Finn, 1984). Attitudes towards the gender segregation of work may be strongly formed by such practices.

Secondly, many children engage in various forms of *voluntary work in the community*. Courtenay (1988), for example, found that 15 per cent of young people in the Youth Cohort Study had done community work during the school day in their fourth or fifth years. Most such work falls into four main areas: environmental projects, and working with disabled people, elderly people, and young children (CSV, 1987). In addition to such school-based activities, other voluntary-work activities may be based around scouts and similar groups.

Thirdly, it is important to recognize that many students while still at school engage in *paid employment* in the form of part-time and holiday jobs. In the Youth Cohort Study, Courtenay (1988) found that 56 per cent had had a part-time job during years 10 and 11, as opposed to only 29 per cent who had had work experience organized by the school. Boys were slightly more likely than girls to have had a part-time job (58 per cent compared with 53 per cent). Finn (1984) points out that such work 'represents a learning experience which, whilst the particular kind of work might be rejected, makes for a continuity between pre- and post-school economic life, and ensures an early exposure to the rigours of the labour market' (p. 44). In particular, it differs from school-based work-experience schemes in the sense that the young people involved have a contractual relationship with an employer which is based on payment for services rendered: they receive a wage in return for sustaining certain levels of job performance, and if they fall below these levels of performance they may be sacked. Traditionally, many of the jobs involved have been essentially juvenile rather than adult jobs (Roberts, 1967) — newspaper rounds being a classic example — and considerable concern has been expressed both about employers' exploitative practices (MacLennan, Fitz and Sullivan, 1985) and about the links between such part-time jobs and poor attendance, behaviour and academic performance at school (Davies, 1972).

More recently, however, Baxter (1988) and Roberts, Dench and Richardson (1987) have found that students with higher levels of academic attainment are now as or more likely to take spare-time employment. Roberts *et al.* suggest that this may be because less-able pupils are experiencing a squeeze on their part-time opportunities, whereas aspiring parents may be starting to encourage school-children to supplement their pocket-money with spare-time jobs, and employers — particularly in distribution and in hotels and catering — are looking increasingly to bright students to fill part-time and temporary vacancies. Roberts *et al.* argue that this may represent a move towards American attitudes and practices, in which part-time employment is regarded as enabling the students to stay-on rather than being an enemy of education. In support of such attitudes and practices, American research has indicated that, while very extensive work involvement amongst some groups is associated with an increase in their rate of dropping out, less extensive work involvement actually appears to lead to increased rates of high-school completion (D'Amico, 1984). There have also been suggestions from other American research that the opportunities provided by spare-time jobs for learning how to interact effectively with others may provide a partial antidote to adolescent egocentrism (Steinberg *et al.*, 1981), though in terms of adolescent psycho-social and moral development there seem to be negative effects as well as positive ones — it can for example lead to the development of cynical attitudes towards work and the acceptance of unethical work practices (Steinberg *et al.*, 1982).

A fourth form of experience of work which merits attention is *helping in family businesses*. This has traditionally been regarded with some suspicion by teachers and others. But Steinberg (1984) suggests that it may have some clear advantages over other forms of experience of work. In particular, adolescents may be more likely to feel that their labour is important, which may increase their sense of responsibility; parents, because they have a stake in keeping their children involved in the family enterprise, may expose them to more diverse tasks and more of the internal workings of the business than would other employers; and working for one's parents may transform the adolescents' family relationships in positive ways. These are all hypotheses which have not so far been tested by research.

Finally, a small number of students may engage in *entrepreneurial activities* on their own account. Some, for example, have been very successful in developing and selling software packages. Other have engaged in other entrepreneurial activities. The dilemmas this can impose were illustrated by a report published in the *Mail on Sunday* (11 March 1984):

> A schoolboy who swopped log tables for log fires has been told to stop making money and get back to the classroom. Darren Murfet, 15, stopped going to school so he could concentrate on the £12,000-a-year business he had built up, recyling industrial waste wood for domestic use. He told teachers he couldn't return to the John O'Gaunt comprehensive in Hungerford, Berks, because he has orders piling up from his 350 customers. Last week his parents were fined £300 for failing to ensure that he attend school.... Darren, a remedial pupil who is legally entitled to leave school in May, said: 'I worked hard to get the business going. I don't want to end on the dole.' But his headmaster, Mr David Lee, said yesterday he deplored the example Darren had set other pupils.

Steinberg (1984) points out that in general, these various forms of adolescent work differ from adult work in one important respect. Drawing upon Mark Twain's definition 'that Work consists of whatever a body is *obliged* to do and that Play consists of whatever a body is not obliged to do', Steinberg points out that the distinction falls short in relation to discussions of work — and particularly of paid employment — during adolescence: 'Adolescent work is generally not obligatory, but voluntary. For the typical adolescent, it is school, not work, that "a body is obliged to do"' (p. 3). It is worth noting that school-based work experience schemes are in an interesting position here: in a sense, it is only by being incorporated into the school that 'work' in its employment-related sense can be incorporated into the realm of obligation.

Steinberg makes a further point which is important in relation to our concerns in this chapter. He defines work as 'any activity in which a young person engages — paid or unpaid, obligatory or voluntary — that places the adolescent, subjectively and objectively, in the role of "worker", adding to or replacing the other primary roles of adolescence, that is, the roles of "family member" and "student"'. But he then goes on to suggest that 'work' is likely to have its most positive developmental impact on the adolescent when the work role itself is merged with another primary adolescent role (that is, with the role of student or family member). Here he draws on Bronfenbrenner's (1979) suggestion regarding the developmental value of connections between the different settings in which children spend time. It is on these grounds that Steinberg explains the hypothesized virtues of children helping in family businesses. More significantly in relation to our main interests in this book, it is also on these grounds that he explains the American evidence that the experiential programmes which show the most consistent impact on students' psycho-social development were those which were more 'school-like' and less 'work-like': 'career intern' programmes in which participants were classed more as students than as workers in their placements, and community-service programmes in which students were learning about community problems (see pp. 51 and 261–2). What seemed to make the difference was the level of integration into the curriculum.

These are important findings, which support the case for structured work-experience programmes in the curriculum. Nonetheless, there would seem to be a strong case for such programmes to take account of students' existing experiences of work. At present such experiences tend to remain totally separate from school-based work-experience schemes. Sometimes they penetrate such schemes, in unhelpful ways:

> Many youngsters contented themselves with extending into school time work in which they had been participating at weekends or in school holidays, and some cases were encountered of pupils 'working' in their own family concerns. Much of the value of work experience is lost if it does not extend the perspectives of pupils (HMI, 1983, p. 13).

If, however, such programmes are to extend the students' perspectives, they need to enable students to draw upon and explore the prior experiences upon which these perspectives are based (Varlaam, 1983).

Box 2.10   A conceptual map of work and related forms of work experience

Form of work	Related forms of work experience	
	Structured by school	Not structured by school
Formal economy		
Paid employment	School-based work experience	Part-time/holiday jobs
Self-employment	Mini-enterprises Work experience with sole traders, co-operatives, etc.	Helping in family businesses Entrepreneurial activities
Informal economies		
Hidden economy	—	Entrepreneurial activities Part-time/holiday jobs
Communal economy	Community-service programmes	Voluntary work
Household economy	—	Household work

Mapping Widening Concepts of Work

If students' experiences of work are to be drawn upon in this way, it may be helpful to conceptualize the main different forms of work within the formal and informal economies, and then to identify the forms of work experience which seem related to each of these categories. A model for doing this is outlined in Box 2.10.

For the majority of adults, *paid employment* provides the main source of their income as well as a prime determinant of their social status and identity. School-based work-experience schemes provide opportunities for exploring paid employment, as do part-time and holiday jobs.

In recent years, however, there has been increasing interest in *self-employment*, in which people work not for others but for themselves. Such people fall into three main groups: first, those who are self-employed and working on their own; second, those who set up businesses employing other people; and third, those who set up workers' cooperatives which are owned by the workers themselves (Watts, 1983b). Opportunities for exploring such forms of work are provided formally by mini-enterprises and by work experience with sole traders, cooperatives, etc.; more informally, they can be provided by helping in family businesses and by students' own entrepreneurial activities.

In addition to these different forms of work within the formal economy, a considerable amount of work is undertaken within three informal economies (Gershuny and Pahl, 1979/80; 1980; see also Watts, 1983b, ch. 9). The first is the *hidden economy*, sometimes called the 'black' economy (we prefer to avoid this term, because of its racist overtones). This covers work conducted

---

Box 2.11   *Narrow and broad definitions of 'work' and of 'experience'*

	Narrow definition	Broad definition
Work	Only paid employment	Also self-employment hidden economy communal economy household economy
Experience	Only direct experience	Also vicarious experience constructed experience simulated experience

---

wholly or partly for money which is concealed from taxation and regulatory authorities: it ranges from undeclared criminal and immoral earnings (e.g. prostitution, drug-trafficking), through office pilfering, to undeclared income earned in particular by the self-employed, by moonlighters and by the unemployed. Schools are likely to disapprove of such activities, but it is important that they should acknowledge the existence of the hidden economy, and it may be fruitful to explore some of the ethical and socio-political issues it poses. Since students' entrepreneurial activities and part-time/holiday jobs are often themselves hidden-economy activities, they can provide a base-point for such discussions.

The second informal economy is the *communal economy*, which involves the production of goods or services which are consumed by people other than the producers, but are not sold on a monetary basis. This ranges from baby-sitting circles or car-pools which operate on the basis of a formal exchange of tokens or credits, through exchanges of skills or of equipment which are part of a relationship of generalized reciprocity between friends, neighbours, etc., to pure gift activities — including voluntary work, and some acts of friendliness or neighbourliness — for which no reciprocity is expected. School-based community-service programmes and students' own voluntary activities are examples of such communal-economy work.

Finally, there is the *household economy*, which covers work within the home that involves the production for internal consumption of goods or services for which approximate substitutes might otherwise be sought elsewhere. Examples include cooking, decorating, child care, home repairs, and garden produce. Again, students' own household work provides instances of such activities. An example of measures that can be taken to incorporate such work within a work-experience programme is outlined briefly on p. 215.

Conclusion

In this chapter we have explored narrow and broad definitions both of 'work' and of 'work experience'. A narrow view of 'work' defines it as 'paid employment'; a broad definition also includes self-employment and the three informal economies. Similarly, a narrow view of 'experience' limits it to direct experience; whereas a broad definition also includes vicarious experience (work shadowing), constructed experience (work visits) and simulated experience (work simulations). These varying definitions are summarized in Box 2.11. In the remainder of this book, we will concentrate in the main on the narrow definitions. This is partly to confine our area of study to manageable proportions, and partly because these are the definitions conventionally adopted by schools. We consider it important, however, that 'work experience' defined in this narrow sense be viewed in the broader context of the other areas we have discussed.

Notes

1   'School' in this connection is defined to cover sixth-form colleges and also to cover courses in colleges of further education and tertiary colleges which are also offered in schools: thus it includes A-level courses in FE but excludes FE vocational courses.
2   We are grateful to Ian Stronach for this observation.

Chapter 3

Some International Comparisons

A.G. Watts

The growth of work experience in Britain in the 1980s has come to be regarded as part of the 'new vocationalism' (Bates *et al.*, 1984; Holt, 1987; Pollard, Purvis and Walford, 1988) and closely associated by some with Thatcherite ideology. It is accordingly important to recognize that work experience has been adopted by schools in many countries, from a variety of ideological perspectives. In this chapter we examine in turn the forms which work experience has taken in Sweden, in other European countries, in the USSR, in East Germany, in Cuba, in Australia and in the USA. Most of the material is taken from secondary sources, and so is not always wholly comparable or equally up to date. We will then conclude by noting some of the implications which can be drawn from this range of international experience.

Sweden

Sweden is probably the West European country which has the strongest tradition of work experience as part of the curriculum of compulsory schooling. It has been a feature of the Swedish comprehensive school since the 1950s. When we looked at the 'PRYO' (practical vocational orientation) system in 1980 (Watts, 1981), it comprised a compulsory two-week period (with an optional extension up to thirty-six days) in grade 9 (age 15–16), preceded by three group visits to different work-places during grade 8. Plans were, however, being made to extend this further. A pilot 'PRAO', (practical working life orientation) scheme had been instituted under which each comprehensive-school pupil was to spend six to ten weeks at work-places: this was to include group visits during grades 1–5 (ages 7–12), the rationale being that attitudes and values began to form in early childhood and

Editor's note: This chapter was written before the unification of East and West Germany.

therefore early contact with the world of work was important from the start of schooling; it also included at least one week's experience during grades 6–9 (ages 12–16) in each of three broad sectors of working life (covering — in the main — manufacturing, commerce and social services respectively). Moreover, there were further opportunities for work experience in the upper secondary school. In the case of the more vocational programmes of study, it was formally integrated into the curriculum (sometimes paid, and sometimes on a day-release basis rather than the block-release basis characteristic of the other schemes). There were also experimental schemes in a number of upper secondary schools under which students on the more theoretical programmes made a number of work visits as part of a 'vocational orientation week', and later had periods of work experience in their chosen area of interest.

In the new school curriculum introduced in 1982/83, the main elements of the PRAO scheme were implemented nationally. Thus all students were now expected to have six to ten weeks in work-places between the ages of 7 and 16 (NSBE, 1984), though this has not always been fulfilled in practice and its distribution between grades has been determined by the local education authority. Some notes subsequently received from Abbott (private communication, 1985) indicated that at the age of 7 pupils were encouraged to spend a day shadowing their father and/or mother at their place of work, and that subsequent projects included studies of workers within the school — the school caretaker, the head teacher, the social worker, the librarian, etc.

Unlike in the UK, the potential careers guidance functions of work experience were initially encouraged in Sweden. Even with the new scheme of three different placements in the comprehensive school, the primary objective was 'to counteract social prejudice in vocational decisions' (NSBE, 1978, p. 4). On the other hand, in order to achieve this broadening of perspective, it was decided that students should not normally be allowed to choose their occupational sectors or work-places. Instead, they have mostly had to accept the places they have been allotted, often as a result of a draw (NSBE, 1984). There has also been encouragement for the adoption of a socially critical approach, with students being expected to ask probing questions about social relations at the work-place, the values of different groups, aims of activities, pay differentials, occupational status, relations between superiors and subordinates, sex roles, and so forth (Reubens, 1977, p. 84).

So far as integration into the curriculum is concerned, the Swedish authorities assert confidently that preparation and follow-up work 'can be done in connection with all school subjects' (NSBE, 1974, p. 13). At the time of the visit made in 1980, however, it seemed that in practice the large group sizes and formal teaching methods tended not to be readily compatible with a 'reflection on experience' model of learning. Moreover, there had been little systematic curriculum development work in this area, and teachers were therefore thrown back on, for example, their own work experience, which in many cases was very limited. Social studies teachers were most likely to feel they had something to offer, and such preparation and follow-up work as was done tended to be carried out by them, supported by the SYO (educational and vocational orientation) counsellor, and with occasional help from other teachers (e.g. Swedish language teachers might help to prepare students for interviewing workers). In a few schools, efforts were made to encourage teachers to visit their students while the students were out on work experience, and in this way to develop the teachers' own knowledge of the local labour market and of working life: since, however, this was voluntary, it was patchy in its effects (Watts, 1981). In the new curriculum introduced from 1982/83 the National Swedish Board of Education issued guidelines on the central concepts related to work experience which were to be embodied in the curriculum at various stages.

Some Other European Countries

In *Denmark*, most students take part in work experience in the final two years of the *folkeskole*. In the past, most of the placements have been found by the Public Vocational Guidance Service, but increasingly they are now being organized by the schools themselves (Plant, 1988, p. 16). As in Sweden, such programmes started in the mid-1950s. It is not uncommon for students to experience several placements. When we visited Denmark in 1980, the programme in one town (Herlev) involved a week for all students in each of the final three years of the comprehensive school. In the first of these years, students were only allowed to select a broad occupational field; in the two subsequent years, they could opt for a particular occupation. A more refined progression model was developed in a pilot project sponsored by the European Commission: this involved progression from 'local work experience' (age 14) through 'limited-choice work experience' (age 15) to 'work experience of one's own choice' (age 16) (see p. 180). These models have since been implemented more widely, and work experience extended both to younger and to older students (Plant, private communication, 1989). Integration into the curriculum in Denmark is helped by the fact that the class–teacher is responsible for guidance and will almost certainly also be teaching both Danish and contemporary studies — and perhaps as much as 60–70 per cent of the total curriculum — for the same group of students (IFAPLAN, 1986, p. 24).

In the *Netherlands*, the term for work experience within vocational training courses is *snuffel-stage* — an evocative way of expressing the sensory nature of the experience. It seems that the Dutch do not include work experience as part of the general curriculum (IFAPLAN, 1986, p. 16). An interesting experimental project was, however, described by Smith (1983; see also de Mulder, n.d.; Van den Bosch, 1983). Entitled *Arbeidserväringsleren* (Learning by Experience in Work), it began in 1977. It had initially been based in seven schools with students aged 15–17, though it had subsequently been extended into sixteen schools, eight of which had developed a programme of work experience with — in each case — as many as six teachers involved in its organization and implementation. The focus of the scheme was on 'the more general relevance of work, its hierarchic structure and relations': to dissociate it from a narrowly 'vocational' perspective, it was located one year before students began specific preparation for a career. Students were required to develop their own 'themes' to explore through the experience: it was emphasized that 'during the work-week, pupils should remain pupils and not become employees', and that 'it is of the utmost importance that pupils exchange and compare their experiences after the work-week'. It was also noted that

> as a result of the organization of the learning-process in small groups and of the fact that pupils' own experiences have become an object of study, the usually passive and consuming [sic] attitude of pupils is changed into an active one: they take part in shaping the learning-process (de Mulder, n.d.).

The teachers involved were drawn mainly from social science, vocational orientation, economics, geography, history, and Dutch. A number of concerns were expressed about integrating this experimental project into the regular school programme.

In *West Germany*, work experience seems to be systematically provided only for the academically less-able students. The *Arbeitslehre* (work-related learning) courses in the high schools normally include work experience as well as work visits. The work-experience placements usually last two to three weeks, or are organized over a longer period on a day-release basis (IFAPLAN, 1986, p. 23). Unlike most other areas of the curriculum, there are considerable differences between the federal states (*Länder*) in the organization and content of *Arbeitslehre* courses. So far as the work-experience component is concerned, two contrasts with work experience in British schools have been identified (Russell, 1982):

(a) In addition to some of the objectives attached to British work-experience schemes, an additional objective is to give pupils an experience of training, in preparation for the apprenticeship they are later likely to enter as part of the 'dual system'. Thus 'in larger firms, whereas commercial placements can take place in an actual work setting, industrial placements may well be located in a training workshop environment with little or no contact with the real work task' (*ibid*, p. 45).

(b) The use of work experience as a pre-selection device is common and, it seems, generally accepted. One result of this is that employers tend to take most of their recruits from particular schools, which in turn encourages informal feedback from employers to schools that may have an influence on the curriculum — e.g. on the nature of mathematical work (*ibid*, pp. 45–6).

In *Luxembourg*, students in the less academic schools have between four and six short placements of two to three days in different firms and industries around age 15. These placements are designed to help students to make their first contact with working life as well as to explore particular occupations (Sauer, 1988).

In *France*, work experience was introduced into the technical high schools around 1980. The students — most of them studying for the *certificat d'aptitude professionnelle* rather than the *baccalauréate* — spent ten to nineteen days with a firm. There was some initial resistance from students on the grounds that it represented exploitation on menial tasks, and was an unnecessary interruption of their studies. In the end, however, the scheme was judged 'a qualified success' (*Times Educational Supplement*, 19 April 1981). In one of the EEC pilot projects, work experience seemed to have a significant impact on the curriculum.

> As a result of both visiting the students while on placement and remarks made by them afterwards, subject teachers became more aware of discrepancies between what students experienced in firms and what was taught in the school. This stimulated discussion in school and with tutors on how the curriculum and the placements could be improved in order to enhance their educational value (IFAPLAN, 1986, p. 15).

USSR

In Soviet schools, work experience has a much longer tradition than in Western Europe, as part of the Marxist theory of 'polytechnic education'. In *Capital*, Marx wrote:

> From the factory system budded, as Robert Owen has shown us in detail, the germ of the education of the future, an education that will, in the case of every child over a given age, combine productive work with instruction and gymnastics, not only as one of the methods of adding to the efficiency of production, but also as the only method of producing fully developed human beings (Marx, 1887, Volume I, ch. XV, section 9).

Work experience was accordingly viewed as an important part of general education, helping growing individuals to develop positive attitudes towards labour, to understand the connection between theory and practice, and to acquire an understanding of their own role in society (see Castles and Wüstenberg, 1979, pp. 32–41; Grant, 1982, pp. 121–3).

The concept of 'polytechnic education' was implemented to some extent after the Russian Revolution. This was mainly in the form of encouraging 'productive' activities within the school, though it also involved encouraging students 'to study the village they lived in by taking part in work, talking to farmers and workers and the like' (Castles and Wüstenberg, 1979, p. 50). During the Stalin era, however, it 'all but vanished without trace' (Grant, 1982, p. 125).

In 1958, Khruschev initiated a series of educational reforms, one of which was that a third of curricular time in classes 9–11 (ages 14–17) should be spent on productive practice in factories or on collective and state farms. As Grant (1982, p. 127) points out:

> the intention behind this was not vocational; schools made arrangements with particular factories, even if few of the pupils had the slightest intention of taking up any of the particular trades on offer, so that they would become used to the realities of working life, and acquire 'respect for work and for people who work'.

This was to be implemented gradually, but soon criticisms began to be voiced, both by educationalists and by factory managers — 'while they were quite prepared to have pupils visit their factories for the occasional "polytechnical excursion", they did not relish having them under their feet for three half-days a week' (*ibid*, p. 128). Accordingly in 1964 the allocation of time to 'productive practice' was reduced from a third to a quarter, and in 1966 such practice was substantially moved back from factories and farms to school workshops and plots. Grant nonetheless notes that some schools decided to continue with the system of external work practice, presumably because they were linked with enterprises which were prepared to provide the appropriate facilities. Also, to counter the tendency for the production practice to slip into a form of pre-vocational training, steps were taken to replace it with a broader 'vocational orientation' focus, under which students could sample a range of jobs in their area, not only to understand how they related to the local and national economy, but also to help pupils make a more informed choice of occupation (*ibid*, p. 128).

The parallels between some aspects of these developments and what was happening in Sweden (see pp. 39–41) are striking. It is also worth noting parenthetically that some of the measures were aligned with the policy introduced by Khruschev to give strong priority in selection to higher education to students who had served a period in productive work (*stazh*) lasting at least two years. Within a year or two of introducing this reform, about 80 per cent of entrants to higher education were *stazhniki*. Similarly, in Sweden, determined efforts have been made to disconnect higher education from continuous schooling by giving generous credits for periods in work (see, e.g.

Kim, 1979): as a result of this, no less than 55 per cent of higher education students in Sweden in 1977/78 were aged 25 and over (Swedish Institute, 1979).

Within the USSR, the emphasis on work experience seems to have continued to wax and wane cyclically. Grant notes that under reforms introduced in the late 1970s the importance of work experience of some kind for *all* students, including the academically able, was reasserted; however, 'the new schemes do not place pupils in actual part-time job situations, but use formal learning programmes located in schools, in production-training combines run by groups of schools, and in factories and collective and state farms' (Grant, 1982, p. 131).

A report in the *Times Educational Supplement* (20 January 1984) noted another set of reforms based on what the Soviet news agency, Novosti, referred to as 'the principle of deep and all-embracing polytechnisation of school': they included lifting the ban on child labour in some lighter occupations for those aged under 16, so that students could opt to work in their spare time; involving children of all ages in 'socially useful labour' within the school; and involving older children at work in factories during their holidays, ploughing part of the money they earned back into the maintenance and development of their schools. The Minister of Education was quoted as saying:

> On the one hand, it is very important for the moulding of the personality, and on the other, it opens up an opportunity for solving many economic problems. It is no secret that the country is short of manpower, and the labour contribution of young people who have received professional skills at school will be useful in all respects.

The repeated embodiment of the same broad ideas in 'reforms' suggests that in practice integrating work experience into Soviet schools has posed difficulties and tensions, and has needed periodic reaffirmation in order to avoid gradual erosion. Clearly, too, the country's labour needs have been an influence on policy. It seems, for example, that many of Khruschev's educational reforms were influenced by the manpower shortages stemming from the massive loss of life and reduced birth-rate during the Second World War. As Grant (1982, p. 129) comments, these reforms 'could all be argued for on social and ideological grounds — and were — but they were also the only way, at the time, whereby the expansion of the [educational] system *and* the needs of the labour force could both be maintained'.

East Germany

Grant (1982, p. 132) noted that, on the whole, the fortunes of polytechnic education and work practice in other East European countries in the period following the Second World War reflected developments in the USSR. He added, however, that there had been some deviations from this pattern, and that

> surprisingly, it has been East Germany, usually thought of as one of the most orthodox members of the bloc, that has departed furthest from Soviet practice; but it has done so by displaying a degree of commitment and consistency through all the vacillations in the USSR. When the time for polytechnical education was cut in Soviet schools, it was *increased* in East Germany; when labour practice in factories and farms was being soft-pedalled in the Soviet system, the East Germans were giving it more emphasis, and making even more of the moral and social arguments (*ibid*, p. 133).

Thus in 1958/59, following Khruschev's reforms in the USSR, the 'school day in production' was introduced in East Germany, which meant that all students from the seventh grade (age 12/13) onwards were to spend one day a week working in a 'socialist enterprise' in industry or in agriculture. There was considerable opposition, not least from parents and students who suspected (rightly as it often turned out) that doing certain jobs while still at school might decide their future occupation (Castles and Wüstenberg, 1979, pp. 81–2). Accordingly, the emphasis subsequently moved away from specifically focused training towards a much broader approach covering a wide range of experiences and processes. The aim was now not only to teach students about production technologies but also to show them the social and organizational structure of a 'socialist' factory. Students were instructed by specially trained polytechnic teachers as well as by foremen and workers, who were released from normal work, and who received instruction in teaching methods. At the same time, however, it was regarded as essential that students should spend a considerable part of their 'school day in production' doing real productive work, in order to form a 'correct' attitude towards manual work (*ibid*, p. 91). Thus in a factory making washing machines, for example, there was a complete assembly line in its 'polytechnic centre', and care was taken for students to change round at set intervals and in a set sequence to experience *all* the relevant tasks (Grant, 1982, p. 133). Indeed, in the final two years of schooling, students were gradually assigned to the regular work teams within the factory (UNESCO, 1981, para. 64).

The rationale for this was closely in line with the original Marxist theory. As an East German publication puts it:

> In the GDR work is brought into the educational process as part of the contemporary technical, economic, and social complex....
> Through direct participation in productive work the pupil becomes conscious of reality and of the value of what he has learned and what he has still to learn. He then finds that school and work as an

occupation are no longer separate categories or areas of life that simply follow one another in time but that the relationship between them makes learning an authentic task in life from the very beginning. He does not suddenly 'end' school and enter something beyond and outside the school called 'life'. If the pupil has taken concrete responsibility in the work process — no matter how simple at the outset — and has had the opportunity to perfect himself in it, he grows into the future more gradually and without a break, and with a full sense of responsibility as a co-owner of his plant and co-ruler of his state (quoted in Steele, 1977, p. 173).

Castles and Wüstenberg (1979, p. 99), however, comment that in practice the East German Government 'has taken the marxist concept of polytechnic education and robbed it of its real content. Instead of "totally developed individuals" capable of creatively transforming society, the aim is the well-trained, hard-working, conformist wage workers.'

Cuba

Many of the concepts of 'polytechnic education', including work experience, seem also to have been enthusiastically adopted in Cuba under Castro. In sharp contrast with the rest of Latin America, Cuba has devised an official 'ideology of work' which emphasizes work as a major individual, social and revolutionary virtue. Important elements in the ideology are: love of work and respect for the worker; the creation of all wealth through work; the dignity of work, especially manual work; the need to overcome the division between intellectual and manual work; and the positive formative influence of work on the individual (Richmond, 1983, p. 102).

To foster this ideology, 'productive work' has been introduced into all levels and types of education in Cuba. Some of the initiatives involve bringing the concept of production into the school. The most notable example is the self-supporting 'schools in the countryside', which by 1985 accommodated about 35 per cent of all students aged 13–17 (Blum, 1985). Thus one such school had about 500 students (250 boys and 250 girls) who lived in dormitories during the week and went home over the week-end. Half the group studied in the morning and worked the citrus fields, under farmer supervision, in the afternoon; the other half worked opposite shifts. The citrus crop was then sold to the government.

In other cases, students carry out 'productive work' in external workplaces. Some urban schools, for example, go *en masse* to rural areas at harvest time for a period of thirty to forty-five days to work on agriculture tasks. Other schools are attached to factories and students work at the factory for several hours a week (Blum, 1985; Richmond, 1983, p. 105).

As well as serving revolutionary pedagogy, the productive work undertaken by students is expected to yield direct economic benefits. Indeed, Castro has advanced the notion that, in an underdeveloped country, 'the application of the principle of universal study is possible only to the extent that work is also made universal'. In practice, as Richmond (1983, p. 104) notes, this idea that education could come to pay for itself now looks much too optimistic. Nonetheless, the economic contribution made by the students is important to the students themselves, as Moorman (1976) observed:

> The study/work arrangements appear popular with the pupils. All those I spoke to — freely and at random — emphasised the sense of fulfilment they got from the responsibilities they were given. It was the visible and concrete contribution they were making to the wellbeing of the country which seemed of most importance to them.

It is also worth noting that the relationship between schools and workplaces is not one-way. Under the *padrino* system, a school is adopted by a nearby work unit such as a factory, which provides various services and voluntary help on such matters as repairs, transportation, and celebrations. These *padrinos* provide children 'with practical, visual confirmation of the workers and peasants as revolutionary altruists' (Leiner, 1975, p. 68). Their workers thus serve as role models of 'a worker who sets an example through his voluntary work, his concern for others, the importance he attaches to education, and his overall social responsibility' (Richmond, 1983, p. 108).

Australia

Work experience in Australian schools developed in the early 1970s, along lines which seem to have been very similar to those in Britain. In Victoria in 1970, only nine schools were engaging in work experience of some kind; but by 1974, eighty-four schools had implemented work-experience programmes (Cole, 1979, p. 33). It was in 1974 — the same year as in Britain — that the Education (Work Experience) Act was passed legalizing and formalizing the programmes. The result of this, and of growing concern about unemployment, was that by 1979 the number of schools running work-experience schemes in Victoria had grown to 524, and by the mid-1980s it was unusual for a post-primary school not to have such a programme (Watkins, 1987, p. 29).

One difference from UK experience is that many students in Australian work-experience schemes receive payment, if usually at a minimal level:

> The students' remuneration for the period of work experience can range from nothing for a governmental or local service organization to $50.00 or more a week. Private employers must pay a minimum

wage of $3.00 per day. This is mainly to satisfy the requirements for Workers' Compensation and a Workers' Compensation form has to be completed for each student and signed by the school principal. To satisfy Workers' Compensation requirements when working for a service organization the students agree to donate any payments back to the organization (*ibid*, p. 29).

The main interest of the Australian work-experience literature from a UK perspective is the greater concern that has been shown in Australia in the ideological underpinnings of work experience. Nash (1980, p. 20) points out that in the schools in which work experience first appeared, it was seen 'as an integral part of a restatement of the purposes of schools'. In particular, this restatement aligned itself with the concern expressed by Coleman (1972) in the USA: it 'recognised the fragmented nature of our society, and was concerned to establish a form of education for children which would reverse the established trend of their increasing isolation from adult culture and society' (Nash, 1980, p. 20). Some of the pioneering schools also saw it as being a means through which students could be assisted to explore their community and critically to examine various elements of society.

Gradually, however, such radical intentions were overtaken by others which were more concerned to socialize the young to the demands of the work-place, so correcting mismatches between school and work. Thus Nash (1980, p. 27) argued that 'although it may be recognised that work experience can serve a variety of purposes, it is the narrow employment purposes rather than the broader educative ones which are being attended to by the great majority of work experience programmes'. Watkins (1980) supported this view, affirming that in practice work-experience programmes acted as an agent of social control, encouraging students 'to forget their aspirations and to inculcate in them the correct attitudes needed for the fragmented, routine jobs of the workplace' (p. 41). Watkins accordingly saw work experience as a means through which the work-force could be more appropriately reproduced, the social relations in the work-place legitimated, and the goals and values of management internalized (Watkins, 1985, p. 57).

At the same time, Watkins' own research indicated the potential within work experience as a means of alerting students to, and enabling them to explore, 'forms of contestation' in the work-place — including both informal and formal forms of employee 'resistance' to employer demands (Watkins, 1987). (The same point has been demonstrated in Canada by Simon [1983] and Simon and Dippo [1987].) As Sharp (1982, pp. 74–5) put it: 'The class dimensions of the workplace, its sexual and ethnic divisions, its hierarchy, the social impact of technology, and the labor process itself are all easier to discuss when students have direct experience of everyday labor routines'. Cole (1983), too, suggests that work-experience programmes should shift their focus from socializing students into prevailing attitudes and values, and instead should focus on the social processes of work and on the relationship between school and work (see also Kemmis, Cole and Suggett, 1983). One of the implications of this is that they should shift their main orientation from *experience* to *enquiry* (Cole, 1987).

USA

The scale and diversity of the American school system makes it difficult to identify a coherent picture of how work experience fits into the system. Hoyt *et al.* (1977) distinguished three broad kinds of programmes:

(a) *Work-study programmes*, which provide economically disadvantaged students with part-time work so that they can earn enough money to remain in school.

(b) *Cooperative education programmes*, which create an active relationship between employer and school, in which both cooperate to prepare the student for particular areas of employment. Typically, the student's day is divided roughly evenly between the school, which focuses on job-related knowledge, and the work site, which offers training in skills and attitudes.

(c) *Experience-based career education* (EBCE), which typically requires sampling of various jobs and sharing of impressions among students. Such programmes tend to be individualized and competency-based: programmes are designed for students to acquire specific academic skills through projects completed mainly at the work-site. The focus tends to be more on work attitudes than on work skills, and occupational choice is also an important focus.

Of these, (c) seems much the most relevant to our concerns. Shatkin, Weber and Chapman (1980, p. 132) point out, however, that 'many individual school programs are difficult to categorise, and terminology is not standardized'.

The American mania for measurement means that they have much more data than do other countries on the effects of work-experience programmes (see Chapter 14). On the other hand, their narrow adherence to classical research paradigms is particularly inappropriate to interventions which are so diverse in nature. As Crowe and Adams (1979) point out, such paradigms assume standardized interventions, the conditions of which can be controlled, and which are designed to lead to predictable effects. None of these elements are present in the case of work-experience programmes. As a result, the use of such methods 'has encouraged us to examine hypothesized effects of programs without learning much about what really happened in the program, what students actually learned, why the program worked or failed, or what features of the program were most and least effective' (*ibid*, p. 88).

Nonetheless, the main results of the evaluations that have been conducted of the EBCE programmes are worth noting. They show that students who participate in the programmes enjoy them and — in comparison with other students — have more positive opinions of their high-school experiences with regard to career preparation. In addition, such programmes have a strong, immediate impact on students' acquisition of information about the world of work, and a positive effect on their attitudes towards both school and work. Their effects on students' academic performance tend to be neutral or even marginally positive, despite the fact that the students are out of the classroom for substantial periods of time. Accordingly, work experience seems to be a way of introducing youngsters to the world of work without compromising their academic progress. In addition, it helps students to feel a greater sense of control over their career decisions. When the programmes are modified to meet the needs of potential high-school drop-outs (i.e. economically disadvantaged and ethnic-minority groups), they appear to help to keep such students in school (Owens, 1982).

A further evaluation study which is worth noting covered a variety of experiential education programmes, including community service and adventure education as well as work experience (Conrad and Hedin, 1981). The programmes which showed the strongest impact on student learning were those which featured a combination of direct experience and formal reflection on the experience. Indeed, the best single predictor of programme success, across all the programme types, was the accompaniment of a regular classroom seminar.

These findings are particularly significant in relation to distinguishing structured work-experience programmes from other forms of adolescent work experience. Steinberg (1984, p. 12) points out that

the actual job experiences of young people in career education and government-sponsored programs are not very different from those of their peers working in the part-time labor force. In all three cases, adolescents typically perform highly routinized, repetitive work with few opportunities for decision-making or learning.

What seems to make the difference, therefore, is the level of integration with the curriculum. Indeed, these findings seem to have stimulated Steinberg to modify his earlier conclusion that, in the light of the research evidence, policy-makers should 'jump off the work experience bandwagon' (Steinberg, 1982).

Conclusion

The only theoretical explanation we have been able to find in the literature of why some countries introduce work experience into schools while others do not, and why some do so at some points and for some groups but not others, is Watkins' suggestion that 'work experience can be related to the periodic economic crises that afflict, particularly, western societies and the consequent legitimation and motivation crises that develop' (Watkins, 1985, p. 54). He links this to the thesis developed by Lazerson and Grubb (1974) in relation to vocational education in the US context: that the cyclical concern with vocationalism is a response to economic crisis. In relation to work experience *per se*, Watkins draws here not only on Australian experience but also on a study by Palmer (1979) of the history of work-experience programmes in the USA and the USSR. Palmer argued that 'work-experience education served similar purposes in both countries':

> During periods when an imbalance between social and economic life
> threatened stability, work-experience was introduced as a stabilizer.
> At other times when contradictions between what society was and
> what it claimed to be were being detailed, work-experience educa
> tion was proposed as a way to transcend this dichotomy. On the
> other hand, work-experience education also served to introduce or
> reinforce social and economic stratification.

The options covered by Palmer's categories are sufficiently broad and varied that they do not do much to clarify the issue. Moreover, Watkins' singling out of Western societies does not seem to be justified by the evidence that we have adduced of the relationship between work experience and economic crises in, for example, Cuba and the USSR. A more illuminating way of examining the question may be to look at countries which have *not* introduced work experience and to ask why this is so. In the case of Japan, for instance, it would seem that the articulation of the education system to the world of work is managed through other mechanisms, notably the elaborate industrial training system, and that this enables the education system to remain within tight academic confines, its main vocational purpose being to act as a selection device (Watts, 1985). In other countries with less conspicuously successful economies, including Third World countries, the same effect seems to appear, but for different reasons: it is as though establishing more operational linkages between the worlds of education and work would risk exposing the tensions between the two which a clear separation is able at least to contain (see Dore, 1976). We therefore suggest that work experience is most likely to be introduced where the relationship between education and work is viewed as problematic, but where there is confidence that the problems may be solved or at least alleviated by seeking new forms of interpenetration between the two sectors.

Our review of work experience in other countries has also illuminated a number of other issues which are currently subjects of debate in relation to work experience in Britain. In the first place, it is clear that it cannot be regarded as a creature of any particular ideology. It has attracted support from both the right and the left of the political spectrum. Moreover, while both the East German and the Australian evidence suggests that it tends to be adaptive in its effects, the Australian evidence also indicates that it has the potential for a more critical stance, and indeed such a stance has been officially legitimated in Sweden.

A second issue is whether work experience should be for all students or only for some. In a number of countries, including France, Luxembourg and West Germany, it seems to be viewed as more appropriate for 'less academic' students; in other countries, it is seen as being valid for all students, including the academically able. Britain is currently moving towards the latter position: this would seem to be supported by the American evidence which suggests that work experience does not have any negative effects on academic performance, and so can be viewed as a way of introducing students to the world of work without adversely affecting their academic progress.

Thirdly, it is noticeable that in several countries work experience is regarded as legitimately making an important contribution to students' career choices. This contrasts with the situation in Britain, where the career 'sampling' function of work experience has been regarded as subsidiary and even rejected altogether in official statements (see p. 20), even though its value is often perceived by students in these terms (Watts, 1983, ch. 6). It is also worth noting, however, that in three of the countries where emphasis was placed on the careers aspect — Denmark, Sweden and the USSR — it was allied with an emphasis on the importance of students experiencing several placements, thereby viewing it as a means of extending rather than narrowing their range of options. In addition, it is interesting that when Sweden moved towards this broadening approach, it decided to cease permitting students to choose their own placement for sampling purposes and instead opted to allocate placements on a random basis (pp. 198–9). The concern to counteract gender stereotyping was given particular importance in this respect.

Finally, the issue of the tension between 'learning' and 'production' is illuminated in a number of ways by the examples we have cited. In Cuba and the USSR, work experience has at times been explicitly legitimated on the basis not only of its learning effects but also of its contribution to production. At other times, however, the learning emphasis has been strengthened, and in some cases this has led towards alternatives based more firmly inside the education system. These alternatives have included practices which strike chords with British practices: the USSR production–training combines run by groups of schools would seem to have clear similarities with work practice units (Jamieson, Miller and Watts, 1988, ch. 6), and the Cuban *padrino* system would seem to have affinities with the concept of the 'working coach' developed by the Grubb Institute (Reed and Bazalgette, 1983). Similar trends towards more education-based alternatives seem to have occurred in East Germany.

The relationship between 'learning' and 'production' is not a simple one. We have noted elsewhere the paradox that if the outcomes of the work are seen by students as being 'for real' — i.e. production ones — the students may be more highly motivated, and the learning yield may accordingly be the greater (Jamieson, Miller and Watts, 1988, p. 159; see also this volume, p. 16). This would seem to be supported by the reactions we have reported from students in Cuba. On the other hand, we also attach considerable significance to the American evidence that the most effective programmes were those that were accompanied by opportunities for reflection and enquiry. While the issue of how best to integrate work experience into the curriculum remains problematic in Britain as elsewhere, this evidence reinforces the view that it is the key to learning effectiveness.

Chapter 4

The Changing World of Work

Ian Jamieson

The existence of work-experience programmes in schools assents to two important facts: first, that work is of central importance in our society; and secondly, that young people and schools are systematically insulated from the institutions and processes of work. Juxtaposed in this sharp way, these two 'facts' do not sit easily together. If it is true that work is of central concern to members of our society (whether they happen to be working or not), then it is strange that schools, whose function is usually understood to include inducting young people into the major aspects of the society, should be so distant from the working world. This chapter will attempt to explain how this separation came about in the UK, and how the world of work emerged as a distinctive segment of modern industrial society, largely distinct from the family household and the institution of schooling.

The major part of the chapter will be spent describing and analyzing the present organization of work in British society, set in the context of the world economy. To comprehend such a description, it is of course necessary to understand how we have arrived at where we are. This is perhaps particularly true in the case of Britain which, it is often argued, bears the strong (and unhelpful) marks of its historical past (cf. Wiener, 1981). History is also important because it can show us in a concrete way that our present arrangements are not set in stone: that the present ways in which we organize work, schooling and family life, for example, can be changed, because at one time they were in fact quite different.

Whatever the curricular frameworks for work experience, for some young people it will be their first direct introduction to the working world outside the home and school. An important question to ask is to what extent the students and their teachers comprehend this complex and changing world. In this chapter we set out to chart its distinctive features and thereby to raise some issues which may be relevant in particular to the preparation and follow-up stages of work-experience schemes (see Chapter 12). The chapter surveys materials on the following areas:

- The gradual emergence of industrial society from pre-industrial and proto-industrial forms.
- Decentralization of work.
- The effect of technology on the work-place.
- Organized labour and the trade unions.
- The small-business and self-employed sector.
- The youth labour market.
- Gender and ethnic divisions in the labour market.
- Values and the world of work.
- The implications of these changes for work experience.

The historical record does not divide itself into neat historical stages like pre-industrial and industrial. History is a Heraclitean flux and historians interrupt the flow by the imposition of 'periods' or 'stages' for their own convenience. We shall do the same in order to draw out the key features of work and working relationships in different historical periods, in full knowledge of the fact that we are doing a certain amount of violence to the continuity of the historical process. It is for analytical convenience only that we consider the form and social relations of work in four broad periods of Western society: pre-industrial, proto-industrial, industrial, and late-industrial (i.e. today). Our analysis is confined to Western society merely because the prime focus of this volume is on work experience in British schools.

Pre-industrial Society

Pre-industrial society presents the greatest difficulties. The convention is to cover a period from the thirteenth century to somewhere around the middle of the eighteenth century: a period of some 500 years. Such societies were agricultural in the sense that the central economic tasks involved working with land, animals and their products.

For this period, both work tasks and occupations defy easy categorization: men, women and children performed a mix of tasks at home and in the local economy, and they possessed a wide variety of work skills. These included a range of agrarian skills, and skills relating to animal husbandry as well as domestic manufacture and repair. Soap, candles, garments, shoes, dairy produce and handicraft products were all made within the household. The essential work unit was, indeed, the household. This meant that work was organized not only on a cooperative basis for the immediate family, but for the extended family as well. People were expected to pool their efforts with both their relatives and their neighbours in the village (Watkins, 1987).

Even in describing this situation, we are using concepts and ideas which would have been alien to the period. The concept of work is a good example. For the great bulk of the population living a rural life and absorbed with agricultural tasks, work and leisure were as one. Not only was there no real distinction between work and non-work, but the home was not separate from the work-place. Similarly, there were not 'two opposed modes of time-consciousness, "working time" and "one's own" or "free time"' (Giddens, 1981, p. 137). Instead the day was filled with activities and tasks which were not artificially divided but which instead related to the seasons, the rhythms of nature and the needs of people.

The nature of work in pre-industrial society and its central location in and around the household had important implications for social relations between members of the household economy. As Pahl (1988) argues, 'in practice households in pre-industrial England, as elsewhere, had to be based on an economic partnership between men and women and other household members' (p. 10). Children were very much part of this equation from an early age — they entered the production cycle in one form or another as soon as they were able. An American historian quoting from an eighteenth-century account of America observed that 'upon the birth of a son, they exult in the gift of a ploughman or a waggoner; and upon the birth of a daughter they rejoice in the addition of another spinster or milkmaid to the family' (Stern *et al.*, 1975, p. 95). Children acquired the skills and knowledge necessary to perform in the household economy from members of their extended family.

Seen from some modern perspectives, such an existence might appear to have a lot of attractions — cooperative working close to nature, and making use of a wide range of skills and knowledge, strikes chords with many who currently feel discontented with their work in large, hierarchical companies that practise an extreme division of labour (for a discussion of such Taylorism/Fordism, see p. 60). But we must beware of the picture of the happy, dancing peasant of 'Merrie England'. Although Pahl (1988) warns us that 'historians find it impossible to evaluate the quality of working life for ordinary people in pre-industrial times', he is sufficiently confident to assure us that 'there was no pre-industrial golden age of satisfying work'.

Proto-industrialization

The term 'proto-industrialization' refers to the argument that there was an intermediate period before the development of the full factory system which is the heart of industrialization (Medick, 1976). This transition phase is typified by the development of work in rural cottage industries in which work was 'put out' by an entrepreneur and taken up by the rural workers to supplement the income they received from their basic agricultural work. In this way, many rural families still continued to work their farms whilst also becoming proto-typical industrial workers who spun or wove materials supplied by the entrepreneurs (Watkins, 1987).

The basic features of the household economy that we have described in the pre-industrial period more or less transferred to this new stage. The workers had a good deal of flexibility and autonomy in their work — they adjusted their hours, effort and tasks to suit their economic situation and the natural rhythms of agricultural work. The sexual division of labour remained very flexible, which is not to say that it was non-existent. Men were often lacemakers and spinners, while women were occupied with the organizing and marketing of the products. In this way, men often took on work conventionally associated with women in the home. The drive to obtain additional income from family work meant that sometimes 'men ... cook, sweep and milk the cows, in order never to disturb the good, diligent wife in her work' (Medick, 1976, p. 312). The irregular work patterns not only meant a high degree of autonomy for the workers but also allowed a degree of flexibility whereby they could 'sub-contract' to children and young people. The very young might draw the wires on the loom, while the older children would be employed as half-weavers — a form of apprenticeship (Watkins, 1987).

This proto-industrialization merged only very gradually into the factory system which centralized production in one place and attracted workers to its location. So widespread was the industrial household model that it has been estimated that even in the early 1840s in England over three-quarters of industrial work derived from these 'diverse, dispersed and unspectacular industries' (Hartley, 1982, p. 268). Chambers (1968) has argued that 'the victory of the factory over the older forms of industrial organization was slow and it was not until the last decades of the [nineteenth] century that it became the dominant form of organization in a majority of industries' (p. 15).

Industrial Society

The essence of industrial society is the factory system — the organization of mechanized production in a single location. This transformation, which began in England around 1750, was slow, and it was not until the second half of the nineteenth century that the majority of the working population were engaged in tasks connected with manufacturing. This meant that craft work, work at home, and contracting all existed side by side with the mill and the factory.

Worker Discipline

One of the central problems faced by managers and workers alike in this new form of work organization was the discipline that was required to run the factory efficiently. Indeed, the slow development of the factory system has been linked by a number of historians (notably Thompson, 1967) to the problems of irregular work habits and the persistence of pre-industrial craft patterns of work in the early factories. Factory owners who had centralized work had great difficulty in educating their workers to differentiate between their leisure time and their work time. In these early factories, the conflict between the timing of work in domestic industry and on the factory floor intensified. Landes (1983) argues that 'from the 1770s on an increasing number of workers found themselves employed in jobs that required them to appear by a set time every morning and work a day whose directions and wage were a function of the clock' (p. 229). Mumford (1973) emphasizes the point in his observation that 'the clock, not the steam engine, is the key machine of the modern industrial age' (p. 271), and it was one of Britain's early industrialists, Josiah Wedgewood, who sought to curtail the unpredictable attendance habits of his employees in his pottery factories by introducing the clocking-in system.

One of the fundamental problems of factory organization was that of discipline and control. Pahl (1988, p. 168) argues that workers were bound to the discipline of wage labour by their expanding needs as consumers and by the lack of alternative ways of maintaining their families and dependants. But it was one thing to ensure that workers came to the factory on time and were docile and obedient to the demands of the management; it was quite another matter to make sure that they worked hard and conscientiously. There were a variety of 'solutions' to this problem, reflected in the wide variety of managerial styles, structures and strategies adopted by industrial employers. Some certainly believed that only be keeping the work-force in poverty and degradation could motivation be assured. Others, like the Quakers and other Nonconformists who had large and flourishing family businesses, were more concerned to use carrots rather than sticks to ensure the commitment of their work-force, and such examples of benevolent paternalism can be found in most industrial nations.

There is an important conclusion to be drawn from these various practices. There is no 'logic of industrialism', i.e. a set of social arrangements that can be read back from the requirements of particular technology. As Pollard (1963) has argued, work in the factories could have been developed along more traditional lines, reinforcing the autonomy of skilled workers (as it did in many 'professional' jobs). Instead the new business class largely decided to 'set to work against them, to reject them as unusable and to crush them, starting afresh with what it was hoped would be a new human material, educated and broken in for new needs' (pp. 52–3).

Industrialization is primarily concerned with the impact of the technology of manufacture on the work-force and society, and the technologies have often confronted the autonomy of skilled workers and traditional modes of organization. These stresses were there at the beginning. It has been argued that the Luddites of the early nineteenth century were not against technology *per se*, but against the breaking of apprenticeship rules and wage agreements, and employer hostility to their unions. The Luddites believed that the new techniques of production enhanced neither the quality of products nor the quality of their own working lives (Webster and Robins, 1986).

Against this background, employers were constantly engaged in seeking out new rationales and techniques to control their work-force. In the early part of the twentieth century, attempts were made to develop a system of 'scientific management' to provide the justification and the means of extending control over the labour process. This line of thought found its clearest expression in the work of F.W. Taylor. The theoretical underpinning of Taylorism was provided by Babbage who in 1835 wrote the following: 'The manufacturer, by dividing the work to be executed into different processes, each requiring different degrees of skill and force, can purchase exactly that precise quantity of both which is necessary for each person' (Babbage, 1971 edn., pp. 175–6). Taylor focused his considerable skills on the work tasks to be performed in order that these tasks might be constructed and performed in the most efficient manner. He used time-and-motion study to effect this and then linked output very closely to pay via wage-incentive schemes. Such procedures were adopted by a large number of manufacturers, and the apotheosis of the system was found at the Ford moving assembly line at Highfield Park, USA, where the Model T Ford was assembled. Two important images of industrialism are embodied in this approach: the extreme division of labour; and the control of the work-force by management as symbolized by the stop-watch and chart of the time-and-motion-study expert.

The picture of industrial management that is portrayed here is one that is virtually omniscient: Braverman (1974) in particular finds little difficulty in writing of the de-skilling of workers and the degradation of work that has followed Taylorism and Fordism. Such a picture is deeply flawed. In particular, it neglects the organized opposition to such managerial behaviour: in Britain, for example, the existence of strong union organization in the major branches of production limited the spread of time-and-motion study (Wood and Kelly, 1982). It also neglects the informal opposition of the shop-floor workers that nearly everywhere frustrated the precise specification of work roles and tasks. Although industrial management was certainly influenced by both Taylorism and Fordism, it is important not to underestimate the success of organized opposition to such practices.

Organized Labour

Workers managed to resist the will of employers by both formal and informal means. The traditional formal mechanism has been through the trade unions — organized labour's method of bargaining with powerful employers. Trade unions had their origins in the pre-industrial period. Although there is some debate about the influence of the feudal guilds on British trade unionism, what does seem reasonably clear is that in every Western

European country the tradition of collective grouping and collective action in social and economic life was thoroughly implanted as part of the old feudal and guild influences.

The influence of the guilds was reflected in the growth of the first trade unions in Britain, which were organized around skilled craftsmen. Two features need to be emphasized here: the craft unions were exclusively for *skilled* workers; and they were almost exclusively for *men*. These craft unions bequeathed two very important legacies to the British trade-union movement. First, as *craft* unions they cut across industries and so effectively prevented the development of industrial unions (where one union represents all the workers in an industry). Secondly, by neglecting less skilled workers, they encouraged the development of general unions which were prepared to enrol unskilled and semi-skilled workers as union members. These origins meant that Britain developed a more complex trade-union structure than in many other countries. This is true even for white-collar trade unions, which mirrored the blue-collar union structure when they began to develop after the First World War.

In 1892, when official statistics were first compiled, trade-union membership totalled 1.5 million (just over 11 per cent of the labour force). It then grew rapidly just before and during the First World War, to more than 8 million members; declined to about half that number by the early 1930s; and grew during the Second World War to reach just over 9 million (45 per cent of the work-force) in the United Kingdom in 1948 (Price and Bain, 1983). This figure remained little changed until the late 1960s: because the labour force increased by some 2.5 million during the post-war period, this meant a decline in union density.

Union membership in the post-war era remained much more common among male employees than among females, and among manual workers than among white-collar workers. Though the number of white-collar workers who were members of a union increased by nearly a million between 1948 and 1968, this did not quite keep pace with the growth in white-collar employment (Brown, 1984). In 1968, union density was almost 50 per cent for manual workers, 33 per cent for white-collar workers, and 28 per cent for female workers (Price and Bain, 1983).

Women and Work

In the early years of industrial manufacture, women and children were used extensively as labour; in the period which we have labelled proto-industrialization, there was a sense in which the household transferred to the factory. By about the middle of the nineteenth century, however, it became unusual for married women to seek paid work. For an atypical period of 100 years until the middle of the twentieth century, households were dependent on a male chief earner who was, in theory, paid a family wage to support his wife and children and possibly elderly dependants as well. The single woman who did work for wages remained in the work-force for only a few years before marriage. Pahl (1988), along with other writers, believes that this shift to the male worker is a complex phenomenon to explain. Why did not the process of industrialization weaken rather than strengthen the sexual division of labour?

> Why should employers care if their employees were male or female, so long as they could pay as little for the necessary skills as possible? It would be, one would think, in the interests of employers to introduce women into what had begun to be thought of as 'male trades' (Curthoys, 1987, p. 10).

There are at least three separate arguments which help to account for the phenomenon in question. The first argument centres on the requirements of male workers. As Pahl (1988) argues:

> If workers are well fed and cared for and are kept in good health they will operate more efficiently. 'Providing for' a wife and children is likely to be a stabilising factor on incipient rebels and is also likely to encourage commitment to employment and a willingness to work hard and long. Furthermore, if workers are individually cared for in individual homes their propensity to acquire and to consume goods and services may be enhanced (p. 13).

A second view suggests that many employers would have introduced cheaper female employees into traditional male trades and occupations if they had been able, but that they were blocked by male trade unions which were anxious to keep up the price of their (male) labour. Some historians have interpreted these actions as male sexism (Barrett and Macintosh, 1980; Hartmann, 1976), whilst others have argued that the exclusion of women from male trades was, in the environment of nineteenth-century industrial capitalism, a defence of the family wage and therefore of the family (Humphries, 1977).

The final approach stresses the humanitarian concerns of individual employers who began to see and feel the contrast between the position of their own wives at home and the degradation of female employment in their factories. Such feelings may have been intensified during the period of the shift to heavy manufacturing, when the conditions were right for the wider diffusion of the bourgeois view that the role of women was in the home.

From the point of view of labour-market participants, the 'costs' of having children have largely been borne by women. When production was located in and around the household, this was not a significant constraint except in the very early years; but when production moved outside the home, the problem of child-care became more significant. As we have seen, in the early days of industrialization many aspects of the household economy, including working children, transferred to the factory. There is a lot of evidence that in this period child and female labour was much valued: employers both in Britain and in America found children and women more industrious, more obedient and more reliable than male labour (Stern, Smith and Doolittle, 1975, p. 101).

Schooling and Work

As the proportion of women in the industrial labour force gradually shrank, so did the proportion of children. The regulation of children's employment, largely for humanitarian reasons but also to protect male employment, began in England at the very beginning of the nineteenth century. In 1802 the Health and Morals of Apprentices Act was passed, and in 1819 a minimum age for factory employment was enacted. As children were gradually withdrawn from full-time employment, so more of them began to attend some form of schooling.

In the context of nineteenth-century England (or America, Canada or Australia — cf. Hurt, 1981) it would be quite wrong to see a sharp dichotomy between schooling and work. The argument for mass schooling in the nineteenth century was largely concerned with the need for social stability. This need was partly a function of the effects of the industrial revolution itself: as the cities filled up, crime and disorder increased, and poverty became more visible (Kaestle, 1976). Of course, social stability, or at least deference and discipline, were regarded by employers as highly desirable attributes of workers. The arguments for education in relation to specific skills were to come much later in the century. Most manufacturing occupations required modest skills which could be rapidly acquired on the job — the more complex tasks were dealt with by the apprenticeship system.

There were many influential figures in the nineteenth century who believed that work and education should be combined. We have already quoted in Chapter 3 (p. 43) Marx's comments about Robert Owen and the merits of combining 'productive work with instruction and gymnastics'. Certainly these arguments were among those used by the proponents of the 'half-time' system of education, whereby children in factories received education for half a day. Such legislation effectively began in 1833, and the half-time system remained until 1918. It covered a wide variety of industries, including textiles, foundries, metal manufacture, tobacco and mining. Views of the 'efficiency' of such schooling varied widely. Some argued that it was as efficient as full-time schooling, which was made compulsory in 1876. The major arguments were that the three hours fitted the attention span of children, and that all that it was necessary for such working children to know could be learned in half-time schooling. Some of the school inspectors took a more jaundiced view and reported children asleep at their desks. There were many, however, who kept alive the spirit of Robert Owen. In 1870, Lyon Playfair looked forward ambitiously to the conversion — under a system of compulsory education for all children — of half-time factory schools 'into useful secondary schools to teach the principles of science and art relating to the actual industries of the half-timers' (quoted in Silver, 1977).

The half-time system was by no means the only schooling available in the nineteenth century. Laqueur (1976) estimated that in 1818 some 6.5 per cent of the relevant population were in school and that by 1851 this had climbed to 13 per cent. Many of these children attended private schools rather than the public elementary schools despite the fact that they had to pay. The reasons for this are revealing. It showed in the first place that working-class parents believed that such schools did manage to teach the rudiments of literacy and numeracy. Of greater significance, however, the private schools were much more part of the communities in which they lived; they understood the difficulties that poor working-class parents had in sending their children to school clean and tidy; and of even greater importance, they understood the complex balance between the necessity of children working to supplement the household income and acquiring the rudiments of an education. The public elementary schools were much less sensitive to these factors and consequently suffered in attendance. Hurt (1981) estimates that on any one day in 1870 half the children of school age would not have been in a classroom of a public elementary school. Instead they would have been at home helping in household tasks, at work, or part of the 'youthful street culture' (p. viii). Attendance was sporadic for working-class children for the whole of the nineteenth century; school had to fit into the 'context of a relationship between the demands of the labour market, the sexual division of labour within the family economy, and the continually asserted strong belief in the right of the parent to control the use of the child's time' (*ibid*, p. viii).

The World of Work Today

The Distribution of Employment

It is common to claim that we are entering a new era or period in which radical changes in the nature of work and its organization are transforming society. The terminology either asserts that we are nearing the end of a period ('late' industrialism or 'late' capitalism), or that we have actually left it ('post-industrialism'). Certainly there are unmistakable signs that some aspects of work, and the distribution of types of jobs, have undergone large changes. Agriculture now employs less than 2 per cent of the population. Manufacturing remained a central employer of labour from the turn of the century to the 1970s, employing roughly 40 per cent of the working population. Rapid changes occurred during the 1970s, however, and by the end of the 1980s employment in manufacturing industry had fallen to only 25 per cent of the working population. As manufacturing has declined in importance, so the service sector (excluding the old public utilities and construction) has grown, so that some 65 per cent of the population is now employed in this sector.

So much is the conventional wisdom, but the traditional categories of the employment statisticians conceal a great deal, and an increasing number of commentators are questioning the wisdom of these traditional categorizations. This is particularly the case with the 'service' sector, which seems to have little coherence as a category. Originally the service sector constituted a relatively small number of people who literally 'served'; today it constitutes occupations as diverse as motor mechanics, computer programmers, nurses and bankers (cf. Gershuny, 1978; Jones, 1982). One of the most dramatic changes which has occurred in manufacturing industry, for example, has been the growth of white-collar 'administrative' jobs which we often presume are the province of the service sector. Between 1948 and 1981, for instance, the proportion of administrative, technical and clerical workers in manufacturing industry increased from 16 per cent to almost 30 per cent (Central Statistical Office, 1983, p. 119). Furthermore, not all aspects of the service sector have grown — private domestic service, for example, has shrunk dramatically.

The enormous absolute and relative increase in the numbers of non-manual workers is probably the most dramatic and important change in the occupational structure. Of the greatest quantitative importance have been the growth in employment in 'clerical' occupations, and the expansion of broadly 'commercial' occupations, e.g. in the financial services sector (Brown, 1984). Until the Thatcher Government began its enormous privatization programme, another important element in the shift to white-collar occupations had been the growth of public-sector employment, which covered about one-third of all employees in 1980. Finally, there has been both a relative and an absolute growth in the number of 'professional' employees, particularly in the number of people in the newer professions based on science and technology.

Decentralization

Many of these long-term shifts can be seen in all highly industrialized societies as mechanization and other technical and organizational developments allow greater productivity first in agriculture and then in the manufacture of goods. There is evidence, too, that some of these changes 'reflect a more general "international division of labour", whereby manufacturing is increasingly being located in the less-developed societies of the world where labour costs are much lower' (Brown, 1984, p. 139). Such changes are not merely a reflection of technological developments, although changes in information technology allow better information flows within a business irrespective of spatial location. The first industrial revolution led to a high concentration of workers in large integrated plants in big industrial towns. This classic pattern is now undergoing fundamental change, as industrialists and economists are beginning to discover some of the 'diseconomies of scale'. This discovery has led to important moves to *decentralize* large areas of industrial production.

The term 'decentralization' is used to cover a variety of related processes. These include the 'expulsion of work formerly carried out in large factories to a network of small firms, artisans or domestic outworkers' (Murray, 1983, p. 260). It also includes the division of large integrated plants into small, specialized production units not necessarily all located on the same geographical site. Finally, it refers to the physical movement of plants away from old industrial areas to new 'green-field' sites, or even location in other countries with lower production costs.

Decentralization is the result of a number of processes. In the first place, developments in information technology make it technically feasible to decentralize. It is also the result of firms seeking cheaper production centres on a world-wide basis. General Motors' 'S' car, for example, was built in its European production network which employed 120,000 workers split up between thirty-nine plants in seventeen countries (Murray, 1983). The West German textiles industry makes extensive use of textile firms in Yugoslavia, where firms send out semi-finished products from Germany to be worked up into the final product. In southern Italy, West German firms making televisions contract out production of complete sets to medium-sized firms around Naples, and these firms in turn put out work to smaller firms in the area.

In Britain, the number of homeworkers and outworkers has continued to grow from an estimated 1.1 million in 1968 to 1.68 million in 1984 (Hakim, 1984). Hakim's study also showed that homeworking and outworking have followed national trends in that they are much more prevalent in the service sector than in manufacturing. Her study further showed that there were roughly equal numbers of men and women employed in homeworking, another sign that professional men are increasingly working from home.

The final reason for decentralization is concerned with the idea of creating a more flexible and malleable labour force. There are several dimensions to this. In Britain, firms are moving to green-field sites and areas of high unemployment with little tradition of unionization and union militancy. In other words, 'the reduction in factory size and the relocation of production are contingent upon the extent to which "unfavourable" industrial relations are an important reason for restructuring in different industries in different countries' (Murray, 1983, p. 263). Prais (1982), for example, suggests that factories in the UK with over 2,000 workers are fifty times more vulnerable to strikes than those with less than 100 workers. In addition to this, firms are trying to achieve flexibility in production by employing a core of polyvalent workers, i.e. people who are able to perform a range of tasks which cut across or extend traditional skill and job boundaries, and then employing a periphery of subcontractors, outworkers, part-time workers (mostly female) and other forms of temporary labour.

New Technology

It is widely believed that information technology (new technology) will accentuate many of these changes and further transform the nature of work in our society. Of course, it is easy to find examples where new technology has made significant changes in the work-place. The printing industry and the trading of financial services are good examples of almost total transformations, but such examples are notable for their rarity. For instance, there are very few current examples in the UK of completely computer-integrated manufacturing (CIM) plants or of flexible manufacturing systems (FMS) (Jones and Scott, 1987). Such systems where the whole business is computerized — manufacturing, warehousing and reordering of parts, as well as the financial and administrative systems — are 'state of the art' systems which are rare even in Japan and the USA. Even at a less sophisticated level, it would not be true to say that new technology has been transforming the work-place. By 1985, there were only 3,200 industrial robots in Britain, used by 740 firms (*The Times*, 17 February 1987). The degree of penetration is considerably higher in countries like Japan, the USA and West Germany, but even here they are not commonplace in manufacturing industry. Certain aspects of manufacturing technology have, however, been more affected by new technology than others. Computer numerically controlled (CNC) machines *are* commonplace, as is computer-aided design (CAD).

It is easier to see the effects of new technology in the world of the office than on the factory floor. It would certainly be true to say that more basic operations have been altered in office settings. This is because the nature of office tasks, centred on information flows, lend themselves to transformation by information technology, and because new technology is relatively cheap compared to that required in the factory. But although word processing, electronic data bases and systems of financial and stock control are commonplace, it is still relatively rare to find fully electronic or paperless offices.

In other parts of the working world not adequately covered by our distinction between the office and the factory, the same general picture emerges. Whilst it is possible to see specific applications of new technology which transform particular tasks — for example, electronic point-of-sale (EPOS) systems in shops, or electronic funds transfer (EFT) in banks, or even the use of expert systems by a widening range of professionals in areas like law, medicine and health — it is not yet possible to talk of a general transformation of the working world. As Jamieson and Tasker (1988) argue, 'the blue-collar and white-bloused workers of 1958 would find the working world of 1988 for the most part instantly recognisable' (p. 13). Such a picture should not surprise us: it mirrors the slow and uneven transformation of the first industrial revolution.

It is very difficult to predict what the effect of new technology will be on jobs and work. The early predictions of a workless society made redundant by the microchip (Nora and Minc, 1978; Sherman and Jenkins, 1979) now look deterministic and simple-minded. Most commentators seem to agree that the high levels of unemployment in many European countries are largely the result of economic recession rather than new technology. For example, a recent study of manufacturing industries by Northcott and Rogers (1985) has shown that, over a two-year period, information technology was directly implicated in some 34,000 job losses in Britain, 30,000 in West Germany and 12,000 in France. Many official estimates of job losses put the figures lower and point to corresponding job gains in industries supplying new technology (Williams, 1984), whilst estimates from the Institute of Manpower Studies at the University of Sussex come to a higher figure by including not only intra-firm displacement but also intra-industry displacement (Rajan, 1985; Rajan and Pearson, 1986).

It is impossible to say what the future employment prospects are for those students who are still at school. Although the number of 'doom scenarios' considerably outnumber those in the camp of the optimists, it is certainly possible to envisage considerable employment being created by the demand for new service products related to information technology (Gershuny, 1986). As Gershuny (1987) argues, 'if we adopt appropriate policies, the new technologies of the eighties need not be job displacing, any more than those of the thirties were' (p. 13). In the end, it is a question of policy not of technology.

If the production of job loss is one of the firmest predictions associated with new technology, then fear of the deskilling of large areas of work is also firmly entrenched in the futurologists' folklore, largely through the influential work of Braverman (1974). The majority of empirical studies of the effect of new technology on work skills fail to confirm the Braverman thesis. What they all show is the *complexity* of the world of work. As Sorge *et al.* (1983) show in their study, foremen, for example, can be downgraded to serve primarily as facilitators, ensuring that jigs, tools and materials are available; or they can be upgraded to use terminals to compile programs and to initiate changes in them. Jones (1982) has shown how the respective roles of workers, supervisors and programmers varied between plants all of which were undertaking small-batch engineering and using similar numerical control technology. The conclusion of the Institute of Manpower Studies enquiries in different industries on the effect of new technology on work skills was that in 50 per cent of the sampled firms the overall effect was neutral, in 30 per cent the net effect was one of reskilling, whilst only in the remaining 20 per cent was the net effect one of deskilling (Rajan, 1987).

Trade Unions

New technology has combined with other industrial changes to limit the scope of worker representation through trade unions. Although the picture was far from uniform across industrialized countries, the period from the mid-1950s to the mid-1970s had seen a big expansion of the scope and influence of worker representation, everywhere except in the United States. In Britain, union membership reached its high point in 1979 with 13 million, representing a density of 54.5 per cent (Lloyd, 1986). Since that point, membership has fallen steadily and in 1986 was only 9.2 million.

The reasons for this decline are to be found in the changing economic and industrial structures of our increasingly global society. Put at its simplest, it can be seen that the kinds of workers on which trade unions have traditionally based their membership — male, blue-collar, full-time and conveniently located on one site — have been in decline for the past thirty years. The kinds of worker which have been steadily increasing over the same period — female, white-collar, part-time and often off-site — are not joining the trade unions in sufficient numbers to make up the deficit.

In addition to these essentially structural characteristics, we should add others. Historically the unions have been strongest where there is a shortage of labour over which they have some control, but in the recent past unemployment has been relatively high and the British government has abandoned full employment as a first priority for its macro-economic strategy. Indeed, the government has attempted to weaken the power of the trade unions in a number of ways, on the grounds that they have been creating barriers to the efficient utilization of manpower and to job creation.

It is generally conceded that Britain's trade unions have been slow to adapt to these new conditions, although it is well recognized that recruiting and organizing peripheral workers and workers in small firms is difficult. Many unions still possess values and structures which are based on the recruitment of full-time, white, male, skilled workers. Furthermore, they possess few full-time officials and have a chronically low income. Evidence from countries like Canada and Sweden, which have experienced the same structural changes in the economy but have not witnessed a decline in trade unionism, show that the unions can survive if they adopt the right strategies and structures. Such strategies may well involve embracing the philosophy of 'business unionism', which entails providing a far wider range of services for their members and acting more like labour subcontractors to management.

Small Businesses and the Self-employed

One area in which trade unionism has never been strong is in the small-business and self-employed world. It is generally conceded that this sector of the economy has been growing in recent years. Certainly it is the case that the small-firms sector has had a lot of political attention focused on it. Storey and Johnson (1986) outline some of the reasons for this: a revival of liberal ideas about the market; a disenchantment with large corporations; worry about competition from abroad, particularly from Japan and the Pacific basin; a belief that the small-firms sector can generate a significant number of new jobs. Features of small business and self-employment which make them look attractive to some politicians include their structure of lower wages, their exemption from some areas of legislation, their greater flexibility in labour relations, and their greater malleability in adapting to new conditions and technology.

One of the problems in examining trends in this area of the economy is that there are no very clear definitions of what is to count as a small business. Numerous size categories for small firms have been used in research, legislation, and support and revenue policies over the years. The landmark report of the Bolton Committee (1971) used a variety of definitions according to sector, the best-known of which are the employment of 200 people or less for manufacturing firms, and a turnover of £50,000 or less for retailing. On these definitions (widely thought to be too high) around 4.4 million of the labour force were defined as being in the small-business sector, with another 1.6 million working in the sectors not covered by the report.

Curran (1986) argues that the census-of-production figures for 1963–81 show a distinct rise in the small-business sector, with 91.4 per cent of all firms being defined as small in 1963, and this figure rising to 97 per cent in 1980, albeit with a reduced importance in terms of output and employment. The self-employed are estimated to have grown 32 per cent between 1979 and 1984, and at 3 million by 1988 represented some 12 per cent of the labour force (CSO, 1989). A range of other developments will almost certainly encourage this growth: these include developments in franchising — 80,000 businesses in 1982 (Curran and Stanworth, 1982) — as well as in producer cooperatives, and in networking (see p. 77).

A recent study of small-business people and the self-employed by Curran *et al.* (1987), using the General Household Survey, produced evidence which contradicted many of the current stereotypes about people who work in this sector. The first finding is that the self-employed are much more numerous than small-business owners with employees — they outnumber them two to one, a figure support by Creigh *et al.* (1986). Small-business owners and the self-employed are under-represented in the 16–25 age group compared with the employed population. The proportion of women who work for themselves rather than as employees of somebody else is 6 per cent (i.e. less than half of the 14.5 per cent among men), and overall three-quarters of those who work for themselves are male. Curiously there are more women than men in the self-employed group aged under 35. The popular view of ethnic minorities being over-represented in the ranks of entrepreneurs is not sustained. The data on the educational background of respondents in the survey is interesting:

In general we can state that male small business owners and self-employed workers possess levels of education *lower* than that for male employees in the sample, whilst female small business owners and self-employed workers possess levels of education *higher* than that for female workers in the sample. (Curran *et al.*, 1987, p. 27)

The Youth Labour Market

It is commonly argued that the process of industrialization has created a gradual isolation of young people from the world of work and the labour market. The fundamental argument has been that as industrialization progresses, jobs become increasingly complex and technical, and require workers with increasing amounts of education and training. An immediate result of this process is that the full entry of young people to the labour market is postponed as they undergo increasing amounts first of education and then of training.

We have already seen that it is too simple to argue that jobs necessarily become more complex and technical during industrialization, although many clearly do. Furthermore, the association of young people with the labour market is much more complex than the term 'postponement' would imply. In fact, recent studies have clearly shown that many young people do participate in the world of work while still at school. In 1982/83, a Joint Low Pay Unit/Open University study of three different areas found that '40 per cent of all the children in the survey were working during term time in jobs other than baby-sitting, running errands, or other unregulated employment' (MacLennan, Fitz and Sullivan, 1985, p. 23); this figure rose to two-thirds if holiday jobs and jobs normally undertaken were included (the survey asked for jobs that were being done in the week of the survey only to be recorded). Other findings from this important study showed that boys were more likely to be so employed than girls, and that employment in the service sector of the economy predominated. Finally, the study showed that the majority of children in the survey appeared to be working illegally, perhaps confirming the view that the *intention* of the state in advanced industrialization is to postpone entry into employment.

When young people leave school and enter employment, they enter the labour market, but this labour market is segmented by age, gender and ethnicity. Dual labour-market theory (Bosanquet and Doeringer, 1973; Doeringer and Piore, 1971) sees the labour market as comprising two distinct sectors — a primary and a secondary sector. It identifies the primary labour market as being characterized by high rates of job mobility, a high degree of job security, and opportunities for career advancement. The characteristics of the secondary labour market are identified as low rates of pay, little or no access to training, a high degree of job insecurity, and little opportunity for career advancement. It has been argued that young people predominate in the secondary labour market, along with ethnic minorities, women, near-retirement-age workers, the unskilled, the poorly qualified and the disabled (Walker, 1982). Such a view seems altogether too simple, however. A significant proportion of young people have traditionally entered skilled trades located in the primary labour market, albeit as apprentices, and many middle-class children have taken a direct route to the primary labour market via further and higher education. Despite these reservations, the central idea of labour-market segmentation remains a useful one (Ashton, Maguire and Spilsbury, 1987).

Although the early job experiences of young people are affected by the vicissitudes of the general labour market, there are some distinctive features of the market for juvenile labour. Certain jobs are closed to young people, either because of legal restrictions or because of certain assumptions made about the young by employers. By contrast, other occupations are thought to be particularly appropriate for the young, e.g. apprenticeships or certain trainee positions. Here young people are preferred because their lower wages offset training costs and they are thought by employers to be more 'malleable' (Pilcher and Williamson, 1988).

One distinctive feature of the youth labour market is its *local* character. Studies have shown that the average distance travelled to work by young people is very low (a matter of two to three miles). The level of income of young people restricts their ability to use public and private transport, and means that they are unlikely to be able to afford to live away from home. Because of this fact, the early experience of work for young people is very much dependent on where they live (Ashton and Maguire, 1986).

Another distinctive feature of the labour market for young people is the existence of government training schemes, in particular the Youth Training Scheme and its successor Youth Training. YTS was introduced by the government as a 'permanent bridge between school and work'. It was aimed principally at 16–18-year-olds, whose labour — since their trainee allowance was paid by the state — was available at a subsidized rate to employers. This resulted in some employers recruiting YTS trainees instead of, rather than in addition to, regular intakes of young people. Some employers also incorporated YTS into their existing training strategies. These arrangements meant that the introduction and operation of the scheme led to reduced opportunities for the regular employment of young people, as employers increasingly relied upon the government to finance the training and employment of young people. In 1986/87, 63 per cent of 16- and 17-year-old school-leavers entered the labour market via YTS (CSO, 1989).

The Youth Training Scheme has made some attempts to combat ethnic and gender stereotyping, which affect the youth labour market as much as they do the market for adult labour. Young women earn less than young men of the same age. This is because young women tend to be concentrated in low-paid occupations like clerical work, selling, catering and cleaning.

Young men are employed in a much wider range of jobs and are more likely to be released by their employer during working hours to take part-time training courses.

The concentration of young women into a limited range of occupations was replicated in YTS. Around 80 per cent of young women were trained in the areas of clerical work, sales or catering, compared to 20 per cent of young men. On the other hand, around 45 per cent of young men on YTS were trained in maintenance, repair and manufacturing, compared to 7 per cent of young women (Pilcher and Williamson, 1988).

For young men, the status of adulthood has in the modern period been achieved through a job and the earning of a wage. For young women, the achievement of adult status has been more closely associated with marriage and children. There is some evidence to suggest that when faced with poor prospects in the labour market, young women may favour achieving adult status in this way (see Pilcher and Williamson, 1988).

Research on ethnic minorities and the youth labour market has consistently shown that, in most respects, their prospects are worse than those of white youth. Black and ethnic-minority youngsters have higher rates of unemployment than their white counterparts, and they also experience longer periods of unemployment. They are two to three times more likely to be unemployed than whites. The over-representation of black and ethnic-minority people in a limited number of low-level occupations and within certain industries means that they are at a greater risk of job loss in a time of economic change. It also means that, on average, black and ethnic-minority people earn less than whites. The existence of YTS seems to have done little to ameliorate this state of affairs.

Two basic causes of the poor labour-market position of ethnic minorities stand out. Discriminatory practices by employers are of central importance. Studies of identically qualified candidates for the same job have consistently found that black and ethnic-minority candidates are less successful than white candidates (Roberts, Duggan and Noble, 1983). Moreover, in periods of high unemployment, young black and ethnic-minority people are also at a disadvantage in terms of their access to jobs via informal networks, such as parents and friends, since unemployment amongst black and ethnic minorities is also much higher (Eggleston, Dunn and Anjali, 1986). Another important cause of racial inequality in the youth labour market is the fact that ethnic minorities tend to underachieve in the education system. In a labour market where qualifications are increasingly important, this obviously affects black and ethnic-minority young people's prospects.

The youth labour market, like the general labour market, is subject to general social, economic and industrial change. The state of the economy is the single most important factor influencing the demand for labour, and the British economy — like the world economy of which it is part — has undergone fluctuating fortunes in the last quarter-century. The late 1960s and early 1970s were times of relatively high demand for all labour. For example, in 1975, of the then 2 million 16–18-year-olds, over 70 percent were in employment; by 1985, an expanded age cohort had less than half of its members in employment. The recession of the 1970s marked the beginning of the decline in the level of youth employment. As we have already noted, output and employment in manufacturing, in which a large proportion of young people have traditionally been employed, declined rapidly. A rapid decline in the demand for labour means that young people, as new entrants to the labour market, are particularly vulnerable. Employers in general aim to cut back their work-forces to the most productive and cost-effective employees, leaving room for skilled and experienced staff only.

Demographic factors have also been an important influence on the supply side of the labour market. The 'baby boom' of the 1950s and 1960s led to a 20 per cent increase in the number 16–18-year-olds between the mid-1970s and the mid-1980s. At the beginning of the 1980s, the boom tailed off and a demographic dip began. The youth labour market is experiencing a drop of almost one-quarter which will last until the mid-1990s. All other things being equal, this should make it easier for young people to acquire jobs.

Social changes have also had an influence on the demand side of the youth labour-market equation. Since the 1970s, the number of women (particularly married women) entering the labour market has increased. Furthermore, these women are often competing for a range of jobs in the secondary labour market which have been the traditional province of young people. It is certainly the case that young people, as new entrants into the job market, have traditionally changed jobs frequently. Higher rates of unemployment have meant that the average number of jobs held by young people in their early years of labour-market participation has declined; however, the rate at which they leave jobs has not altered to the same extent (Pilcher and Williamson, 1988, p. 24). Another social factor which has influenced the labour-market participation of young people is their increasing participation in the education system beyond 16. Whereas in 1975, 25 per cent of 16–18-year-olds were in full-time education, by 1987 this had risen to 45 per cent (CSO, 1989).

Finally, we need to take note of a widespread set of beliefs that many employers have of young people as potential employees. These beliefs have often been coalesced and described as a deficiency theory of young people. On this view, young people are deficient in a range of qualities which would make them 'good workers'. The key qualities appear to relate to a set of *attitudes* towards employment which centre around an ethic of hard work and obedience. The hypothesized absence of such qualities is variously attributed to the nature of 'modern' schooling, and/or the shift in cultural values which took place during the 1960s. Politicians of the political right have termed this culture the 'permissive society' or, more pejoratively, 'yob culture'. A letter to *The Economist* from an English entrepreneur summed up this general view, suggesting that a key to solving the British economic problem was 'getting the education system to produce literate, numerate people who are taught the good old Protestant ethic' (quoted in Rose, 1985, p. 15). Careful historical studies suggest that complaints about the qualities of the young, particularly the lack of a work ethic, are hardly new (Rose, 1985). It is worries about the lack of a work ethic, and the belief that it can be 'caught' or acquired — or at least its importance appreciated — through contact with the work-place, that are some of the principal arguments that persuade employers and government of the value of work experience.

Gender and the Labour Market

It is fashionable to portray women workers as increasing their infiltration into the male-dominated world of work and beginning a slow transformation of work itself. The facts of women's role in the work-force of modern British society are more sobering. As Purcell (1988) persuasively argues, 'the overall pattern of gender segregation in British employment has remained surprisingly stable, despite the increase in female economic activity rates, the introduction of equal opportunities legislation, occupational diversification and industrial restructuring' (p. 160). In 1984, women made up 43 per cent of the total labour force; of these women, 69 per cent were married (Dex, 1985). Forty-five per cent of women's jobs were part-time. The average earnings of women are well below those of men in all major industrialized countries, including Britain: in 1983, the ratio of women's to men's full-time hourly earnings in Britain was 73:100 (Dex, 1988). Some changes have occurred in the scale of this differential, and the ratio is higher in the 1980s than it was in the 1950s and 1960s, but the basic nature of the differential persists.

Women tend to be concentrated in certain occupational categories. For example, they provide a large proportion of the labour force in semi-skilled factory work; they also occupy more than 70 per cent of jobs in clerical and related activities, and a similar proportion of jobs in catering, cleaning, hairdressing and other personal services (EOC, 1984). The occupational segregation of women is not only horizontal (they work in different occupations) but also vertical (where they do work in the same occupation, men tend to occupy the higher grades) (Dex, 1988). The Women and Employment Survey of 1980 (Martin and Roberts, 1984) and the General Household Survey (OPCS, 1984) found that 63 per cent of women were in jobs done only by women and that the equivalent figure for men was 80 per cent. But Sloane's (1987) work on the New Earnings Survey suggests that vertical occupational segregation is far more important than horizontal segregation in explaining women's lower earnings than men's.

Breaking into 'new' occupations appears to be more difficult for women than for men. Breakwell and Weinberger (1987) found that women were handicapped by the prejudices of employers, who regarded 'token women' as liable both to experience and to cause problems. There are no strictly comparable data for men, but an interesting study by Wharton and Baron (1987) showed that 'token men' appeared to derive occupational and psychological benefit from being in this situation.

It cannot be argued that trade unions have been conspicuously helpful in championing the cause of women workers. In 1979 the TUC published a ten-point charter to promote 'Equality for Women within the Trade Unions' in affiliated unions, but it had what was euphemistically referred to as a 'mixed response' among unions (EOC, 1983). Differences in union membership between male and female employees have often been assumed to illustrate women's lesser commitment to paid work and their greater political conservatism, but an examination of the distribution of male and female trade-union membership and political attitudes reveals that the organization and market situation of the industry, plant size and hours of work are more reliable correlates of union membership than is gender itself (Purcell, 1988). Part-time employees, for example, are less likely to have access to or belong to a trade union.

One of the distinctive features of women as employees is that they are generally perceived as having a career option which men do not have — marriage and motherhood. This option, however, involves dependency. It is certainly the case that part-time employment is normally undertaken by people who are primarily dependent on someone else and who undertake a considerable additional burden of household work. In general, there is still marked segregation of household duties by gender. Gershuny (1987) has shown that the core routine domestic tasks are primarily the responsibility of women, with men being more likely to perform non-routine tasks. Time-budget analyses by Gershuny and Jones (1987), using data from a total of seven surveys, do show almost a doubling of male routine domestic work between 1974/75 and 1983/84, albeit from a low base; during this period, female involvement in routine tasks declined, while female involvement in non-routine tasks increased (as it did for men). There has thus been some blurring of the sexual division of labour, but we are still a long way from the symmetrical family that was announced by Young and Willmott (1973).

Values and the World of Work

There is little doubt that employment structures, the organization of work, and work tasks themselves, have all undergone and are still undergoing a considerable transformation. In the industrial period, we have tended to conceptualize work as a male occupation carried on outside the home in the formal economy. Industrial, economic and social change have led us to challenge this simple conception. It is possible to identify four main challenges. The first emanates from the increasing employment of women in the economy and the challenge mounted by feminism to our patriarchal structures.

The second emanates from close studies of the economy which reveal not one formal economy, but several interpenetrating economies — including the hidden, domestic and communal economies. Thirdly, new technology has certainly made possible some radical changes in the organization of work. Finally, historically high levels of unemployment have led some to challenge many of the practices and values associated with work in modern Britain.

Feminism has looked hard at the values which, it is argued, are embedded in patriarchal systems of employment and male-dominated organizations. Rose (1988) is among many who argue that 'one of the most important structural effects of growing women's employment may well be on the employment values of *men*' (p. 150 — emphasis in original). Feminism has been one of the factors which has caused us to re-examine what is to count as work in our society. In the household economy — which we have defined earlier (p. 37) as covering the production within the home of goods or services that might otherwise have been bought for cash through the formal economy — it is, as noted above, women who perform most of the labour. This work is neither remunerated, nor does it appear in our national accounts, and yet it is clearly vital for the efficient operation of the formal economy.

The concept of the household economy raises fundamental questions about our whole conception of work and employment. Most interest in recent years has been focused on the hidden economy, which — as noted on pp. 36–7 — covers work that is not declared for tax purposes, or work that is illegal in itself, like theft or embezzlement. A wide variety of different activities can be grouped under this label, including 'moonlighting', which several studies have shown is common among teachers (Alden, 1981)! For Britain in the late 1970s and early 1980s, estimates of the size of the hidden economy ranged from 2 per cent to 15 per cent of GDP, with the most commonly suggested boundaries being between 5 per cent and 8 per cent. In addition to the household and hidden economies, we have noted (p. 37) the concept of the communal economy: that is, unpaid work and exchange which is paid for on a neighbourhood, kin or minority-interest basis.

The relationship between these economies is complex. It appears not to be the case, for example, that as the official economy contracts, more work is transacted in the household economy. Pahl (1984) has shown that it was precisely those households which had access to cash from the official economy that had the most opportunities to engage in informal self-provisioning activities in the household economy. Many schoolchildren work in all four economies — household, communal, hidden and formal — and yet in terms of the work-related curriculum and work experience organized by schools, it is often only the formal economy which is recognized, despite the fact that most students will have had least exposure to this economy (cf. pp. 36–7).

It is true that new technology could radically alter our traditional conception of work. The examples which are often presented are the Rank Xerox executives networked into the company main-frame computer whilst working from home, and the women computer programmers of F International who similarly work as independent contractors from home. Handy (1984) amongst others has done much to popularize this new conception of work, and if such ideas become more prominent, it may well be the case that there will be an increasing blurring of the divisions between the household, communal and formal economies. But much of Handy's work remains futurology: the workers of Rank Xerox and F International are tiny in number, and so far show no signs of significant growth.

The final factor which has challenged our traditional conception of work is unemployment. Mass unemployment both affects and reflects the way in which work society is organized. Between 1979 and 1982, unemployment doubled to just under 3 million. By the end of the 1980s it stood at around 2 million, although numerous changes to the ways in which the figures were calculated made comparisons difficult. Youth unemployment during this period remained high because of the characteristics of the youth labour market (see pp. 71–5). For every 1 per cent increase in male unemployment, the youth rate tended to rise by 1.7 per cent (Ashton, 1986).

The fact that we are so much concerned with unemployment, and that the unemployed suffer psychologically and socially as well as economically whilst being out of work, indicates how important work is in our society. Yet paradoxically, a widely-held view on the political right and amongst some employers is that significant numbers of people are not really looking for work at all. This view is linked to, but not confined to, the criticisms made of young people in particular (cf. pp. 74–5). It can be seen as part of a more general thesis that as a society we have in some way 'abandoned' the work ethic. Theories of abandonment claim that we once had a strong commitment to work as a moral virtue but that this has now been discarded.

Rose (1985) charts this view from the 1960s when managers and business commentators began to report a fall-off in attachment to work. Between 1968 and 1973, he argues, concern began to turn into alarm. Such impressionistic evidence was given some backing by the work of Inglehart (1977). He argued, on the basis of international comparative research, that a 'silent revolution' in values had been occurring among people growing up after 1945, with a substantial minority of these young people holding a 'post-materialist' view of the world, and other groups showing some signs of having been affected by post-material values. There is even some evidence from international studies of work values that the British might possess a set of values about work which are distinctive. These studies seem to show that the British have little intrinsic motivation to work and emerge as the nation least likely to regard work as centrally important in life (Rose, 1988). The major difficulty with the thesis that a significant abandonment of the work ethic has occurred is that there is very little evidence to suggest that we ever possessed it in the first place. As Rose (1988) has argued, 'work discipline and productivity in the nineteenth century... did not generally depend upon a moral commitment to work among labourers and semi-skilled workers. Industrial discipline could be upheld by fear and need' (p. 139).

A more likely source of the worries about the work ethic felt by some employers and politicians is to be found in the structural transformations of the economy. Service industries now employ 63 per cent of the work-force, and one of the features of employment in this sector compared to manufacturing is that much of the work done cannot be so easily checked as in manufacturing. Employee discretion and autonomy tend to be widened at the same time that consumers are being empowered to demand higher standards of service. Furthermore, a lot of service tasks are growing more complex. Many workers who have been brought up in the 'low trust' (Fox, 1974) culture of manufacturing industry dominated by Fordism — which assumes that workers are either irresponsible, unintelligent or lazy, and usually all three — are transferring their values to the service where these values become more socially visible. Worker behaviour that is deemed to be 'irresponsible' in the factory is hidden away from the public, only revealing itself, if at all, in substandard finished goods; a similar type of behaviour in a shop is instantly revealed to the customers.

Conclusion

Much of this chapter has been concerned with mapping the changing picture of the world of work from the pre-industrial period to the present. Such an exercise relates directly to world-of-work learning (see Chapter 2) and demonstrates what a rich area of knowledge this is, combining aspects of many different subject disciplines. It shows in particular that history as a school subject can use the work-place as an important resource and can place the present experience of work undertaken by students on work experience in an illuminating historical context.

The real value of the historical perspective, however, is that is emphasizes the fact that our arrangements for work are constantly changing. The work-place which is experienced on work experience was different in the past and will be different in the future. Students can be encouraged to seek explanations of a wide range of phenomena they encounter during their placements and can be referred back to the origins of certain practices. The pattern of trade-union organization is a particularly good example.

Work experience, if integrated within an educational framework, can thus raise important questions for young people about both the nature of work and our society's current arrangements for work. Our analysis helps to show why it is that most young people think of industry in terms of *manufacturing* industry (Jamieson and Lightfoot, 1982), because it is manufacturing industry that has dominated the modern historical period. One of the advantages of work experience, assuming that placements reflect the modern industrial structure, is that young people are likely to learn that manufacturing is not now the dominant sector in the economy. A danger of work experience, on the other hand, is that it might reinforce the view that work is synonymous with paid employment transacted in sites outside the household. This — as suggested in Chapter 2 (pp. 36–7) — would be a limited and limiting view.

Our analysis of the modern picture of British industry thus implicitly raises the question of whether the distribution of work-experience placements reflects the modern world of work, and to what extent the configuration of placements used by a particular school is influential in fixing students' perceptions of British industry. Whatever the answers to these questions, it is important that schools consider their distribution of work-experience placements in relation to the local, regional and national economy. It is particularly important that schools should have a clear view of those elements of the world of work that tend to get neglected or at least under-represented in work-experience programmes. These include the self-employed and small-business sector, which we have shown is of growing importance in the economy. They also include the domestic household, both as a site for work which usually goes unrecognized and unpaid, and as site for paid work where varieties of homeworking take place.

It might be argued that the growth of the small-business and self-employed sectors as an element of industrial change has made it more difficult for work-experience organizers to sample adequately the distribution of work-places. It is likely that other changes have had a similar effect: for example, the spatial decentralization of industry out of some of the older industrial areas towards green-field sites creates obvious problems for schools which have not adapted quickly to changing population shifts. The growing labour-market segmentation into primary and secondary labour markets, and core and peripheral work, raises another set of difficulties for work-experience organizers. Both in terms of the sets of competences likely to be possessed by young people, and the interests of employers of young people, the temptation must be to place young people on work experience in the secondary labour market and in peripheral jobs. Whether this raises any problems must depend on the curricular framework for the work-experience programme (see Chapter 2).

If schools thus find certain changes in the organization of work difficult to embrace in their work-experience programmes, it can also be argued that some features of work placements tend to be deliberately ignored or played down. Trade unions are a good example of a key feature of many workplaces which is often ignored by work experience. Other features of workplaces can also confront schools with difficulties. Gender segregation is something which schools are enjoined to confront by both central and local government, but the gender-segregated labour market remains a powerful fact of economic life, as we have shown. In Chapter 11 (pp. 202–5) we consider the ways in which some schools attempt to deal with this issue.

This chapter began by pointing out that in pre-industrial society 'work and non-work or leisure were as one' and that, on one reading at least, the history of the development of work has been a history of the gradual compartmentalization of work. It is certainly the case that the formal education system has become gradually detached from the formal organization of work. As noted in Chapter 1, however, we are beginning to see a reintegration of these two structures. Our conception of what constitutes work is being widened to embrace a wider range of activities — most importantly, many of those transacted in the household. Education also has begun to expand its conceptual territory and is no longer being thought of exclusively in terms of schooling. More and more work organizations are beginning to embrace the idea of lifelong learning. More specifically, with the development of the education–industry movement, the world of work and that of schooling have drawn closer together. Schooling is beginning to be seen as a site for a growing range of work and work-related activities, whilst an increasing number of learning activities are being sited in the work-place — including, of course, work experience.

Part II

Organizational Issues

Chapter 5

School-based Organization

Andrew Miller

Initially, all work-experience schemes were organized by individual schools. In recent years, a number of LEAs have set up centralized schemes covering all the schools in a particular area or across the LEA as a whole: these will be discussed in Chapter 6. In many areas, however, schools still organize their own work-experience programmes. In this chapter, we examine the diversity of forms which such school-based organization can take, and raise the main questions which schools need to consider when planning and reviewing their work-experience schemes. We begin by identifying the main advantages and drawbacks of school-based organization. This is followed by a discussion of the four main dimensions of work-experience organization: policy, resources, tasks and roles. Then the question of school-based, school-focused in-service training is introduced. Issues related to the timing and duration of work experience are addressed in the final section. Other organizational issues which are pertinent both to school-based and to LEA-based organization are dealt with elsewhere: matching students to placements in Chapter 11; and monitoring and student log-books and diaries in Chapter 12.

Pros and Cons

Some schools run their own work-experience schemes because there is no central organization in their LEA, and therefore they have no alternative. This is most often the case in rural areas where schools, population and employment are geographically dispersed. Consequently, the need for central coordination is reduced, because the lack of overlap between the 'economic hinterland' of each school means that there is no competition for work placements between schools. In areas where there is an LEA-organized scheme that is voluntary, in the sense that schools can opt in or out, some schools choose to maintain their own schemes. This reluctance to join the LEA scheme may be the result of an unwillingness to change a 'successful' programme, or to give up particular placements into a central pool (see

p. 119). Special schools in particular often prefer to build up close relationships with specific employers, frequently through parents and governors of the school. Independent schools, too, usually organize their own schemes.

In maintaining their own work–experience organization, schools can gain a number of potential advantages (for a discussion of LEA-based versus school-based organization, see Fitzgerald and Bodiley, 1984; Jamieson and Lightfoot, 1982; Miller, Jamieson and Watts, 1989). First, they can develop their own documentation and publicity material to suit their distinctive needs. This has the added advantage of enabling such materials to be viewed as part of the wider 'marketing' of the school as a whole to parents and employers. For example, Burleigh Community College in Leicestershire has developed its work–experience programme as part of an 'Open Door' programme which seeks to involve parents and employers more in the life of the school (Berkeley, Braham and Miller, 1990). All stationery and documents carry the 'Open Door' logo.

Second, schools can build closer links with particular employers, because the tasks of liaison are undertaken by the school coordinator rather than by an LEA coordinator. Some employers prefer to have close links with one or two schools rather than take students from a number of schools within an LEA (see Chapter 8).

The third advantage is that schools are able to devise their own work–experience aims, and to organize the scheme in such a way that the likelihood of achieving the aims will be maximized. Often centrally-organized schemes assume a set of aims that are common to all schools. This can cause difficulties to schools which have distinctive aims in mind. If, for example, these aims require directing students to particular placements, this may not be possible in a centralized system, which is usually based upon students' 'free choice' of placements (see p. 198). In school-organized schemes, the aims can be set within a sympathetic organizational framework.

A fourth advantage is the greater control which schools have over the phasing of organizational tasks and in particular over the timing of when particular groups of students go out on work experience. In principle, this allows the work-experience programmes to be timed to permit the optimum curricular framing, i.e. at a point in the school year which allows a full programme of preparation and follow-up closely linked to the curriculum. Such autonomy also, however, permits schools to time their schemes in order 'to minimise disruption', and so to place them for example at the end of the summer term when there is little opportunity for adequate debriefing and follow-up. If other local schools do the same, this can lead to a 'bunching' in demand for placements at such times, with a resulting overload on employers, and a reduction in the number of students obtaining their first choice of placement.

A final advantage is the greater flexibility which schools have over the duration of the work placement. Centralized schemes may use one-, two- or three-week blocks, but often find it difficult to respond to demands for different combinations of these patterns from participating schools. The questions of the timing and duration of work-experience programmes are discussed further towards the end of this chapter.

These potential *benefits* must be set alongside the possible *drawbacks* of school-based organization. The first and most obvious set of drawbacks concerns the resourcing of work experience. School-based organization can be very time-consuming in terms of the demands of finding placements, administering the scheme, and maintaining links with employers. It also requires, for example, ready access to a telephone and secretarial support. Local management of schools should encourage school managers to consider whether the staff time and other resources used in administering work experience would be better deployed elsewhere in the school, and whether cost savings can be made by asking the LEA to provide this service.

A second set of drawbacks concerns the demands on the expertise of the staff responsible for work-experience organization. When schools take on the responsibility for finding and vetting placements for health and safety, this is not only time-consuming but also requires specialist knowledge (see p. 129). Schools may prefer to look to the LEA to provide such expertise rather than having to develop it within their own staff.

In most schools which organize their own schemes, the organizational systems have evolved over a period of time in an incremental or *ad hoc* way. The process of rethinking work experience should involve taking stock of the *status quo* and subjecting it to critical scrutiny. In order to do this, it may be helpful to examine each of the four main elements that comprise the system. The first is the school's work-experience *policy*: such a policy may be made explicit in a written document, but is more likely to be implicit and based upon custom and practice. The second is the *resources* used in operating the system. The third is the set of *tasks* involved in administering the programme. The fourth is the allocation of *roles* and associated responsibilities for managing the system. It is to these elements that we now turn.

Policy

Currently few schools have discrete work-experience policy statements (HMI, 1990). In most cases, the work-experience system has developed over a number of years without an apparent need for a policy document. Why, therefore, might schools now want to develop a policy statement for work experience? The main purpose is to ensure that all the parties involved — teachers, employers, students and parents — share a common understanding of the main aims of the programme and of how they are to be achieved. Is work experience an entitlement for all students? How does the organization of work experience relate to the school's equal-opportunities policy, if it has one? In what ways is work experience linked to the whole curriculum of the school? What is the philosophy regarding parental and employer involvement

---

Box 5.1   *A school–industry policy statement including work experience*

- All students must select an activity which will give them experience of industry and/or enterprise.

- Equal access available to all activities irrespective of students' gender, race or physical ability.

- Students are actively encouraged to consider activities beyond the limits of traditional gender roles.

- All members of the teaching staff are involved in the delivery of the programme.

- Local industry and commerce is given every opportunity to be involved in the planning of the programme, the preparation of the students, and the evaluation of the whole programme and the students' individual achievements.

- A wide variety of work-related activities is offered to the students to cater for all interests and the full ability range within the college.

- All aspects of the programme are centred within the academic curriculum and work undertaken within the programme can be assessed as GCSE coursework.

- The students' experiences are closely linked to the pastoral and profiling curriculum of the college.

- All students are encouraged to build upon the experiences gained within the programme with further work-related activities.

- The programme is to be seen as only one part of a 'whole-school' commitment to partnership between education and industry.

Source: Allen (1989).

---

in the scheme? Who is responsible for planning, implementing and monitoring the programme? What resources are available to support it? What is the procedure for keeping the programme under review?

Some schools have included such work–experience policy statements as a section in their whole-school policy documents. Others have developed a specific policy document on industry links which includes work experience. For example, Hope High School in Salford formulated a policy titled 'Industry Across the Curriculum' (Hope High School, 1989). A member of the senior management team, the Industrial Curriculum Coordinator, had responsibility for monitoring the implementation of the policy. Again, Ifield Community College in West Sussex developed a policy statement setting out the key principles upon which its school–industry-links programme was to be based (see Box 5.1), after negotiation with twenty of the major employers participating in its work-experience programme. The college's Industry Month programme was based upon a whole-school approach which was closely linked to the curriculum (see p. 170).

What other information might a school work-experience policy document contain? Some schools have included targets and performance indicators, in order to facilitate the measurement of progress towards set goals (see Chapter 14). This practice is based on the assumption that although policy goals may be valuable in themselves, they are not the only ingredient in successful curriculum change. A policy document could also incorporate the other three aspects of the work-experience system. Firstly, it might indicate the resources available to aid the implementation of the policy, including capitation, secretarial support, time allocations, and staffing. Secondly, it could set out the roles, responsibilities and operational relationships of the key staff involved. Thirdly, it might establish a critical path for the main tasks involved in work-experience organization against a timetable of the school year.

How can such work-experience policy documents be developed? In general, the policy goals are most likely to be achieved successfully if the various parties who have to implement them have themselves been involved in their development. At Ifield Community College, for example, the policy was developed on the basis of extensive consultation with teachers and employers. Some school policies have been based upon general LEA guide-lines, although HMI (1990) found that most LEAs 'offered little constructive advice on the determination of objectives and setting training strategies to attain such targets' (p. 3).

Resources

Few schools have attempted systematically to identify the resources used in their work-experience programme and to calculate the costs involved. Curriculum costing is in general at a rudimentary stage of development, but the advent of Local Management of Schools (LMS) may give a boost to such accounting processes. The accurate costing of work-experience programmes would enable schools to describe more accurately the ways in which resources are allocated. It would also raise awareness of the consequences of policy decisions upon resources and costs (Cumming, 1988).

What are the chief resources and costs involved in running a school-based work-experience programme? Although the resources used to mount such a programme can be readily identified, attaching costs to some of the items is more problematic. In terms of organization alone, the main resource will be the *work-experience organizer(s)*. In some cases, a special incentive allowance may be allocated for this purpose. Alternatively, responsibility for work experience may be attached to a senior teacher, a head of year or a head of department, with no extra payment being made (Bates, 1989).

The main cost is often perceived as being the time required by the organizer to administer the scheme. A widely-quoted estimate was as follows:

> For a group of 100 pupils from one subject area within a school, including contacting firms from an existing list of organisations which are already involved in one way or another with school-industry collaboration, a teacher is likely to need one day a week for

one and a half terms. Our experience is that it is doubtful whether this time could be reduced by more than 50 per cent even when the scheme has been running for a number of years (Jamieson and Lightfoot, 1982, p. 136).

More recently, some school evaluations have endeavoured to calculate the number of hours used in carrying out the various tasks involved. For example, Deeside High School in Clwyd had two school coordinators who ran a 'Work Appreciation Scheme' (Parnell and Roberts, 1988). It was estimated that they spent a total of 300 hours on the scheme, these being divided as follows: contacting employers — 60 hours; administration — 60 hours; preparation of students — 30 hours; dealing with queries from employers and students — 10 hours; supervision of placements — 120 hours; and evaluation — 20 hours. Using the 1,265 hours of 'directed time' as a basis, this constituted the equivalent of around 0.25 of a teacher over a full year — higher than the Jamieson and Lightfoot estimate.

The *other human resources* involved in school-based work-experience organization are the time of staff monitoring the placements, and of ancillary staff supporting the administration of the scheme. In many schools the supervision of students is undertaken by staff who have been freed from other teaching commitments. Typing and other secretarial support may be provided, in which case this involves direct and/or opportunity costs.

The *non-human resources* can be divided into consumable and non-consumable items. Consumable costs may include: the travelling expenses of students and of visiting staff (though students' costs may be covered by employers — see p. 134); the telephone and postage costs; and the printing/photocopying costs of the extensive documentation required, including pro-formas, preparatory and follow-up student materials, log-books and diaries. Some schools have calculated the costs of these consumable items, and have sought sponsorship to meet them. For example, Burleigh Community College calculated that its work-experience documentation cost an average of £1.20 per student (Berkeley, Braham and Miller, 1990), and asked major local employers to meet the costs of up to fifty students each. Non-consumable items may include computer hardware and software used to establish a database of placements (although hardware is unlikely to be solely dedicated to work-experience organization). Again, sponsorship may be sought for such facilities.

Tasks

What are the main tasks involved in the organization of work experience in a school? Some writers have distinguished between administrative, educational and pastoral tasks (e.g. Holmes, Jamieson and Perry, 1983). It is acknowledged, however, that in practice the different tasks associated with school-based organization are difficult to disentangle. For example, a meeting between the work-experience coordinator and a student to discuss the application form on which the student has selected three possible placements could be viewed in a number of ways. It could be seen as an *administrative* task of allocating the student to a suitable placement. Alternatively, it might be seen as a *pastoral/counselling* task in helping the student to gain maximum personal benefit from the placement, or as an *educational* task in linking the placement choice to curriculum subjects which the student is studying. Here we will describe the main tasks involved in administering work experience which are focused primarily on communication with employers, parents, teachers and the LEA, rather than with students. The main tasks which involve communication with students are discussed in Chapters 11 and 12.

Box 5.2 provides a summary of the main tasks involved in work-experience administration, based upon case-study material (Berkeley, Braham and Miller, 1990; Fitzgerald and Bodiley, 1984). The chart indicates some of the main tasks associated with the four stages of work-experience organization: preliminary; pre-placement; placement; and post-placement. Each task has as its object communication with one or more of the main parties involved, and is classified according to the most common methods used by organizers in carrying it out.

Communication occurs in three main ways: through *letters and documents*; through *telephone* conversations; and through face-to-face contact in *meetings*. Inevitably the quantity and quality of such communication vary widely within and between schools. Some schools have used desk-top publishing to improve the appearance of their information leaflets. This is particularly the case in schools which regard work experience as an important opportunity to market the school and what it stands for. Thus, as noted earlier (p. 86), Burleigh Community College used the theme of the 'Open Door' to run through all its work-experience documentation. Geoffrey Chaucer School in Kent established a working group of employers, parents, students and teachers to review and rewrite information packs for parents, for employers and for students. Yardleys School in Birmingham presented a frameable 'certificate of thanks' to employers offering work-experience placements (Berkeley, Braham and Miller, 1990).

Although written communication is important, many coordinators testify to the need to make personal contact via the telephone, and through visits and meetings. One of the main drawbacks of school-based organization is the time-consuming nature of the process of adding placements to the databank. This often means canvassing employers by letter or 'cold-calling', and visiting the work-place to discuss placement details and carry out a health-and-safety check.

Some schools have used various forms of meetings as a way of building up relationships with employers and/or with parents. For example, the work-experience coordinator at Ifield Community College made regular visits to discuss the industry-links programme with employers, and invited

Box 5.2 Tasks of the school-based work-experience coordinator

WHAT?	HOW				WITH WHOM				
	Administration/ paperwork	Letter	Telephone	Meeting	Employers	Parents	Other teachers	Students	LEA
A. Preliminary tasks									
1. Canvassing for placements		*							
2. Negotiating placement tasks			*	*	*				
3. Vetting placements for health and safety			*	*	*				
4. Informing employers about the scheme		*	*	*	*				
5. Informing parents about the scheme		*		*		*			
6. Gaining parental consent		*				*			
7. Investigating student medical problems	*					*			
8. Updating placement bank/database	*								

Task	1	2	3	4	5	6	7	8
B. Pre-placement tasks								
9. Allocating students to placements	*	*					*	*
10. Debriefing staff/staff INSET	*							*
11. Gaining LEA approval			*	*				*
12. Completing log of placements	*			*				
13. Confirming placement details					*	*	*	*
14. Organizing pre-visit interviews				*	*	*		
C. Placement tasks								
15. Dealing with queries/problems		*		*	*	*	*	*
16. Compiling staff visit roster	*					*	*	
17. Visiting placements			*	*	*		*	*
D. Post-placement tasks								
18. Dealing with queries/problems		*		*	*	*	*	*
19. Collecting and processing employers' assessments	*			*	*		*	
20. Organizing follow-up meetings				*			*	
21. Preparing an evaluation report				*			*	

93

them to visit the school during 'open mornings' when they could attend lessons and talk to staff and students (Berkeley, Braham and Miller, 1990; see also p. 170). Parents' evenings prior to work experience are increasingly common, sometimes with employers present and students from the previous year's scheme displaying their work. Meetings may also be held after the placement. For example, Burleigh Community College organized a parents/ tutors afternoon and evening to discuss the outcomes of work experience immediately after the debriefing morning with students. Swanshurst School in Birmingham held a presentation evening for parents at which students talked about their experiences. Carlton-Bolling School in Bradford provided a student-organized buffet lunch for work-experience providers as part of a GCSE Home Economics module.

Roles

In allocating roles and responsibilities for work-experience organization, there are three main issues that need to be considered. First, what is the optimum relationship between the curricular frame and the organization of work experience? Second, what are the benefits of a team approach to work-experience organization? Third, what are the advantages and disadvantages of having more than one set of organizers for work experience in a school?

In many schools, responsibility for work experience has traditionally rested with the Head of Careers and the careers department. The rationale for this — often implicit rather than explicit — is that the teachers responsible for the curricular frame should also be responsible for the organizational work. As we have noted in Chapter 2 (pp. 17–21), the curricular frames adopted for work experience have tended to multiply in recent years. Box 5.3 illustrates the different members of staff who might be given responsibility for work-experience organization in relation to particular frames.

When academic subjects provide the main curricular frame, the departments which are likely to assume responsibility for pre-16 work experience are those with a relatively 'weak' knowledge frame — for example, English and Humanities. Testwood School in Hampshire provides a good example of organization by an English department (Vicary, 1989; also see p. 158); Cheslyn Hay High School in Staffordshire offers an example of organization by a Humanities department (Cattell, 1989). The responsibility for organizing work experience for students following vocational courses in schools might rest with the CPVE or BTEC Coordinator, or with the staff delivering particular options such as CPVE Art and Design (see p. 166). Where there is a world-of-work-learning frame, work experience could be organized by the Coordinator for Economic and Industrial Understanding, who might also have responsibility for coordinating other work-related activities in the school so as to promote curricular continuity and progression. Finally, a

Box 5.3   Some possible locations of responsibility for school-based work-experience
           organization

Curricular frame	Possible responsibility for work-experience organization
A. Academic subjects	Head of English Head of Humanities Head of Modern Languages Head of Technology
B. Vocational courses	CPVE Coordinator BTEC Coordinator
C. World-of-work learning	Coordinator for Economic and Industrial Understanding
D. Careers education	Head of Careers
E. Personal and social education	Head of Year Deputy Headteacher (Pastoral) Community Liaison Officer

personal and social education frame suggests that responsibility could reside with the relevant Head of Year or with the Deputy Headteacher with pastoral responsibilities. Some schools have appointed full-time Community Liaison Officers, whose brief includes work-experience organization as part of their responsibility for community placements and schools–industry liaison.

As noted in Chapter 9 (pp. 166–7), schools tend in practice to use more than one curricular frame when choosing their aims and when planning preparation, briefing, the experience, debriefing and follow-up (see also Chapter 12). We have also found that school-based coordinators working alone on organizational tasks tend to feel hard-pressed and isolated. These factors, along with the trend towards developing policies and development plans for work experience, suggest the desirability of a team approach to the organization and curricular integration of work experience. A school work-experience team could have a team 'leader' or 'coordinator' who would have overall responsibility for organizational matters, and a number of team members representing different curricular interests in the programme.

Some schools have analyzed the obligations and responsibilities of each party involved in implementing the scheme. Box 5.4 shows one school's attempt to define the various roles and the tasks associated with each. It is noticeable in this example how the curricular and organizational tasks are intermingled within individual roles. This marks a significant difference from LEA-based organization, where there tends to be a clear separation between organizational and curricular tasks, the former being viewed as the proper responsibility of the LEA and the latter of the school. It is also worth noting

Box 5.4   Allocation of roles and tasks: an example

The Coordinator — overall responsibility for the organization and smooth running of the scheme; link between school/careers office/parents/employers/students; arrange parents' meetings; arrange INSET; allocate placements; arrange monitoring; ensure aims and objectives can be achieved; counsel students.

Careers Office — introduce and sell the idea of work experience to employers; recruit employers; establish guidelines; suggest programmes of work; arrange insurance; health and safety; support the school.

Careers Teacher — implement JIIG–CAL programme and interest profile; inform students of placements allocated; ensure students understand the scheme and know where and how to redress problems; ensure parental involvement and consent; link between coordinator and careers teacher and students; advise suitability/unsuitability of particular placements; oversee letter to employers; check arrangements for preliminary interview and placement; counsel students; use role-play, simulation and other techniques to solve problems and worries; debrief and evaluation; thank-you letters.

Year Tutors — support the form tutor and stand in as necessary; counsel students; debrief and evaluation.

Pupils — complete JIIG–CAL and interest profiles; complete work-experience choice form; contact employers; preliminary interview; work experience; debrief and evaluation; thank-you letters; working party for following year.

Parents — support work experience as an important part of the curriculum; attend parents' meetings; sign consent form and appreciate its implications; ensure their children treat work experience seriously; inform school if placement is unsatisfactory.

Monitors (teachers visiting placements) — visit at least once during placement; telephone calls as appropriate; complete a report form for each student; inform coordinator if placement is unsatisfactory; debrief and evaluation.

Headmaster/Deputy Headmaster — establish ethos for work experience within the school and among staff; integrate with the curriculum; support meetings and INSET; debrief and evaluation.

Subject Teachers — develop work experience as a resource for classroom study and/or examination coursework.

Office Staff — typing and duplicating; telephone and reception (often the first point of contact for concerned parent or worried employer: sympathy for and knowledge of the scheme essential).

Employers — treat work experience as a valuable educational exercise; provide a suitable and sympathetic environment for the pupil; set standards to enable achievement; devise suitable tasks; inform school if placement unsatisfactory; complete report form for each pupil.

Source: Material submitted for the Rover Award for Quality in Work Experience 1989.

that the role allocation in Box 5.4 suggests unresolved overlaps between the roles of various different people involved in counselling students, in debriefing and in evaluation.

There are four main potential benefits in a team approach to work-experience organization. First, there are more resources available, which in principle reduces the burden upon individuals, while at the same time making more activities possible. For example, individual pre-placement and post-placement counselling becomes manageable once profiling tutors are involved (see p. 169). Second, it shares the 'ownership' of the programme, which tends to create greater commitment among the staff. This can reduce opposition to the use of curriculum time for preparation, briefing, debriefing and follow-up. Third, the involvement of other staff in the programme tends to facilitate subject integration, encouraging them to consider how they might use work experience to promote subject-specific knowledge and skills (HMI, 1990). Fourth, a team from diverse teaching backgrounds will tend to have a greater variety of teaching styles and experiences, which can enhance the quality of the curriculum experience for students.

A number of schools have more than one locus of responsibility for work-experience organization. There are two main situations in which this occurs. First, some subject departments which have used work experience as part of a GCSE course, such as Business and Information Studies or Child Care, have retained responsibility for organizing their own placements. Second, in some schools there is a division of responsibility between pre- and post-16 work-experience organization. For example, the Head of Careers and the pastoral team might organize work experience for students in years 10 and 11, while the CPVE team organizes work experience for year 12 students.

The first case can be justified on the grounds that it facilitates close subject integration of work experience. If, however, the school has a policy of making pre-16 work experience concerned with the broadening of occupational horizons, to insist on business-studies students going to an office placement imposes limitations on their choice, and may conflict with the school's broader aims. Potentially, too, it could lead to conflict between the subject department and the school organizer over liaison with the employers concerned and over who is to have priority in allocating students to placements. This illustrates the need for careful coordination of policy and practice in such a case.

The second case is justifiable if the school intends to stress the differences between pre- and post-16 work experience. Some would argue that having different teachers organizing the programme increases the chances of a change of approach, which may be motivating for students. Others would counter that it makes it more difficult to ensure planned progression and curricular continuity. Again, such problems can be avoided by effective communication and cooperation between the different organizers (or teams of organizers) within an overall whole-curriculum framework.

School-based, School-focused INSET

Team and whole-school approaches to work experience encourage staff to come together for school-based, school-focused in-service education and training (INSET). It is often difficult to draw the line between planning meetings, briefings, and INSET. This is evident in the way in which one-day

INSET days have been used increasingly for planning and briefing sessions. What counts as INSET hinges on whether a narrow or broad definition of 'education and training' is adopted. Certainly the involvement of staff in working groups, planning aspects of the work-experience programme, can produce valuable learning outcomes in terms of knowledge, understanding and capability for the individuals concerned.

Some schools have developed particular forms of school-based INSET focused on specific aspects of work-experience organization and curricular integration. For example, Ifield Community College involved thirteen heads of department with a group of employers over the course of three sessions in *developing their whole-school approach* (see p. 170). Block whole-year work experience usually involves a team of staff, most commonly the form tutors, in *preparing and briefing students*: this can require preparatory sessions. Some schools have provided INSET on *counselling skills* to help tutors to undertake matching using 'counselled choice' or 'guided choice' rather than 'free choice' strategies (see Chapter 11). Developments in *assessment* have meant in some cases the involvement of tutors in INSET linking work experience to the school's system of recording achievement: Garth High School (see p. 169) offers a good example of such a process. Probably the most common form of whole-staff INSET on work experience is sessions held to brief teachers on their *monitoring visits* to students on placement (see pp. 221–5).

The approach of one school to school-based, school-focused INSET is shown in Box 5.5. The work-experience coordinator at this school distinguished between tutor, subject teacher, and employer INSET. The INSET for tutors included briefings on how to operate the system, and a half-day session with inputs provided by the LEA Safety Officer and the school's Equal Opportunities Coordinator. The subject teacher INSET took the form of planning meetings; while the employer INSET comprised a structured reverse-shadowing experience in which the employers followed the student day.

Timing and Duration

The timing of work experience in the school year and the duration of the period of work experience are organizational issues which can have a profound influence upon the quality of curricular integration. A recent evaluation of work experience in TVEI pilot schools revealed the extent of the problem:

> With few exceptions in the schools that we have visited, work experience was subordinated to academic timetabling requirements. Work experience was no more than an addition, occurring at the end of term or the end of the academic year, when the possibilities for its integration into the curriculum were, at best, limited (Barnes *et al.*, 1988, p. 88).

Box 5.5   A school-based INSET programme

Teacher/Tutor INSET

Tutor INSET is led by the school coordinator who uses colleagues from local industry and the Local Education Authority in the delivery of this part of the programme. There are eight meetings for tutors:

1. *Introduction*
   A discussion as to the worth of work experience for our students. Commitment of the Year Head and tutors. Objectives for programme decided upon.

2. *The Procedure*
   A discussion on the procedures to be followed and introduction of the catalogues of placements and the associated tutorial.

3. *The Application Form*
   Introduction of the form and the method of filling it in.

4. *Tutor Comments*
   Meeting between coordinator and each tutor to discuss student choices and complete relevant section of the form.

5. *Tutorial on Placement Information*
   Discussion on delivery of job description and completion of maps.

6. *Briefing on Tutorials*

7. *Half Teacher Day* (one week before placements)
   Taken up by:

   (a) introduction to monitoring form and discussion as to completion;
   (b) allocation of visits;
   (c) briefing by Local Education Authority and Safety Officer;
   (d) briefing by school Equal Opportunities Coordinator;
   (e) introduction of log-book;
   (f) general discussion.

8. *Debrief Session*

   (a) sharing of success;
   (b) collation of monitoring forms;
   (c) preparation for evaluation sessions;
   (d) catch-net for problems arranged.

Subject Teacher INSET

1. *Meeting between English Department and Coordinator*
   Discussion continued and involvement of work experience as part of English curriculum before and after work experience.

2. *Meeting between Art Department and Coordinator*
   Discussion of proposal for Art Exhibition related to fourthy-year work experience/world of work.

3. *Meeting between Business Studies Department and Coordinator*
   Discussion of Business Studies GCSE work to be included in log-book.

Employer INSET

Finham Park sees work-experience as a two-way process. Over recent years many employers have visited students during the school day and last year several employers followed our student shadowing programme, i.e. employers followed the student day.

(a) Registration.
(b) Lesson One of employer's choice.
(c) Break with students.
(d) Lesson Two of employer's choice.
(e) Lunch with students.
(f) Registration.
(g) Lessons Three and Four of employer's choice.
(h) Debrief with senior management of the school.

Source: Finham Park School, Coventry.

These findings echo earlier work which found a strong relationship between the academic attainment of students and organizational arrangements for work experience (Fitzgerald and Bodiley, 1984, pp. 40–7). There is still a widespread view among classroom teachers and senior management in schools that work experience should not be allowed to interfere with the examination courses for higher-attaining students.

One effect of this view is that work experience is frequently timed to coincide with other events, such as activities weeks, which similarly disrupt the timetable and which tend to occur before Christmas or at the end of the summer term. These preferences on the part of schools are reinforced by the fact that they often conveniently match those of employers, who can use 'extra pairs of hands' to cover busy times like Christmas and periods like the summer when there may be staff absences on annual holidays (Jamieson and Lightfoot, 1982, pp. 142–3).

A particularly common arrangement is for work experience to be timed to occur after school examinations at the end of years 10 or 11. HMI (1990) found that the end of the summer term in year 10 was the most popular time, because it interfered least with preparation for GCSE and the completion of GCSE assignments. Work experience after examinations in year 11 was less common but still occurred, even though some students had already left the school by this stage.

Perhaps the clearest sign of a change in traditional academic attitudes to work experience would be if senior staff with the power to influence time-tabling decisions ceased to pose the question 'What is the optimum timing and duration to minimize disruption to learning?' and instead began to ask 'What is the optimum timing and duration to maximize learning?'. Putting the question this way means that the placement period needs to be seen as one part of an overall programme which also involves preparation, briefing, debriefing and follow-up. This cycle can take up to a year to complete, and ideally should not include undue interruptions. Placing the work experience at the end of year 10 may postpone the debriefing and follow-up stages; placing it at the end of year 11 is likely to rule them out altogether. More-over, addressing student learning means that the learning objectives associated with the particular curricular frame(s) which the school has chosen become paramount. In order for work experience pre-16 to be integrated with GCSE courses, it must occur well before examinations and final course-work submissions in year 11. HMI note the benefits from locating work experience during the autumn or spring terms in year 11:

> The students were acknowledged to be more mature at that time and, where a progression of work-related experiences had been organ-ised by the school throughout the secondary years, more able to appreciate the experience in context. It was noticeable that higher quality reflective written work was produced by students on work experience in year 11 (HMI, 1990, p. 14).

In recent years there has been a decline of day-release schemes in which students undertake work experience for a half or full day per week over a number of weeks. There are two main reasons for this decline. First, there is some evidence that such arrangements have proved unpopular both with employers and with students (Jamieson and Lightfoot, 1982). Second, day release can only work without disrupting the teaching programme when a small number of students are absent at any one time: the trend towards work experience for all students has thus made day-release arrangements less popular. Some schools, however, still operate day-release programmes for particular courses or particular groups of students. For example, special schools often prefer a day-release structure (HMI, 1990, p. 14). In post-16 pre-vocational and vocational courses, too, half-day-a-week or one-day-a-week placements for the duration of the course enable college-based work to be linked to a progression of work-place experiences (*ibid*, p. 7). Day release might also be suitable for community-work placements where the intention is for students to build up relationships with the young or the elderly over a period of time. A good example of day release for vocationally-linked community placements is given in Chapter 9 (p. 167).

The main debate now is not over the relative merits of day-release or block-release patterns, but rather over the optimum duration of work-experience placements. The most common periods are one week, two weeks and three weeks. The HMI enquiry pointed to an emerging pattern in schools:

> Schools embarking upon their first venture into work experience were inclined to set aside one week but thereafter acknowledged their desire to provide a second as soon as practicable. Two weeks was considered by most schools the minimum necessary to provide students with the opportunity to assimilate into their new surroundings and also to be objective about the activity. A third week was often shown to be beneficial but was not essential in order to fulfil a goodly number of the objectives of work experience (HMI, 1990, p. 14).

This raises the question of which learning aims are achievable in placements of differing lengths. In our view, there are six aims for work experience which are more likely to be met on a three-week rather than a one-week placement. The *sampling* aim, which allows students to test a vocational preference, is best met if students can undertake as many as possible of the work tasks associated with a particular job: this can more easily be achieved over a longer period. Again, it is unlikely that students will be able to acquire the skills and knowledge related to a particular occupational area, associated with the *preparatory* aim, unless they are able to some extent to take on the role of a young worker on a longer placement. The preparatory aim is indeed most commonly a feature of pre-vocational and vocational courses, where

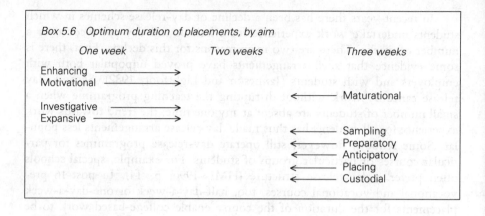

Box 5.6 Optimum duration of placements, by aim

day-release (often totalling more than fifteen working days) is still widely used. Longer placements are also useful to the *anticipatory* aim, in enabling students to experience the rhythms of work, including the repetitiveness of certain tasks. The same is true of the *maturational* aim: three-week placements allow relationships to be established, and skills and confidence to be developed. So far as the *placing* aim is concerned, placements are more likely to lead to a job offer if time is available for both parties to make a proper assessment of what each has to offer the other. The somewhat dubious *custodial* aim will also clearly be promoted through placements which remove the students concerned for longer periods from the school.

At the other end of the scale, the one-week placement is more likely to leave individuals in the role of *student* rather than allowing them to assume the role of young *employee* (cf. p. 29). This is reflected in the kinds of aims which can be met from a one-week placement. In our view, there are four aims which can be met appropriately, though not exclusively, by placements of this length. Such placements are often adequate to promote the *enhancing* aim, with students collecting information that is related to a specific subject (though this may depend on the complexity of the information required). A one-week block is, for example, often appropriate when students are carrying out specially constructed tasks as part of a 'taskweek' approach to work experience (see pp. 28–9). Similarly, students can often effectively undertake research into the world of work for an assignment as part of the *investigative* aim in a short period of time. A week is also frequently sufficient for work experience to have a *motivational* effect. Finally, the *expansive* aim which can involve students working in non-traditional areas is probably best achieved through short placements. This is based on the pragmatic assumption that students will be more willing to try non-traditional placements if they are of relatively short duration.

Our analysis of the optimum duration of placements by aim is summarized in Box 5.6. There are of course other considerations that will be involved, including the opportunity costs of longer placements in terms of other curricular experiences foregone. At the same time, it is worth noting that the amount of administration involved is much the same on long placements as on shorter ones. The desire to overcome the limitations of one-week and three-week placements, while retaining the advantages of both, probably accounts for the increasing popularity of two-week models, noted by HMI (see p. 101).

Conclusion

We have described the main features of school-based work experience at the moment. However, a number of pressures and demands upon schools are likely to affect the prevailing patterns. In particular, initiatives emanating from government (see Chapter 1) are likely to influence all four of the elements of school work-experience organization we have explored: policy, resources, tasks and roles.

So far as *policy* is concerned, many schools have developed institutional development plans as part of the requirements of the Education Reform Act 1988. TVEI Extension has encouraged schools to develop policies for schools–industry links in general, including work experience. The demands of the National Curriculum have persuaded schools to look at the existing relationship of work experience to the curriculum, with a view to developing and implementing a coherent policy. Local Management of Schools and the enhanced role for governing bodies stemming from the Education Reform Act 1988 are also likely to create demands for written policy statements on school-based work experience in order to facilitate monitoring and accountability.

Second, Local Management of Schools will tend to place the *resources* required for work experience under the spotlight. There will be pressure to cost schemes accurately, and to seek sponsorship to meet some of these costs. However, the development of local education–business partnerships may provide schools with additional resources to offset any decline in funding from governmental sources.

Third, demands from parents and from employers can create additional *tasks* for school-based work-experience organizers to undertake. Parents might request greater involvement in the scheme, resulting in additional parent/staff meetings. Some employers may try to improve the quality of work experience by insisting on teacher placements prior to accepting students from a particular school on work experience (Berkeley, Braham and Miller, 1990).

Fourth, there will be increased demands upon school-based work-experience organizers stemming from the greater curricular integration arising from the implementation of the National Curriculum, and from moves to provide work experience for the great majority of pre-16 students as well as a greater use in post-16 courses as part of TVEI Extension. This is likely to encourage more schools to develop a team approach to work-experience organization and coordination. A team approach will promote a clarification of *roles* and a clear division of labour among members of the team.

Chapter 6

LEA-based Organization

Andrew Miller

This chapter examines the variety of systems which have been established for the organization of work experience within local education authorities. It begins by outlining various models of LEA-based work-experience organization, and discussing the constituent elements of an organizational system for work experience. Case-studies from Doncaster, Newham, and Coventry local education authorities are then presented to illustrate three of the models. Organizational issues arising from the case-studies and other evidence are examined in the final section. Issues which pertain equally to school-based and to LEA-based schemes — such as the timing and duration of work-experience programmes — have already been discussed in Chapter 5 and will not be given further coverage here.

Organizational Models

In recent years, many LEAs have come to assume greater responsibility for the organization of work experience. Particularly in metropolitan areas, which often have a small number of secondary schools in a compact geographical area, such a policy has made sense in terms both of the efficient use of resources and of rationalizing the demands made upon local employers (Cope, 1983). By 1979 a DES survey of LEAs reported that one-fifth of schemes were centrally coordinated, usually by the Careers Service (DES, 1979a, p. 174). The growth of Project Trident provided added impetus to LEA-based organization (Kerry, 1983): by 1988 it was offering a work-experience organization service to over thirty-five LEAs in England and Wales. In the late 1980s, the increased demand for work-experience places in relation to developments in the curriculum and various central government initiatives (see pp. 7–10) placed additional pressures upon school-based work-experience organizers. In particular, the spread of TVEI pilot projects resulted in many areas in consortium-based forms of work-experience organization, and TVEI extension subsequently created the demand, resources and opportunity in many LEAs to centralize work-experience organization on an authority-wide basis.

Behind this centralizing tendency lies the increase in demand from schools for work-experience places, and the desire on the part of LEAs to meet this demand without overburdening individual employers. LEA-based organization can overcome the two main drawbacks of school-based organization noted in Chapter 5 (p. 87): lack of time and lack of expertise. The employment of full-time specialists to organize and coordinate work experience can relieve school-based work-experience coordinators of a major part of the administrative burden involved in finding and allocating large numbers of placements. In principle, LEA-organized programmes could seek to retain the advantages of school-based organization for the individual schools concerned: more targeted marketing, closer links with employers, more flexible aims, and more control over the phasing, timing and duration of the programme (cf. pp. 86–7). It is more common, however, to find LEA schemes which seek to standardize, rationalize and coordinate.

The benefits of central organization can accrue to the LEA, to employers, to students, and to schools. It allows the LEA to adapt the scheme more easily to meet changing LEA priorities and policies. The resourcing and content of INSET programmes can be more easily focused. Quality control is facilitated, as monitoring and evaluation processes can be more readily established. Employers can benefit because the central LEA contact acts as a mediator of demands, requesting placements only at pre-arranged times of the year, and using standardized procedures. Students and schools can benefit from the greater range and wider pool of placements that can be made available under a centralized scheme. The benefits of central organization are particularly likely to be reaped, and the bureaucratic disadvantages minimized, when the work-experience organizers are in close touch with link teachers in the schools and are concerned with educational as well as administrative functions (see p. 91).

There is a range of ways in which LEAs have responded to the tasks of surpervising, coordinating and organizing work experience (see Box 6.1). LEAs may choose to provide minimum resourcing simply to supervise the legal requirements of work-experience schemes. Beyond this, support for school-based work-experience organizers may be provided through a register of approved placements which have been vetted by, for example, the Careers Service. In order to rationalize demands upon employers, the LEA may further decide to coordinate when individual schools send out their students. An extended degree of centralization occurs when schools are obliged to submit their work-experience schemes for LEA approval. In all these cases, the locus of operational responsibility remains with the schools.

In some cases, though, the major burden of establishing and administering the system of work-experience organization may be taken on by the LEA, and located within the Careers Service (see the Coventry LEA case-study below) or within the advisory and support services (see the Newham

---

Box 6.1   Main types of LEA-based work-experience organization

1. LEA supervision

   Type A — LEA supervises legal requirements only.
   Type B — LEA supervises legal requirements and maintains a register of approved placements.

2. LEA coordination

   Type C — LEA supervises as in Type B, and coordinates the timing of when individual schools send students out.

3. LEA 'in-house' organization

   Type D — The Careers Service coordinates and organizes work experience.
   Type E — A seconded teacher acts as the LEA's work-experience organizer.
   Type F — A hybrid model, with LEA coordination and organization in some areas, or for students taking certain courses, but not others.

4. 'External' organization

   Type G — Project Trident organization and coordination across the LEA.
   Type H — Project Trident in some areas, but school-based organization in other areas.
   Type I — Project Trident in some areas, and LEA 'in-house' organization in other areas.

5. 'Partnership' organization

   Type J — A seconded industrialist is appointed by the local Chamber of Commerce or Local Employers Network (LEN) group.
   Type K — A seconded teacher or industrialist is appointed by a local education–business partnership.

Source: Adapted from Elsom (1987).

LEA case-study below). In many instances, LEAs have chosen the option of engaging the services of Project Trident, which appoints seconded industrialists to operate the system (see the Doncaster LEA case-study below): in some cases Project Trident may cover the LEA as a whole; in others, it covers only particular areas. The development of the Compact initiative and the rise of education–business partnerships (see pp. 7–8) provides a model similar to Project Trident, where the Compact/partnership work-experience organizer may be an industrialist or an LEA secondee, and where the LEA is a partner within the scheme rather than the sole proprietor.

The introduction of LMS creates possibilities for a 'half-way house' between school-based and LEA-based organization: i.e. consortium-based organization. This occurs where a group of schools decides jointly to organize and coordinate work experience. TVEI has in some cases encouraged the formation of such consortia.

The organization of work experience in an LEA can be viewed in some respects in terms of an economic market for services (Miller, Jamieson and Watts, 1989). The schools represent the consumers of the service, and employers represent its suppliers. In school-organized work experience, the market is unregulated, with competition between schools for scarce services

— that is, popular placements. Demand tends to be seasonal, and concentrated at particular times of the school year. This excess demand results in pressure upon employers and shortages of popular placements. Placements tend to be allocated either on the basis of 'first-come-first-served' or on the strength of the special relationship built up between employers and schools — for example, through twinning arrangements. On this analysis, the purpose of LEA-based organization is to intervene in the market in order to rationalize demands upon the suppliers by coordinating demand according to a set of principles other than 'first-come-first-served'.

An interesting recent development is the awareness among employers of the so-called 'demographic time-bomb' which, coupled with the spread of education–business partnerships and Compacts, has increased the possibility of the market for work experience becoming an extension of the youth labour market, as work experience is used to a growing extent for recruitment purposes (see Chapter 8). In this sense the employers could come to be viewed increasingly as customers rather than suppliers in the work-experience market.

The Components of Work-experience Organization

Work-experience organization, therefore, constitutes a system for matching the demands of the education system with the supply of available placements in the local economy. The main components of the system can be analyzed using the same four-fold model adopted in Chapter 5: policy, resources, tasks and roles. These combine to convert inputs into outputs. Inputs to the system include offers from employers of work-experience placements, demands from schools for these placements, and funding from the LEA. Outputs can be seen in terms of the numbers of students attending work placements in a given time-period.

Regarding *policy*, the growth in work experience in recent years has led many LEAs to produce policies and guidelines on work-experience practice. Such documents can vary from short statements of policy to comprehensive guidance on all aspects of work experience including both administrative and curricular matters. An example of the latter is that provided by Salford LEA through its Careers Service. Its policy statement is a model of brevity: 'It is the policy of this Authority to offer the opportunity of work experience to all pupils and students in Salford'. The policy is supported with a detailed account of the responsibilities of all parties involved, and includes a system of two-level training to ensure that these responsibilities are understood (see p. 129). The handbook, in addition to dealing with legal and insurance issues and including standardized pro-formas, also covers the integration of work experience into the curriculum.

Regarding *resources*, the *human* resources of the system include the work-experience organizer(s) together with ancillary support staff, and the school-based link teachers. The experience and training of the people who are operating the system will influence their perceptions of the purpose of work experience in schools, and of their role in terms of its balance between administrative and educational tasks. *Non-human* resources include the time, space and finance allocated to the system.

In most schemes there is also a common pattern of *tasks* which form part of the system. These tasks may involve the work-experience organizer in carrying out a number of *roles*. Such roles can be grouped under four core roles for the purposes of our analysis: a pioneer role in establishing the system; a leader role in coordinating and supporting other people in the system; an administrator role in maintaining and operating the system; and a monitor-evaluator role in searching for ways to improve the system.

During the initial start-up period, the *pioneer* role involves establishing the basic system, and creating pro-formas and information materials about the scheme for employers, students, teachers, and parents. Placements must be located, which involves persuading employers to offer work placements of a particular type, for a particular period of time, on a number of occasions during the year. Employers must be acquainted with the aims and objectives of the scheme, and the work-place has to be vetted for reasons of health and safety. Negotiation skills are important when agreeing on suitable induction procedures, work tasks, job descriptions, 'fringe' benefits for the student, research time, and feedback and assessment roles for the employer or supervisor. Once the placement 'bank' is established, either in the form of a file of job descriptions or on a database, information about the scheme needs to be disseminated to schools, parents, and employers.

The *leader* role is important when the organizer has to provide professional development and coordination. The work-experience organizer must operate a procedure for allocating blocks of time during the school year when each participating school can send students out. There are times of the year when demand is at a peak — for example, after examinations in the summer term, when year-10 students are eligible and many schools wish to give year-11 students an experience of work prior to embarking on their post-16 education. Such a procedure must be seen to be fair and open to change each year, so that favoured slots can be distributed evenly over time.

The work-experience organizer will rely on the support of the school-based link teacher for the smooth operation of the system. It is therefore important that the link teachers are offered training, support, and networking, in order that new ideas and good practice can be shared. This may include examples of good practice in the integration of work experience into the curriculum (see Chapter 9). The work-experience organizer may assume the role of leader in relation to this professional development work.

The *administrator* role involves a major set of tasks: sending to schools details of available placements; informing students and parents about the scheme; obtaining parental permission. Information must be sent to employers informing them which placements are required, at what times, by which school, and by which student. Matching involves taking information about the student which is perceived to be relevant, and matching this to the available placements; rematching of displaced students may be necessary in some cases. Teacher visits also need to be organized to monitor students' progress.

The *monitor–evaluator* role can involve collecting, storing and retrieving data about each placement. This may include an employer assessment of the student, and a monitoring sheet on the quality of the placement compiled by the visiting teacher. The evaluator role can also include writing a summative report on individual school schemes, and/or upon the scheme as a whole.

These four core roles of the work–experience organizer are central to the effectiveness of the work–experience system. The pioneer role ensures successful start-up, and the administrator role involves system maintenance. The leader role produces effective coordination and use of the system. The monitor–evaluator role prevents the system from ossifying by providing information to aid the process of change.

The four roles can all be performed by the central coordinator of work experience, but in some cases the roles may be shared. For example, school-based link teachers may take on a pioneer role in finding a proportion of their own placements. The training dimension of the leader role may be assumed by the local schools–industry coordinator. Aspects of the administrator role may be devolved to individual schools through the establishment of a computer network linked to the central database. Box 6.2 summarizes the main tasks associated with the core roles in LEA-based work-experience organization.

Case-studies of LEA-based Organization

In this section, we examine three case-studies of work-experience systems. They illustrate diverse and interesting practice, as well as raising a number of issues which are discussed in the concluding part of the chapter. The first case-study (adapted from Miller, 1989b) describes the operation of the major 'external' organizer, Project Trident, in Doncaster LEA. It is a representative example of the Type H organizational model (see Box 6.1). The second case-study (adapted from Miller, 1989c) is an account of the Careers Support Unit in the London Borough of Newham, which is an example of Type F work-experience organization. The final case-study (adapted from Miller, 1989a) illustrates the system evolved by the Education–Industry Unit in the City of Coventry, including its computerized system for recording placements and matching students. It is an example of the Type D organizational model, where the organizers are part of the Careers Service. Box 6.3 summarizes some of the main points of difference between the three case-study models. They provide a snapshot of the form the models took during the

Box 6.2   *Organizational roles and tasks*

1. The pioneer role

   (a) Creating the organizational system
   (b) Informing employers and teachers about the system
   (c) Persuading employers and teachers to participate in the system
   (d) Finding the placements
   (e) Vetting the placements for health and safety
   (f) Negotiating suitable job descriptions
   (g) Establishing the database or 'job-file'

2. The leader role

   (h) Coordinating the timing of each school's placements
   (i) Training of school-based link teachers to use the system
   (j) Supporting teachers in the curriculum integration of work experience
   (k) Networking school-based link teachers
   (l) Initiating improvements to the system

3. The administrator role

   (m) Communicating information about placements to schools
   (n) Obtaining permission from parents
   (o) Matching available placements to student choices or scheme criteria
   (p) Informing employers about students
   (q) Briefing students on the administrative aspects of the scheme
   (r) Organizing the teacher visits
   (s) Rematching displaced students

4. The monitor–evaluator role

   (t) Collecting data about the placement and the placement experience
   (u) Monitoring the balance of placements and the quality of individual placements
   (v) Evaluating individual school schemes and the scheme as a whole

(*Note*: The tasks of the school-based work-experience coordinator are discussed on pp. 90–4).

1988/89 academic year. All three have continued to evolve since then in response to local and national developments.

Case-study A: Project Trident in Doncaster

Background.   Project Trident had organized work experience in Doncaster since 1977. The LEA paid a fee to the Trident Trust, which arranged for the secondment of a Project Director to operate the Trident system. The LEA provided an office and administrative support. The demand for placements came from the twenty-six secondary and special schools that participated in the scheme. Participation in the scheme was voluntary and most schools had chosen to join in over time. Increasing demand from schools had resulted in the need to enlarge the supply of placements. In 1982, there were 70 employers participating, but by 1987/88 this had risen to 733 employers, providing 1,138 jobs, for an annual total of 6,599 placements. The balance of

Box 6.3   LEA case-studies: a comparison

	Case-study A: Doncaster	Case-study B: Newham	Case-study C: Coventry
1. Main organizer	Project Trident	LEA Careers/ Industry Support Unit and school work-experience organizers	LEA Education– Industry Unit, located within Careers Service
2. Type of LEA-based organization	Type H	Type F	Type D
3. Participation by schools	Voluntary	Voluntary	Compulsory
4. Coordination of school programmes	Coordinated	Not coordinated	Coordinated
5. Nature of placement bank	List of job descriptions	Small central database and school placement banks	Computerized central database
6. Personnel	Seconded industrialist(s)	Seconded teachers, part of Careers/ Industry Support Unit	Seconded teachers, part of Education–Industry Unit; plus administrator seconded from industry, part of Careers Service

jobs, according to the classification used by Trident, was 197 jobs in manufacturing industries, 684 jobs in service industries, and 257 jobs in public services. The outputs from the organizational system were the number of students completing the standard Trident three-week work placement in a given year. During the 1987/88 academic year, 244 year-10 students, 2,095 year-11 students and 141 sixth-form and further-education students were placed.

Organizational roles.   In her pioneer role the Project Director had approached headteachers collectively, then individually, to explain the standard Trident organizational model. This model involved whole year-groups going out for three-week blocks of time. Employers had been recruited from the Yellow Pages, through talks to the local Round Table, and through schools. A set of standardized job descriptions had been compiled for use by schools in the process of job choice and matching.

The leader role involved coordinating the blocks of time when students would be sent out. The year was divided into seven three-week blocks, with demand from schools being heaviest during the autumn term. The Project Director endeavoured to block schools together from different parts of the LEA in order to avoid too much overlapping demand for particular employers and jobs. Typically, in any one time-block, three schools sent out 180 students each. The Project Director supported the school-based link teachers, often Heads of Careers, through personal contact and through the distribution of support materials in the form of a teachers' and a students' handbook. Work-experience INSET was provided through the local schools–industry coordinator.

The administrator role required the Project Director to visit the school to explain the organizational process to students, and to deliver a set of job descriptions from which students could prioritize three or four. Students with special needs had a more limited range of placements to choose from, often in construction, parks, garages, and kitchens. The students completed application forms, teachers' comments were added, and the Director then matched students to placements. Agreement forms were sent to schools with details of each student's placement, and parental approval was obtained and returned to the Trident Office. After the placement, students returned report forms to the Trident Office, providing some brief feedback upon their degree of enjoyment of, and opinions about, the placement. The Trident Director collected the employers' assessment reports: these helped in 'credentialling' some students, who obtained YTS places and jobs as a result. Project Trident was also operating a Record of Achievement for students successfully completing work experience (see pp. 255–7).

The role of monitor–evaluator involved collecting data about aspects of the scheme in order to improve it. Changes in the quality of placements were monitored through a system of cards which were completed by teachers on their visit, and collected by the Project Director. A comparison between present and previous cards could reveal any deterioration in quality. In practice, only four placements had been taken off the list because of the unsuitable nature of the tasks; others had withdrawn voluntarily. Such a monitoring process enabled job descriptions to be kept up to date.

For the purposes of writing the annual summative report on the scheme, the Director collected some statistical data. These included the range of student choices, and the number of students receiving first, second, third, fourth, and alternative choices. During 1987/88, two-thirds of students obtained their first or second choices. Matching was more difficult at times of peak demand when there were more students chasing a limited pool of placements. Demand for placements was very skewed, with high demand for jobs in retailing, schools, and offices. Job descriptions specified the location and name of companies so that popular ones could be identified by students. In general, the work-experience choices of students bore little relationship to the distribution of available jobs in the area. The extension of TVEI and the advent of the Doncaster Compact had led to demand from the schools for a mix of two- and three-week blocks for work experience, and this seemed likely to require changes to the organizational system.

The school-based link teacher. The role of the school-based link teacher was not only to liaise with the Trident Director over the administrative aspects of the scheme, but also to deliver the educational and pastoral frame through which the scheme was integrated into the curriculum. At Don Valley School, for example, the link teacher was the Head of Careers, and work experience occurred within a careers-education frame (see Chapter 2 and also pp. 163–5). In terms of the administrator role, the link teacher arranged a 'job shop' display of all the available placements. Forms entered one at a time to study the job descriptions, and to make their choices with the guidance of the link teacher. The teacher's knowledge of the placements and the students enabled him to spot possible mismatches, and to advise students against making certain choices.

A second important task for the link teacher was the organization of the teacher visits during the placement. A large poster was placed in the staff-room with the names of students, jobs, location, and contacts. Form tutors had the first 'pick', up to a maximum of ten students, for the visits, which commenced from the Friday at the end of the first week. The teachers were briefed to talk to the students, to record any problems, to look around the work-place, to foster further links, and to engage in good public relations for the school.

A third task involved in-school evaluation of the scheme through the use of a student evaluation form, and the preparation of an annual summative evaluation report.

Case-study B: Work experience in the London Borough of Newham

Background. The organizational model for work experience in Newham had evolved during the 1980s. At the start of this period an 'external organizer' had been engaged by the LEA to administer the scheme, but the failure of schools to 'own' such a model led to the appointment of a Careers Support Teacher to develop what was described as a 'democratic model' of work-experience organization. Additional resourcing from the LEA permitted the establishment of the Careers/Industry Support Unit, which broadened the work to include schools–industry links in general. Thus work experience was seen as one in a set of work-related activities, and the demands made upon employers for a variety of links could be more easily rationalized. Schools could ask the central team for help in establishing or expanding their work-experience programmes. The prime responsibility for organizing work experience, however, remained with the school.

Although there were 100 employers offering 350 placements on the central database, it was the team's policy not to offer more than 50 per cent of the total places required to each participating school. In this way, school-based link teachers had an important role to play in the finding of placements, and in all aspects of administration. The shared administration of the scheme had enabled the central team to concentrate on raising quality, through curriculum and professional development. Despite the team's emphasis on quality, the quantity of work experience had risen twelve-fold between 1982 and 1990, from 226 to 2,700 student placements.

Organizational roles. The leader role had involved producing comprehensive guidelines for all the LEA's teachers organizing work experience. An important goal for the team had been to change the attitudes of teachers, from perceiving work experience as mainly for the less able to regarding it as an entitlement for all. Student diaries had been developed for 14–16 and 16–18-year-olds. A central set of curriculum materials on the world of work had been created, and was loaned to schools as a travelling library.

The team had played an important role in promoting equal opportunities through work experience. Although one-quarter of Newham's population were classed as being from ethnic-minority backgrounds, the placement bank had few ethnic-minority employers. A 'positive action programme' involved the team in linking with local black networks and 'cold-calling' by visiting work premises in targeted areas. Equal-opportunities and anti-racist policies were accorded a high priority in the LEA work-experience guidelines.

Thus the leader role had been particularly important in the Newham organizational model. New school-based link teachers were given training and support for the equivalent of half a day for half a term. This involved working alongside the link teachers, demonstrating good practice in telephone links with employers, and finding placements through Yellow Pages or through cold-calling. The aim was to foster independence, not reliance on the central resource, and at the same time to promote quality and good practice. This encouraged schools to develop their own network of local employers. In the small-business world of the East End of London, many employers preferred to have close links with one or two schools, rather than contacts with all the LEA's schools.

A rapid turnover of staff had meant that this package of support and training had been in constant demand each year. The team had been heavily involved in meeting INSET needs in response to curriculum changes. Thus, for example, the arrival of CPVE with its compulsory work experience, which did not necessarily involve careers teachers, had brought a new need. The unit had also networked the school-based link teachers through regular meetings in order to share good practice.

School-based, school-focused INSET had generally involved an examination of aims and objectives, and an investigation of ways of involving different curriculum areas. INSET sessions with teachers and employers had explored differing perceptions of work experience. Increasingly, work-experience INSET was integrated with other forms of schools–industry INSET — for example, on work simulation and work-based projects.

Coordination had not been a major function of the unit, and schools had been able to choose their own favoured time to send students out. 'Bunching' occurred at the peak times of June/July, October, and February, and de-mands upon employers tended to be uncoordinated, unless they were on the central database. Subsequently an annual calendar was developed within which schools 'democratically' opted for specific two-week blocks.

The administrator role of the team had been minimized, although there was a range of tasks associated with meeting school requests for placements from the central database, and maintaining up-to-date information on these placements.

The monitor–evaluator role was again a shared responsibility between the central team and the school organizers. Monitoring was carried out through the teacher visits, and students were involved in evaluation through a pro-forma in the centrally-distributed diary. In addition, specific evaluation projects had been set up to respond to identified problems. For example, the team leader had found that employers made many assumptions about stu-dents' experience, knowledge and skills, and that these often proved to be baseless. She had also discovered that supervisors were inadequately briefed, and that many were poor at explaining to students their work tasks. This had led to the appointment of a seconded teacher to investigate 'quality' place-ments, with a view to producing guidelines to help employers improve the structure and process of work placements.

The school-based link teacher. The link teachers were given training and support by the team. In addition, they were provided with student materials, which covered preparation, briefing, debriefing, and follow-up. As we have seen, they were encouraged to build up their own network of employers, and this meant that in such cases they were responsible for checking the health and safety of work-places. They were also responsible for the matching process and for promoting the LEA equal-opportunities policy within the scheme. The teacher visits, monitoring, assessment, and evaluation were all the responsibility of the schools, although the guidelines produced by the central team offered pro-formas and ideas on all these areas.

Case-study C: Work experience in the City of Coventry

Background. All work experience in the City of Coventry was organized through the Education–Industry Unit, which was housed within the Careers Service headquarters. The unit was well resourced and staffed by two seconded teachers acting as Education–Industry Development Officers, a

Coordinator for Work Experience, and administrative support. In addition, there were centrally-based careers officers, who worked with the unit on employer placement liaison, and school-based careers officers, who worked alongside the school link teachers. Apart from work experience, the unit had responsibility for teacher placements in industry, and all other aspects of schools–industry links. Central to all the work of the unit was the computerized register of employers, which listed some 5,000 placements across the city.

Organizational roles. The pioneer role had involved establishing the large central database of work placements, and the production of a series of documents to inform teachers and employers about aspects of the scheme. The comprehensive catalogue which was produced annually showed the vast range of placements which were available to students. Individual employers were not named in the catalogue, and students were encouraged to apply for particular occupational areas instead. This avoided heavy demand for particular employers and the resulting disappointment for large numbers of students. Over time, through personal contact and through INSET, the unit had involved headteachers, governors, and advisers in the scheme, thereby raising the status of work experience in the city.

The leader role included managing the annual planning process, which involved schools in submitting their proposals to the unit. The unit matched the total demand with the estimated supply of placements at different times of the year; where necessary, dates were renegotiated. Training for teachers was an important aspect of the unit's work, both for the link teachers, who had to administer the system and to liaise with the Coordinator for Work Experience, and for other teachers involved in the educational and pastoral dimensions of the scheme. The unit had been particularly active in disseminating new and interesting practice relating to work experience, through support materials and INSET.

The administrator role was a specialist function undertaken by the Coordinator for Work Experience. School-based link teachers and school-based careers officers used the catalogue and helped students complete a detailed application form, which contained detailed matching criteria (see Chapter 11). These were passed to the Coordinator, who interrogated several fields on the database in order to find suitable placements. Rather than matching each student with a particular placement, he presented the schools with a range of possibilities for each student. Interim bookings were made with the selected employers. The schools then had to consult with students on placement suitability, bookings were confirmed, and all students attended a preliminary interview.

Matching student demands with available placements was a continuing problem. The school curriculum and the courses on offer did not reflect the economic base of the city. Each year hundreds of placements were unused, and yet there were shortfalls in other categories. Demand was especially high for placements in service industries, caring, information technology, business–management–related work, sport and leisure, and tourism. In contrast, there was a large proportion of placements in manufacturing, engineering and fabrication where demand was low, largely because of their traditional image involving dirty, heavy work.

The unit in its monitor–evaluator role had encouraged all schools to engage in monitoring and evaluation on their own account. The declared purposes of the monitoring visits by teachers were: to check on the student's welfare; to see if the programme met the agreed objectives; to ensure that students were aware of health and safety issues; to check that the administrative arrangements were smooth; and to help students with their Records of Achievement. In addition, teachers completed a monitoring report form, which involved assessing the placement, and drawing the attention of the unit to any health-and-safety or other issues that needed to be followed up. The unit had encouraged schools to produce pupil profiles based on the experience, and link teachers to produce annual evaluation reports. LEA advisers had also been involved in visiting students during and after placements to evaluate the effectiveness of the programme.

The school-based link teacher. The link teachers had an important role in providing the educational and pastoral frames for the programme, and they were also involved throughout in administering the scheme in their school. The guidance and counselling role of the teachers was emphasized in this model, and the application form was viewed as the key to successful matching and beneficial experiences for students. The teacher and careers officer in the school, apart from liaising with the Coordinator for Work Experience over placement allocation, had to arrange for student interviews and teacher visits.

At the time when this case-study was being prepared (1989), it had been decided that the system was to become more decentralized, with all schools having access to the centralized database via terminals. The central unit would continue to maintain the register, but more time would be devoted to improving the quality of placements through contact with employers.

Issues

In this section three main aspects of LEA-based organization are discussed. The first concerns the problems associated with managing the change from school-based to LEA-based organization — in particular, the question of territoriality. The second relates to the different organizational models illustrated in the case-studies. In this connection, three central issues are addressed: the background of key personnel; the question of 'ownership' and the division of core roles between the central unit and the school; and the flexibility of the system to respond to changes within related aspects of the

LEA organization. Finally, there is a discussion of ways of evaluating LEA-based work-experience organization.

Managing the Change from School-to LEA-based Organization

During the pioneer stage of a centralized scheme for the organization of work experience, all work-experience coordinators will be faced by similar management-of-change issues. Central administration, whether in-house or external, threatens the autonomy and status of school-based organizers, who commonly tend to be Heads of Careers. Yet their cooperation is essential if the new system is to work.

In particular, during the initial phase of building the central register, schools may be asked to 'give up' work placements which they may have used for several years. This represents a challenge to the phenomenon of territoriality: the tendency of some schools to regard particular placements as their 'property'. Territoriality seems to result from two main factors: the time and effort spent in obtaining the placements; and the sense of ownership associated with placements derived from the school's own parents and governors, or from local twinning arrangements. The main argument against putting such placements in an LEA 'pool' is that the quality of the placement is determined by the special relationship with the school. There is also a concern that other schools may 'spoil' the placement, through inadequate preparation of students. Although some schools do have exclusive use of certain companies for placements, such exclusivity is sometimes imaginary rather than real, as other schools will often be using the same company at different times. Some organizational models, such as that of Newham, allow more latitude to schools to retain their placements and so do not threaten the autonomy of the school in the same way as schemes which seek to control the vast majority of placements.

In one LEA, not represented in our case-studies, the threat to school autonomy was taken further. One of the aims of shifting from school-based organization to a compulsory LEA-based organization was to encourage good practice in the form of greater curricular integration of work experience. Schools were accordingly instructed to submit their proposals for work-experience schemes — including the curriculum objectives, and preparation and debriefing outlines — to the LEA's central unit for its approval. Such an approach caused resistance, because it was seen as challenging school autonomy not only on organizational but also on curricular matters, and as elevating the professional judgment of the central coordinator over that of the teacher organizers.

Another problem facing the work-experience organizer during the start-up period is whether the scheme will cover all schools and be compulsory, as in the Coventry case-study, or whether it will be voluntary, with schools opting in over a period of time, as in Doncaster and Newham. The former approach is likely to meet with more opposition, and will probably require greater initial resourcing, than the incremental approach to change. The incremental approach is particularly likely to work in shire counties, where there is little overlap between the work-experience 'hinterland' of individual schools, and therefore less competition for placements. Both approaches can benefit from the support of clear LEA policy guidelines.

Once the central organizational model is in place, its success will be judged by the practical demonstration of efficiency and effectiveness when compared to school-based organization. It is the case that many larger companies prefer dealing with a single point of contact within an area, between a named individual within the company and a named individual in the education service. Smaller companies, including some branches of larger companies (such as building societies), are more likely to prefer direct and personal contact with a particular school. It seems reasonable that centralized schemes should be flexible enough for individual schools to establish and retain some placements which are based upon employer preferences and close personal links.

Organizational Models

In our case-studies we illustrated two examples of LEA-organized, and one example of externally-organized, work experience. The geography of the LEA is an important variable when choosing an appropriate organizational model. It is accordingly worth noting that our examples are all drawn from relatively compact metropolitan areas.

At the same time, the degree of centralization varied between the three examples. The *laissez-faire* approach of the Newham scheme was voluntary, did not involve all schools, and did not attempt to coordinate the timings of when schools sent students out. Both the Doncaster and Coventry schemes, on the other hand, included coordination and administration as key elements. In Coventry all schools were included within the scheme as part of the LEA policy, whereas in Doncaster schools had opted in over time, and some schools organized their own work experience.

The personnel responsible for LEA-organized work experience can be careers officers, seconded industrialists or teachers. In general, it will be easier for teachers, who will often be leading practitioners, to become involved in the non-administrative aspects of work experience, particularly the in-service education and training of teachers. External organizers, and secondees organizing work experience in partnerships and Compacts, are often industrialists. This gives them an advantage in dealing with employers, but makes it more difficult for them to play a leading role in the curriculum aspects of work experience, and in the professional development of teachers. These latter dimensions will often not be a part of the contract which external organizers have with the LEA: this usually focuses on the administrative tasks associated with work experience. An optimum solution might involve a team of people from a range of backgrounds working together. In Coventry, for example, the Coordinator for Work Experience who dealt with administration was a seconded industrialist, the Education–Industry team who played a leader role in INSET were all seconded teachers, and in the schools the careers officers worked with the school-based link teachers to operate the programme.

The question of 'ownership' of work experience was raised in the Newham case-study. It may be that external organization makes it easier for some schools to maintain low-status 'bolt-on' work experience, since the external organizer can be blamed for any deficiencies in the scheme. Clearly, the Newham approach to the role of the central unit, and to the division of organizational tasks, leaves considerable ownership vested in the schools; conversely, it does not coordinate demands upon employers in the same way as in the other schemes we have examined. Ownership can be a product of school-based, school-focused INSET, and it is here that some LEA organizers have an advantage over external organizers.

The issue of ownership should not, however, be regarded as an inevitable by-product of a particular model of work-experience organization. What needs to be clarified in all LEA-based models is the role of the school-based link teacher and the division of tasks between the central unit and the school. The tendency in some schemes for there to be a sharp division of labour, with the 'educational' dimension left to the schools and the 'administrative' aspects dealt with by the central unit, appears to exacerbate problems of ownership, responsibility and accountability. A partnership model, with elements of the four core roles being shared between the central organizer(s) and the school link teacher(s), seems most likely to ensure shared ownership of the scheme.

The final issue concerns the degree of flexibility of the organizational model. It is often difficult for external organizers, who have a contract to deliver a particular model of work experience in an LEA, to respond rapidly to changing demands from the education system. The work-experience unit will often be attached to, but separate from, other parts of the education service dealing with employers and schools–industry links. Such a unit will generally not have access to in-service budgets or decision-making. In contrast, the case-studies of Newham and Coventry demonstrate the flexibility of these particular LEAs' units to changing curriculum demands, and the leading role played in improving practice in the schools. This flexibility resulted in part from the reduction in their administrative burden, through devolution to schools in the case of Newham, and through the application of new technology and the appointment of a specialist administrator in the case of Coventry. It is also, however, clear that there are considerable advantages in linking all personnel concerned with industry links in one unit, in terms of offering a coordinated approach to implementing LEA policy, and to INSET provision.

Box 6.4 *A framework for evaluating LEA-based work-experience organization*

Targeting	• Are the needs of the schools and students clearly defined and understood?
	• Have the intended clients been clearly identified?
	• To what extent do the needs of schools come before the needs of employers?
Inputs	• Are there resources available at a sufficient level and in a suitable form to meet the needs identified?
Process	• Are the standards required by statute, professional practice and efficient administration met in the delivery of the scheme?
Output	• Are the services being delivered consistent with the original goals, procedures and standards?
Outcome	• Do the services provided meet the needs of the client groups?
	• Are there unanticipated outcomes?
Efficiency and review	• Is the overall deployment of resources balanced and consistent with the objectives of the LEA?

Source: Adapted from Spittle (1989), after Lishman (1984).

Evaluation

In the light of the pressure for a rapid growth in the number of work-experience placements, some LEAs have reviewed their current organizational arrangements in order to make a judgment about their ability to respond to changing circumstances (Spittle, 1989). The organization of work experience in one London education authority was evaluated using a framework comprising six areas: targeting; inputs; process; output; outcome; and efficiency and review (Lishman, 1984). Box 6.4 illustrates some of the key questions that could be included in an evaluation of LEA-based work-experience organization. Where the evaluation highlights problem areas, a decision must be taken on whether to adjust practice within the current organizational system or to change to a different model of organization. In this case, it is appropriate to undertake a feasibility study in order to find the optimum alternative. Such a study should include: *technical* issues to do with the likely impact upon the quality and the quantity of work placements; *economic* issues concerned with start-up funding and costings compared to the current model; and *political* issues to do with who will benefit or lose from the change and the extent to which perceived gains are certain (Spittle, 1989, p. 33).

Conclusion

The expansion of demand for work experience, analyzed in Chapter 1, has led to pressures for greater resourcing and coordinating of schemes. LEAs have adopted different strategies in response to these pressures. In some cases, a piecemeal approach to change has seen work-experience organization hived off from related LEA functions, mirroring the 'bolt-on-to-the-curriculum' syndrome often found at school level (see pp. 154–5). In other cases, the development of whole-LEA and whole-school policies and strategies for links between education and industry have produced a more systematic integration of work-experience organization with school–industry work and INSET provision, across the authority as a whole. The harmonization of administrative and curriculum support at LEA level for work experience has enabled schools to respond to increased demand and, in many cases, to improve the quality of their programmes by sharing good practice via INSET and local networking.

During the 1990s, however, this centralizing trend may be reversed. LMS and the opting-out of some schools from local authority control may mean that some schools will choose to organize and administer their own work-experience schemes in areas where these functions were previously undertaken by the LEA. It is likely that many schools will continue to recognize the benefits of the administration costs being borne centrally, and of cooperation with neighbouring schools over the timing of schemes. LEA-based organization of work experience will tend to be viewed as a service to the schools, which will free teachers to concentrate on the educational and pastoral aspects of the scheme, rather than its administration.

In terms of the market analysis we introduced earlier in the chapter (pp. 107–8) the role of the LEA as coordinator and broker of work experience in an area may therefore decline. But this is unlikely to result in a return to the 'free market' of the past. It is more likely that the increasing organization of the supply-side market among the employers will intervene to take on certain functions, particularly those concerned with meeting the needs of employers — for example, the rationalizing and coordinating of supply. In the event of either a continued LEA role in coordinating demand together with an employer-led coordination of supply, or the development of an education-business partnership, the regulated work-experience market of the late 1990s should be well placed to ensure work experience for all students.

Chapter 7

Legal Issues

A.G. Watts and Anthony Johns

Because work experience is designed for educational purposes, but takes place on employers' premises, it involves a variety of difficult legal issues. Some of these are common to all out-of-school experiences. But work experience and work shadowing are distinctive in these respects because not only are they *off-site* activities: they are also *out of sight* of teachers, and not just occasionally but routinely so (see Box 7.1). In effect, LEAs and schools 'franchise' some of their educational and custodial responsibilities to employers (Law, 1986). Moreover, since work experience in particular involves the performance of work *tasks*, it becomes subject to statutory restrictions relating to the employment of young people.

The current position regarding school-based work-experience schemes is regulated by the Education (Work Experience) Act 1973. This was designed primarily as *enabling* rather than *restrictive* legislation: its declared aim was 'to enable education authorities to arrange for children to have work experience, as part of their education in the last year of compulsory schooling'. It was accompanied by DES Circular 7/74, which provided general guidelines on school-based work-experience schemes (including references to those involving students over compulsory school age): this was superseded in 1988 by the DES booklets *Education at Work: A Guide for Schools* (DES, 1988a) and *Education at Work: A Guide for Employers* (DES, 1988b). An increasing number of LEAs are supplementing these documents with their own guidelines.

This chapter does not attempt to provide an authoritative guide to the legal issues involved in work experience and how they can best be tackled. It does, however, attempt to define the main issues and to discuss some of the problems they pose. In particular, it will discuss issues related to *permissibility* in terms both of age and of employment sector, to *discrimination* in terms of sex and race, to *health and safety*, to *insurance*, to *costs*, and to *protection of children*.

One of the problems with the complexities of these matters is that they consume so much time and anxiety. Some teachers are clearly deterred from getting involved in work-experience schemes by uncertainty about such legal

Box 7.1	The basis for the legal status of work experience in relation to some other educational activities (especially work-related activities)	
	On-site	*Off-site*
In-sight	(Normal classroom work) Work simulations (most)	Work visits
Out of sight	(Some library work) (Some playground activities) Mini-enterprises (at times)	Work experience Work shadowing

questions as liability in case of accidents. Moreover, such issues sometimes command so much attention that they may leave little energy for the issues which, we contend, are ultimately much more important in terms of legitimating work experience as an educational activity: the *curricular* issues to which much of this book is addressed. Yet it is essential that the legal questions be covered, not only in order to remain within the law, but also to reduce the chances that good curricular practice will be undermined by malpractice in the work–place.

Permissibility

The Education (Work Experience) Act 1973 states that

> the enactments relating to the prohibition or regulation of the employment of children shall not now apply to the employment of a child in his last year of compulsory schooling where the employment is in pursuance of arrangements made or approved by the local education authority ... with a view to providing him with work experience as part of his education.

The restriction to the 'last year of compulsory schooling' means that students whose sixteenth birthday falls between 1 September and 31 January can begin work experience from the end of the spring term in year 10, but that those whose birthday occurs between 1 February and 31 August can only do so from the beginning of June (DES, 1988a, p. 13). In practice, therefore, the restriction is normally interpreted as permitting work-experience schemes to take place from half-term in the summer term of year 10. Many schools like to locate their schemes during these few weeks at the end of year 10 rather than in year 11, because of the pressures of public examinations during the latter. The result is a considerable 'bunching' of demand into the space of a few weeks, which in turn greatly increases the difficulties of finding a sufficient supply of places to meet the demand. Concentrating schemes close to the end of the summer term can also have the effect of severely reducing opportunities for the crucially important debriefing and follow-up stages (see Chapter 12).

The case for reducing the age limit is strengthened by the pressures for curricular integration (see Chapter 9). If work experience is to be fully integrated into two-year GCSE courses, for example, insisting that they be confined to the latter stages of such courses makes little sense. There are of course concerns about the age at which students are likely to be responsible enough to be acceptable to employers. But there would seem to be a strong argument for bringing the limit forward until at least Easter or even Christmas of the fourth year. In Scotland, under the Self Governing Schools etc. (Scotland) Act 1989, the legislation has already been amended to bring it forward to 1 May.

In addition to age restrictions, the Education (Work Experience) Act also prohibits employment in certain locations and forms of work. This includes work in sectors subject to a statutory restriction based on age limits which exclude students of compulsory school age, and also work on ships (as covered by Section 1[2] of the Employment of Women, Young Persons and Children Act 1920 and by the Merchant Shipping Act 1970). The Act also applies to work-experience students various other statutory restrictions relating to the employment of young persons. This used to include a large number of different items of legislation, ranging from the Children and Young Persons Act 1933 to the Licensing Act 1964 (Johns, 1987), which restricted the hours which young people of school age could work and also excluded them from certain places of work like mines and quarries. The Employment Act 1989, however, repealed much of this legislation, leaving greater responsibility to LEAs and schools to ensure that students do not work excessively long or unsocial hours. It left in place a string of restrictions on young persons working in certain processes or with machinery (e.g. locomotives) considered dangerous by the Health and Safety Executive. In addition, employment in betting shops and many licensed premises (e.g. bars) remains restricted to people over 18.

The 1989 Act has also rescinded the provision in the Children and Young Persons Act 1933 for local authorities to proscribe further forms of employment through by-laws. In some quarters there were already doubts about the extent to which these regulations applied to work experience, and indeed a document issued by the Department of Health and Social Security in 1976 (LAC/76) expressly 'disapplied' them in this connection. Nonetheless, DES Circular 7/74 stated that 'so long as the by-laws are in force, authorities and schools should have regard to their spirit and intention when selecting occupations for work experience schemes' (para. 13). Such by-laws have in some cases, for example, prohibited students being employed in catering establishments, and this has been interpreted in some areas as applying even to school kitchens. Now, it seems, these restrictions will disappear.

In short, the constraints on permissibility in terms of hours and types of employment have been considerably reduced, while those on age have not.

Discrimination

So far as discrimination is concerned, work experience is covered by the Sex Discrimination Act 1975 and by the Race Relations Act 1976, which declare that it is unlawful for a local education authority in carrying out its functions to do any act which constitutes sex or racial discrimination respectively. It also seems likely that work experience is subject to equal-opportunities legislation related to employment, and to associated codes of practice — notably the Code of Practice for Elimination of Discrimination and the Promotion of Equality of Opportunity in Employment issued by the Commission for Racial Equality in 1983. Such codes do not have the force of law, but can be taken into account by the relevant judicial bodies in any litigation based on the legislation.

The legislation covers both direct and indirect discrimination. *Direct* discrimination consists of treating a person, on sex or racial grounds, less favourably than others are or would be treated in similar circumstances. *Indirect* discrimination consists of applying a requirement or condition (e.g. in terms of dress or language) which, though applied equally to all groups, is such that a considerably smaller proportion of a particular sex or racial group can comply with it, and it cannot be shown to be justifiable on other than sex or racial grounds. There are, however, some exclusions which in effect permit some degree of positive discrimination in the case of women's cooperatives, black theatre groups, and the like.

During 1987 the Commission for Racial Equality tested the applicability of the legislation to work experience by bringing a case against an electrical repairs company in Croydon for refusing work-experience placements to two pupils of West Indian origin because they were black: proceedings were brought for inducing, or attempting to induce, the school to discriminate against the two boys by not sending them to the company. A declaration was granted by Westminster County Court that a contravention of the Race Relations Act had occurred, and the defendants were ordered to pay costs. CRE subsequently sent a circular to LEAs urging them to issue guidelines in schools about these aspects of the Race Relations Act. It added that 'if a school was to give way to discriminatory pressure or to comply with discriminatory instructions it would almost certainly be contravening Section 17 of the Race Relations Act'.

Discrimination may take place both in relation to the allocation of placements and also *within* placements. Our own fieldwork produced several examples of cases where LEA work-experience organizers had been confronted with discrimination issues. In some cases, the LEA had decided not to send any students to the placement: an example was where a firm was not prepared to allow girls to work in a certain department, for fear that they would 'disrupt' the male employees. In other cases, the employers had been prepared to change their policy: thus a department store which had been reluctant to let a Muslim girl wear trousers during her work experience was persuaded to permit her to do so.

An important issue is how proactive schools and LEAs should be in pursuing cases of these kinds. A common practice is to be reactive, relying on complaints from students, parents, etc. Some LEAs, however, systematically follow up all cases in which students who have offered themselves for interview have not subsequently been offered a placement, to ensure that the rejection has not been on discriminatory grounds.

Health and Safety

Health and safety have been major issues in relation to work experience in the Youth Training Scheme, where a number of fatal accidents have occurred. They have been given much less publicity in relation to school-based work experience, partly perhaps because such schemes have been less controversial politically, and partly also because students on them are less likely — in view of the relative brevity of their placements — to be exposed to tasks involving major dangers. We have not yet come across any examples of a fatal accident on school-based work-experience schemes, but certainly there have been a number of examples of less serious accidents.

The legal position in this respect, as outlined in the DES guidelines on work experience, is that LEAs and schools have a common-law duty to look after children in their care, and also have a duty under Section 3 of the Health and Safety at Work Act 1974 to ensure that they do not expose pupils to risk to their health and safety. They accordingly are expected to 'take reasonable steps to satisfy themselves that the placements they arrange will be safe' (DES, 1988a, p. 9). In particular, the DES recommends that 'before agreement is reached on possible placements/visits, a representative of the school should visit the premises to appraise their general suitability from a health and safety point of view' (*ibid*, p. 15).

Implementing this recommendation causes considerable problems to work-experience organizers. There are first of all difficulties in finding the time to make such visits to the large number of placements that may be involved in a scheme. Not infrequently, such visits are only made when the student is already in the placement. A device adopted by some LEAs, on the advice of the Health and Safety Executive, has been to classify placements into two categories: those which are considered suitable in terms of health and safety without a special visit, subject to the employer's completion of a health-and-safety questionnaire; and those which should be visited. Workplaces in the second category which have previously been used for work experience without problems may continue to be used for a period without a special visit, subject to completion of the questionnaire. Even such arrangements, however, may leave a considerable volume of visit requirements.

Box 7.2   An LEA training programme on health and safety

Salford LEA organizes two levels of training, to enable schools to participate in its Work Experience Scheme.

Level 1 training aims to promote an understanding of the aims and objectives of the Scheme and to explore its curricular implications and associated administration.

Level 2 training develops the skills to enable the teachers to set up and submit work-experience places for approval by the Careers Service. It includes a one-day training course, which covers various aspects of visiting employers, including health and safety requirements. This is followed by four half-day visits to companies, with careers officers. Among the objectives of these visits are: to enable the teachers to understand the criteria for acceptance of a work-experience placement, including health and safety considerations; to appreciate the standards necessary for each of these criteria; and to demonstrate the application of these standards under the observation of the careers officer.

Source: Salford LEA.

Such problems are exacerbated if students are encouraged to find their own placements (see p. 191).

In addition to these logistical difficulties, teachers and LEA organizers are often anxious about whether they are sufficiently skilled to know what to look for in making such visits: they are not, after all, factory inspectors. The DES guidelines state that 'LEA/school representatives should have for this purpose a basic grounding in health and safety, and access to specialist advice' (p. 15). HMI (1990) note that one of the merits of LEA-based organization (see Chapter 6) is that 'some one from that organisation carries out the inspection on everyone's behalf': the fact that this person is likely to have built up a degree of expertise over time means that he or she 'may well be able to satisfy a court that "due care" has been taken should the need arise' (p. 16). An alternative strategy adopted by some LEAs is to set up training programmes for this purpose: an example resting heavily on Careers Service expertise is outlined in Box 7.2. But many teachers involved in work-experience schemes have not been involved in such programmes, careers officers are not necessarily qualified either, and the specialist advice mentioned in the DES guidelines may not always be easy to find when the factory and health-and-safety inspectorates are under-staffed even in relation to their mainstream duties.

In this situation, monitoring of placements is often not as thorough as schools and LEAs might like. This may mean that some students are placed in situations which are not as safe as they should be. Conversely, it can also mean that schools and LEAs may be excessively cautious about certain broad areas of work, and that this may rule out some placements which might be perfectly satisfactory. In one LEA, for example, the Health and Safety Executive pulled several pupils off labouring placements on a new building site because in their view the supervision was inadequate. As a result, the LEA decreed that no pupils could work on a new building site, and this caused the cancellation of well-tried placements with tradespeople like plumbers, electricians, painters and carpenters who at times worked on such sites.

One response to the problem of achieving effective monitoring is to 'beef up' the formal written agreement with the employer. The DES has recommended that employers should in general be asked to make written undertakings that 'no pupils will be allowed to do work which is either prohibited by law or too hazardous for the young and inexperienced', and that 'the employer will give pupils the full range of health and safety protection which would be available for young employees' (including provision of protective clothing, etc.) (DES, 1988a, pp. 16–17). The latter point has since been reinforced by the Health and Safety (Training for Employment) Regulations 1990, which state that all those receiving training or work experience from an employer in the work-place are deemed to be employees for the purposes of health and safety legislation.

Some LEAs issue their own health-and-safety check-lists: an example is shown in Box 7.3. A problem with such lists is 'what do they leave out?': the check-list that covers every eventuality is elusive. Other LEAs accordingly prefer a general letter or undertaking on the part of the employer.

In principle, however, good practice needs to go beyond such written statements. The DES guidelines suggest that there should be detailed negotiations between schools and employers, and that this should cover three areas in particular. The first is the activities which students are to engage in, whether there are any areas which should be proscribed to all (or to particular) students, and what needs to be done to ensure that students do not stray into them. The second is whether there are any students who need special arrangements — for example, on medical grounds such as asthma, colour blindness, epilepsy, hearing impairment or other disabilities — and if so, what information and advice the school will give the employer. The third is what arrangements are to be made for briefing (both by the school and by the employer) and for induction, training and supervision. An example of a check-list for an employer's induction programme is shown in Box 7.4.

Once the student is on the placement, the basic legal responsibility for health and safety resides with the employer. If, however, there is an accident, the school/LEA and the employer may jointly or separately be considered liable for damages if negligence can be proved. This leads us to the major issue of insurance provision.

Insurance

The DES guidelines (DES, 1988a, p. 22) identify five main types of risks that may arise in the course of work experience:

(a) Injury to the pupils themselves.
(b) Injury to others on the premises (employers, visitors, customers, etc.).

Box 7.3   An LEA health-and-safety check-list

Have you registered the site with Health & Safety Executive or Environmental Health Office? YES/NOT NECESSARY
   REASON

Do you have a written safety policy?
Do you display the Statutory Notices?
Do you have an established fire drill?
Do you have your fire exits signposted?
Do you have assembly points?

Do you provide a safe place of work?
Do you provide safe access to the place of work?
Do you use flammable materials?
Do you display the regulations broadsheet?

Will safety training (use of tools, materials, electricity, chemicals, lifting techniques) be
   included in the trainee's induction to your business?
Are your machines safely guarded as current regulations require?
Will the student be adequately supervised?
Will you provide the necessary safety equipment?

Will you provide the following facilities:
   WC?   Washing?   Barrier creams?
   First aid box?   Clothing store?

Please give employer's liability insurance company
   Policy No.   Expires

Please give public liability insurance company
   Policy No.   Expires

Have you informed your insurance company that you have a student on work experience?
If not, will you arrange cover?

Do you have an Accident Record Book?
Do you know about RIDDOR?
Do you have a record of RIDDOR accidents?

Do you have DES Education and Work Booklet Guide for Employers?

I certify that the information given above is correct _____ Date _____

Source: Avon LEA.

(c)   Injury to others not on the premises (including customers and members of the general public).
(d)   Damage to or loss of employers' property.
(e)   Damage to or loss of other property.

Broadly speaking, there are three parties that may wish to cover themselves by insurance. *Employers* on the one hand, and *LEAs/schools* on the other, may wish to cover themselves against compensation for injury or damage where their own liability can be proved. In addition, steps may also be taken to insure the *student* against compensation for accidents where no such liability is proved.

So far as employers are concerned, the majority carry insurance policies

---

Box 7.4   An employer's induction check-list on health and safety

The company's induction programme for work-experience students is very similar to that given to YTS trainees, with emphasis being placed on Health and Safety — a factory being a very different environment from a school. Points to be covered include:

1. Responsible for own sensible behaviour.
2. Smoking areas.
3. Emergency exits — where they are and to keep unobstructed.
4. Handling heavy goods correctly.
5. *All* accidents must be reported.
6. Meeting points for fires.
7. Keeping tidy work-place.

The necessity of keeping good time is also explained to the students, to ensure supervisors know where they are, particularly in the event of accident or fire.

A principle of the scheme is that no student will operate hazardous machinery, or work in a hazardous environment. No special or protective clothing is therefore necessary, except in the mechanics department, where it is issued as necessary.

Source: Jaeger Tailoring Limited, Kilmarnock.

---

which now cover most of the risks involved. This has not always been the case. DES Circular 7/74 warned that:

> As pupils participating in work experience are not employed under a contract of service they are not entitled to the benefits of the National Insurance (Industry Injuries) Act in the event of injury through accident; nor is the employer under an obligation under the Employers' Liability (Compulsory Insurance) Act 1969 to insure against his liability to them.

The 1988 guidelines, however, state that:

> The Association of British Insurers, the British Insurance and Investment Brokers Association and Lloyd's of London have agreed as a matter of convention that pupils on work experience placements in conformity with the Act [the Education (Work Experience) Act 1973] should be treated as employees for the purposes of insurance against personal injury (i.e. they will be covered by the Employer's Liability policy), providing always that the insurer has had notification ... (DES, 1988a, p. 23).

The Employer's Liability policy should also cover injuries etc., caused to employees by pupils; injuries etc., caused to others should normally be covered by the employer's Public Liability policy; damage etc. to the employer's property should be covered by its Material Damage policy.

Despite this, schools are strongly advised to ask employers for written confirmation that their policies do include cover for work-experience students, and that any necessary notifications to insurers have been given. Even then, problems may occur. If, for example, a school adopts a 'wider concepts of work' approach (cf. p. 30ff), and arranges for some students to undertake placements with voluntary bodies, it may be that such bodies have no insurance cover of these kinds. Government establishments may not be covered by insurance but instead may underwrite themselves; they are, however, bound by the same common-law duty to employees as are other employers, and should be requested to give similar written assurances. Sometimes insurance cover may impose some restrictions on the tasks which can be carried out: one school, for example, found that students on a physiotherapy placement would not be able to place their hands on patients because National Health Service insurance would not cover any accidents which might ensue.

Rather than undertaking the burden of checking up on employers' insurance policies, and to relieve employers' anxieties on this matter, some LEAs prefer to indemnify employers for any claims made against them. Even where this is not the case, LEAs/schools may have residual responsibilities which they must cover themselves. Two such cases noted by the DES (1988a, pp. 22–3) are those arising in the course of transport to the workplace, and those arising from negligence — for example, in matching students to placements or in ensuring adequate supervision. Again, these may be covered by existing policies — damage to employers' property or to other employees, for example, may be covered by existing Third Party insurance — but this should be checked. In the case of at least one LEA, it was decided simply to meet claims, since risk analysis suggested that this was likely to be less expensive than the necessary insurance cover would be.

All of the arrangements discussed so far, it should be emphasized, offer compensation only for accidents in which it can be shown that injury or damage resulted from negligence on the part of employer and/or the LEA/school. Often, however, no such negligence can be proved: either the student is responsible, or there is no demonstrable fault on anyone's part. Such risks can only be covered by Personal Accident Insurance (PAI), and it is important that parents are made aware of this. Some LEAs and schools now offer all parents of work-experience students the opportunity to take out PAI policies on their children's behalf, though these vary considerably in the level of cover. Others have taken out general PAI policies under which students injured while on work experience are automatically compensated for accidents which are neither the employer's nor the LEA's responsibility: in some cases, such policies may even cover cases which *are* the employer's or the LEA's responsibility, in which case any payments made under the policy will be independent of and additional to any compensation as a result of litigation or admitted liability.

This may, however, leave open the issue of liability for damages or for injury to others for which the student is clearly responsible. In one case, for example, a student in a placement with an auctioneer dropped a valuable piece of antique pottery: in the event, the employer stoically agreed to bear the loss. In another case, a student working in a garage misused a blow torch, resulting in a major fire, and considerable damage to the employer's premises and to customers' cars: in this case, the insurers agreed to regard the student as an employee and to meet the employer's claim under its Material Damage policy. In both cases, however, the students could have been liable, had the employers and insurance companies concerned taken a tough line.

Further complications have arisen from the growing interest in organizing work-experience placements in other European countries (see European Work Experience Project, 1989). In such cases it seems that the usual regulations regarding school trips apply to the journeys involved, but that the relevant country's law applies once the student is in the work-place.

On the whole, our general impression is that the number of insurance claims made for accidents on school-based work-experience schemes is remarkably low. This does not mean that insurance issues should be skimped: it is clearly essential that they are given the attention they need. But certainly it would seem desirable to try to find some simpler system than the present one, which requires that such issues take up much more time and energy than they should.

Costs

A further set of legal issues relates to financial matters. The DES guidelines state categorically that 'as work-based activities, including work experience, are part of pupils' education, employers should make no payment for work performed, whether to the pupils, the school or the authority' (DES, 1988a, p. 12). Some employers, however, feel that they should provide some financial reward in exchange for the services performed by the students. A particularly common practice is to pay 'overtime' for work done after normal school hours. This can, however, cause complications in relation to insurance and other matters by altering the legal basis from that related to work experience to that related to part-time employment.

It is also not unusual for employers to cover the costs of transport or lunches. The DES guidelines endorse such practices, and also state that where employers do not pay such costs, 'the school should consider whether any arrangements for transport or meals are needed, taking into account the position of those pupils receiving free transport to school and/or free meals' (*ibid*, p. 12). HMI (1990) reported that some LEAs provided a nominal sum per student to be spent at a school's discretion, while others met the costs in full. Many students, though, continue to pay their own costs.

The Education Reform Act 1988 could cause problems in this respect. Under this Act, activities which take place wholly or mainly within school time must be provided free of charge. It is still open to schools to solicit voluntary contributions from parents, but it arguable that parents are entitled to claim travel expenses for work experience if they so wish. One teacher commented: 'I am awaiting with trepidation the first phone call from a parent suggesting that we fund transport costs!' At another school, a Governors' Meeting attempted to avoid such claims by defining work experience as an activity that was extra to the school's normal curriculum and could only proceed if parental contributions covered the costs involved. This seems contrary both to Government policy on work experience (see p. 9) and to good curricular practice as we are defining it in this book; it is particularly open to challenge where work experience is a contractual part of a TVEI programme.

The introduction of Local Management of Schools (LMS) through the same Act seems likely, at the time of writing (1990), to make such issues even more problematic. Given greater responsibility for their own budgets, schools are likely to become more concerned about the direct costs which work-experience schemes involve (see pp. 89–90). These already include considerable telephone and postage costs, travel expenses for teachers' visits to work-places, and sometimes safety clothing and footwear (one Glamorgan school spent nearly £900 on safety boots in 1989). If not only insurance but also students' travel costs were added to this, some schools might be discouraged from running such schemes (particularly European schemes).

Protection of Children

Finally, work experience is also affected by DES Circular 4/86 on 'Protection of Children: Disclosure of Criminal Background of those with Access to Children'. The Circular outlines procedures for checking with local police forces the possible criminal background of those who have 'substantial opportunity for access to children'. It states explicitly that:

> The arrangements for checking with the police should also apply where appropriate to students and others engaged for limited periods of practical work as part of their training or for work experience. Local authorities will need to take this into account in the arrangements they make with educational and other bodies for providing training and work experience (para. 4).

Particular attention is paid to situations where the position involves 'one-to-one contact', though the Circular also states that where there is 'close supervision' the contact might not necessarily be regarded as 'substantial access'. How is all this applied in the case of work experience? Does it mean that the vetting procedure needs to be applied to all the employees in the work-place with whom the work-experience student might come into significant contact? If so, the sheer labour involved, together with employer (and employee) resistance, would be likely to lead to a massive reduction of work-experience placements. Also, does the Circular mean that in the case of students who go on work experience in a nursery or primary school, the students themselves need to be vetted?

Conclusion

We have attempted to outline some of the legal issues which apply to school-based work-experience schemes. Many of them are still a source of some confusion; others seem to require an inordinate amount of time from those responsible for organizing such schemes. Yet dealing with these legal issues does not ensure the *quality* of work-experience schemes: it merely removes some of the obstacles to such quality. There are parallels here with Herzberg's (1966) theory of work motivation: the legal issues only address the 'hygiene' factors, not the 'motivators'. It is accordingly important that they should not consume more attention than they merit. If work experience is to become a fully integrated part of the school curriculum for all students, as the Government has declared it should, greater clarification and stronger, simpler structures for implementing the law are urgently needed.

Chapter 8

Employers' Perspectives

A.G. Watts

Employers' perspectives are crucial to the success of work-experience programmes. The delivery of work-experience placements depends on employers being willing and able to provide them. Moreover, the form the experience takes is determined at least as much by the employer as by the school or the student. One of the unique features of work experience is that it is part of the curriculum and yet is normally delivered outside the direct supervision of teachers. Other parts of the curriculum may use 'adults other than teachers' in a supportive role; in work experience, however, employers in effect *deliver* the curriculum for a period of time. Accordingly, their perspectives are likely to be strongly influential on what happens during this period.

In this chapter we will therefore examine the *motivations* of employers in taking part in work experience, some *issues* related to these motivations, and the *roles* employers can play in work-experience schemes. We will draw from two small workshops for employers which we organized in 1987/88: one for large national employers; and one for local employers in part of north London (Brent). We will also draw from a number of secondary sources, including three small-scale studies of employers' perspectives on work experience: two in the UK (Hodge, 1987; Shilling, 1989); and one in Australia (Watkins, 1988).

Employer Motivations

Benefits

Why do employers support work experience? To suggest that their motives are purely philanthropic would be naive, as is demonstrated in the business adage 'there's no such thing as a free lunch'. But clearly the motivations vary considerably between employers. Often they are vague and ill-defined. In

---

Box 8.1   *Potential benefits to employers*

1. *Social contribution*: helping to build a national 'climate of assent'.
2. *Community involvement*: helping to build a local 'climate of assent'.
3. *Employee satisfaction*: giving individual employees a 'warm glow'.
4. *Educational influence*: stimulating educational provision to meet employer needs.
5. *Publicity*: advertising the company and its products or services.
6. *Recruitment*: screening potential recruits.
7. *Labour power*: providing additional staff resources.

---

general, however, at least seven possible benefits to employers from participation in work-experience programmes can be identified. These are listed in Box 8.1. We will examine each of them in turn.

Some employers view work experience as part of their *social contribution*. This applies mainly to large companies and is based on the desirability of building and maintaining a 'climate of assent' — or a 'licence to operate' as a BP document (Marsden and Priestland, 1989) terms it. The underlying assumptions here appear to be three-fold: that a strong and healthy society is likely to be 'good for business'; that it is good public relations to be seen to be making a contribution to the betterment of society; and that such considerations may provide opportunities to infuse wider aspects of society with values which are congruent with, or at least supportive of, the market system. A focus for such activities is provided by the Per Cent Club: a group of some 200 leading companies which are committed to contributing at least 0.5 per cent of pre-tax profits to social projects. Work experience may be seen as one way in which companies can make their social contribution.

The same kinds of arguments are used at a more local level to support the notion of *community involvement*. They are enshrined in terms like 'prosperous high-streets need prosperous back-streets' and 'a healthy company needs a healthy community' (IFAPLAN, 1988, p. 14). They are concerned with maintaining a local 'climate of assent' and with developing the local reputation of the company or organization on the assumption that this could — often in indirect and intangible ways — lead to business benefits. Such motives may be less prominent in large cities than in towns and rural areas, where the sense of community and the closeness of social relations tend to be stronger. They may form part of a proactive policy. Alternatively, they may operate in a more reactive way: thus Shilling (1989) found a couple of cases where individuals felt that the position of their firm in the local community, and their own position on local training boards and parent-teacher associations, meant that they were obliged to involve themselves when approached (p. 138) — they considered that they could not afford to be seen to be responding negatively. In these respects, one of the attractions of work experience to small companies in particular is that it is a means through which they can be seen to be 'doing their bit' within modest and containable limits.

Work experience may be viewed by some employers in more personal terms as a way of providing *employee satisfaction*. Some employees will have children in local schools: they — and other employees — may experience a 'warm glow' in being able to use their position in the organization to enhance local children's education. Fostering such feelings can help to promote employees' morale and their allegiance to the organization. Employers themselves may be influenced by similar considerations: Shilling (1989) cites several cases in which small employers were motivated by memories of the inadequacy of their own 'preparation for work' while at school and by their concern for their own daughters/sons; while Marsden (1989a) notes that in devising strategies for increasing education–industry links, 'education's strongest asset is the sheer challenge, stimulation, pleasure and responsibility of working with young people' (p. 85).

In relation to such considerations, work experience may be seen in less altruistic terms as a means through which employers can exert *educational influence*. The basic assumption here is that if employers have certain expectations from the education system, they may need to establish a stake within that system to ensure that these expectations are met. This is the core rationale for business–education partnerships in general (e.g. CBI, 1988). It also applies to work experience in particular. Hodge (1987), for example, noted that some employers believed that making work experience available to students could be an effective way of encouraging teachers to adapt their practice more to industry's needs. This was particularly apparent among electronic/technology companies, some of which had little confidence in the nature and content of the work being developed in schools: they believed that where students had seen these areas in 'real life', the students would be able to correct perceived misinterpretations at the school level. More generally, some employers view work experience as being an opportunity to ensure that at least part of students' educational experience is concerned with developing the skills, attitudes and values which employers regard as important. This includes such basic matters as 'learning to come on time and dress properly' (see Watkins, 1988, p. 86). Employers frequently do not trust schools to inculcate such attributes.

The four benefits discussed to date are all relatively long-term and difficult to measure. While not wholly altruistic, they are not based on narrow and direct self-interest. Instead, they are concerned with various forms of 'enlightened self-interest'. The remaining three benefits, however, are more short-term, more measurable and more specific.

One is *publicity*. Hodge (1987) notes that 'work experience was a way of advertising both the company and its products in the locality, which was particularly useful to small firms involved in marketing their goods or services to the public' (p. 3). Shilling (1989), too, cites cases in which employers regarded work experience as a way of spreading their name and improving their image. This could have pay-offs in terms of consumer awareness or in terms of attractiveness to potential recruits.

A further benefit focuses on *recruitment* in a more direct way. While viewing work experience as a form of educational influence may be seen as a means of raising the quality of the *pool* of recruits from which they will eventually draw, some employers view it in more immediate terms as a means of making contact with some *individual* young people who may be potential future employees. Thus in Shilling's (1989) study, fifteen out of twenty companies mentioned that work experience provided a steady flow of potential labour which could be closely screened for its suitability. Again, Watkins (1988) in his Australian study noted that most employers viewed work experience as a way of sifting potential employees, enabling them to 'try before you buy'. This could produce substantial savings in recruitment costs in terms of time, paperwork and money; it could also be more effective than other recruitment methods, because it provided an unrivalled opportunity to view the potential recruits in the real work situation. Several firms in Watkins' study stated that they 'kept good work-experience students on file': if vacancies arose, they initially contacted students who had impressed (*ibid*, p. 88). The same practice was adopted by around half of the employers in a study of TVEI work experience in the UK (Fuller, 1987).

Finally, some employers view work experience in even more immediate terms as a way of providing additional *labour power*. Shilling (1989) points out that those who doubt that work-experience students can provide productive labour should note the practice in some firms of giving some form of remuneration — whether in the form of money or of tokens or 'presents'. This was reflected in one of our workshops, where employers said that they 'felt bad' about the general formal practice of non-payment, and that some payment 'would ease our conscience'. For those who readily view this use of students' labour power as capitalist exploitation, it is interesting to note that in Watkins' (1988) study the most obvious examples of benefits from cheap labour were not in private firms but in such sites as schools and child-minding centres, where teachers frequently used comments such as 'I do not know what I would have done' without the work-experience student taking a reading, sporting or other group.

The Cost–benefit Calculation

These various benefits need to be balanced against a number of costs. Such costs fall into three main categories. The first is *administration*: this includes the time taken up in planning, preparation, organization of placements, and follow-up. The second is *training and supervision*: this is likely to be particularly time-consuming at the earlier stages of a placement. The third is *direct costs*: this may include travel allowances and lunch allowances. In some cases there may be additional costs: for example, from having to rectify mistakes made by the students.

Our impression is that few if any employers calculate the costs and benefits of work experience in a rigorous quantified way. Some believe that the immediate direct benefits to employers outweigh the direct costs. Others believe that the direct benefits are exceeded by the direct costs, but that the 'loss' is more than covered by the longer-term and more intangible benefits. The key difference between these two groups is that business contraction may affect the support of the latter group, but is unlikely to affect the support of the former — indeed, it may prompt them to increase their involvement (Shilling, 1989, p. 142).

The lack of formal cost–benefit calculations is linked to the fact that few employers as yet have written policies on work experience. Large companies sometimes have broad policies about schools–industry liaison, but policies on specific activities like work experience tend to be left to local management. A few companies are, however, developing codes of practice. Such codes are important as a means of *legitimating* the positive responses of individuals lower down in the organizational hierarchy, and of *stimulating* more positive responses from people who might otherwise have responded negatively. They also provide a way of maintaining standards in the company's work-experience provision. In the light of the recent growth of work experience and its greater institutionalization (see Chapter 1), such practices are likely to grow. An interesting side-effect may be the importing of practices derived from other areas of employer activities: one employer, for example, has argued strongly and articulately that the competence-based approach already in operation as part of the Youth Training Scheme should be applied to school-based work experience (Berkeley, 1988).

As employers' involvement grows, their motivations may change. In Shilling's (1989) study, for example, the recruitment motive played little part in employers' initial rationale for being involved, but became a strong 'reason for continuing' (p. 146). Fluctuations in employers' motivations may also be related to changes in the labour market. Thus Ball and Gordon (1985), in a more broadly-based study of employer liaison with schools, noted that the reduction in school-leaver recruitment in the early 1980s had led some employers to replace the recruitment rationale for their school-liaison activities with a broader rationale based on social contribution, community involvement and educational influence. Conversely, the growing concern in the late 1980s about the 'demographic time bomb' of shortages of school-leavers (NEDO, 1988) led to a move back to the recruitment rationale.

The same kinds of differences also seem likely to occur between different parts of the country. Thus in areas where there are labour shortages, the recruitment motive is likely to be strong; whereas in areas of high unemployment, other motives are likely to prevail. In general, it seems probable that such differences are particularly liable to affect involvement in work experience in smaller companies, which — because they tend to be financially more vulnerable and 'nearer the margin' — are inclined to be more concerned with short-term benefits and less responsive to longer-term goals.

In addition to the motivations of *employers*, the motivations of *employees* need to be taken into account. An important characteristic of work experience is that it involves a wide range of employees in contributing to the curriculum: this is very different from employers' contributions to school-based activities, which tend to be the preserve of narrow groups of managers. Hodge (1987) points out that the person responsible for organizing work experience and liaison with schools, and for accepting and deploying students on work experience, can often be distant from the employees with whom the student will actually work. This can pose difficulties if the employees do not see the relevance or value of work experience and view the student as a nuisance or as a 'skivvy'. On the other hand, as we have already noted, employees may bring strong positive motivations of their own, particularly if they have a concern for young people and a link — perhaps as parents — with the local school.

The motivations of *trade unions* are important, too. Unions have sometimes been resistant to work experience, partly because of their concern that it may be used as a source of 'cheap labour'. Indeed, at national level, the Trades Union Congress for some time strongly resisted the extension of work-experience schemes (see Watts, 1983a, pp. 9–10), and it was only in the late 1970s that it moderated its position. Its change of policy was due in part to its recognition of the opportunity provided by work experience to contribute to students' understanding of the role of trade unions. Smith and Wootton (1988) pointed out that it can do this from two interrelated viewpoints: first, from the organizational perspective of the appointed union representative in the work-place; and second, from the individual perspective of the union member. In work experience, opportunities for the latter are likely to present themselves more frequently than the former.

Issues Related to Employer Motivations

Some of the employer motivations we have identified can pose difficulties in terms of the educational aims of work-experience programmes. The recruitment motive can be particularly problematic in this respect. If companies start to apply this motive in a strong way, it may affect the kinds of schemes they are prepared to support: Hodge (1987), for example, notes that such employers were often ambivalent about work experience for students aged 16–18, since these students would probably not enter the labour market until after higher education and might then be seeking very different levels of work from those available within the company. Recruitment motives are also likely to have a considerable impact on procedures for matching students to placements: employers with such motives may begin to expect some form of pre-selection to take place, so that the students are plausible candidates for the area of work in question. This may subvert other aims which the school has in mind. In addition, it may mean that students begin positively to opt for such placements, as information about them percolates through on the 'grapevine': Hodge (1987) points out that this could become a potential vehicle for discrimination against particular groups of students, and that schools would need to monitor it carefully.

Widespread adoption of the recruitment motive could have further effects. If combined with 'pairing' or 'twinning' between particular companies and particular schools (see Shilling, 1989, pp. 150–1), it could restrict opportunities for students from other schools. It could also serve to encourage early entry into the labour market at the expense of further education and training, and so act against the employer's own longer-term interests (Marsden, 1989b). In this respect, it is interesting to note that the recruitment motive seems to have become relatively respectable in Compact schemes (pp. 7–8), which are crucially based on the notion that the promise of a job is educationally motivating, and in which employers make a commitment to provide ongoing education and training for their recruits (see Flockhart, 1988).

The educational influence motive, too, may contain problematic elements. Cole (1983) notes that firms which are concerned with using work experience as a way of changing the *behaviour* of young people can be seen as being involved in an act of socialization rather than of education. Again, Watkins (1988) points out that attempts to tie the curriculum to work and its immediate requirements limit school learning to the existing state of the economy, and leave little room for self-reflection, for intellectual growth, or for self-realization. They not only reproduce but legitimate the existing structures of work organization. Education comes to be seen not as a way to improve society, but rather as a means of ideological fine-tuning and of preparing the student to meet present industrial and occupational needs.

On the other hand, Watkins goes on to note that work experience *may* offer to students the chance to develop reflection and critical insights into the social relations of work. It can indicate areas of contestation and resistance: for instance, workers objecting to, and acting against, certain features of the work structure. It can also provide students with experience of class relations, hierarchies, and inequalities in the distribution of rewards in the work-place: teachers can then adopt a critical framework through which these experiences can be articulated and evaluated. Such approaches, if made too explicit and visible, may however lead to conflict with the employers concerned, who may feel that their attempts at educational influence have been thwarted and subverted.

Particular employer motivations may have implications for the nature of work-experience placements and the way in which they are structured. Thus employers concerned with using work experience as additional labour power might be happy to restrict placements to boring, repetitive tasks, whereas employers seeking benefits with a stronger public relations flavour would be

---

Box 8.2   Employer roles

1. *Recruiter/selector*: helping to choose which students are to fill the placements.

2. Job designer: determining which tasks and responsibilities are to be given to the students.

3. *Trainer*: inducting the students into the work organization, and showing them how to carry out the tasks allocated to them.

4. *Supervisor*: ensuring that students are coping with the tasks they have been given, and carrying them out competently.

5. *'Godparent'*: providing personal and emotional support.

6. *'Model'*: modelling what it is like to be an adult in the working world.

7. *Assessor*: evaluating students' performance in their work role.

8. *Debriefer*: helping students to review their progress and to reflect on what they have learned from the experience.

---

likely to provide a more varied and more carefully structured experience (Shilling, 1989, pp. 140–1). Again, shorter placements might mean that there will be less chance of the students' labour power making a significant contribution to output; on the other hand, they might make it possible to see a wider pool of potential recruits.

In the end, the aims of employers need to be reconciled through negotiation with the aims of teachers and of students. If this is not done, it is easy for misunderstandings and conflicts to occur. For instance, the teacher may regard work experience in investigative terms (see p. 19) as an opportunity to learn about the structure of industry, whereas a student may view it as an opportunity to test a career choice, and the employer as an opportunity for cheap labour. In this situation, each party is likely to block the achievement of each other's aims, leaving all sides frustrated and angry. There are market considerations involved here: where placements are in short supply, schools are more likely to feel forced to accede to employers' wishes; where they are relatively plentiful, schools may feel in a stronger negotiating position. In principle, however, the more each side understands what each other is trying to do, the more opportunity there is to reconcile the aims of the different interests involved, and the greater the trouble taken to ensure that the experience is able to accommodate any agreed divergence of aims, the more successful the work experience is likely to be.

Employer Roles

In the course of a work-experience placement, employers or their employees can play a number of different roles (Box 8.2). Some of the roles can be played in ways which are very similar to the roles they would play in relation to normal employees: some are specific to, or can be adapted to take account of, the distinctive needs of work-experience students.

The first role is that of *recruiter/selector*. Some employers choose to delegate this role to schools or to work-experience coordinators, and to accept whoever is nominated by them. Some, however, feel that students on work experience should be treated as much like other employees as possible, and accordingly should be encouraged to apply formally for the placement and to undergo a selection interview. This is particularly likely in the growing number of cases where schools encourage students to find their own placements. Such applications and interviews provide opportunities to help students to learn how to present themselves more effectively. In some cases the interviews are in reality 'mock interviews', since there is no real competition for places. In other cases, though, there may be several students interested in a placement: if employers choose to see them, real selection may be taking place. Some teachers and employers argue, however, that the 'selection' aspect of the interview should not be played up too strongly, and should be presented as 'matching' rather than 'choosing', to avoid students starting their work experience with the experience of failure.

The second role is that of *job designer*. It involves determining which tasks and responsibilities are to be given to the students concerned. This may be predetermined before the student is known; alternatively, it may be adapted to the abilities and needs of the student in question. It may also need to be adapted to take account of the curricular aims and objectives of the scheme (see Chapter 2). In some cases, employers may seek to involve students in the selection and planning of their tasks. A preliminary interview, whether undertaken for selection purposes or not, can provide a valuable opportunity for such negotiation between employer and student about how the placement is to be structured (see pp. 217–9).

The third role is that of *trainer*. There are two parts to this. General *induction* training covers the nature of the organization and the way in which it operates: this includes any rules and regulations in the work-place (e.g. health and safety), the length and times of the working day and of work breaks, and any standards or codes of behaviour (i.e. unwritten rules). *Task-focused* training is concerned with showing the students how to carry out the tasks allocated to them. In most cases, the tasks are of a simple nature, and 'sitting next to Nellie' is the most common training method used here.

The fourth role is that of *supervisor*. This is concerned with ensuring that students are able to cope with the tasks they have been given, and are performing them competently. It may provide opportunities to redesign tasks, or add new tasks, possibly again in negotiation with the student concerned.

The fifth role is that of *'godparent'*. This term has been used in some youth training schemes (see e.g. Gregory and Rees, 1980) to apply to ordinary adult workers who take a 'pastoral' responsibility for particular trainees but act independently of the trainees' immediate supervisors. A few organizations may have adapted it for use with students on school-based work experience. But even where it is not formalized in this way, it may occur on an informal basis, whether as an extension of the supervisor role or separate from it. Such a 'godparent' role can help the students to deal with any emotional difficulties they may be having in adjusting to the work-place. Often it is carried out in meal-breaks and the like. The role is frequently given to, or claimed by, workers who have a rapport with young people, either because they have children of their own of that age, or because they are involved in youth work or similar voluntary activities in the community. A variant of the role, used for example in the USA in a New York scheme, is the use of a 'buddy' system in which students are allocated not just to a supervisor but also to someone closer to their own age who can provide a more informal support to them.

The sixth role is that of 'model'. This again may or may not be linked to the supervisor role, but encompasses the wider notion of modelling what it is like to be an adult in the working world: 'This is what the real world is like.' The concept has been formalized in the notion of the 'working coach': ordinary men and women in ordinary jobs who can help young people to learn to accept responsibility for themselves as they take up adult roles in society (Reed and Bazalgette, 1983). It can, however, operate in more informal ways.

The seventh role is that of *assessor*. Schools may ask employers to assess students' performance; employers may also wish to carry out assessments for their own purposes, particularly if they are regarding the work-experience placement as a means of screening potential recruits. Because school-based work experience is brief, some employers consider that the amount of 'real work' is likely to be too limited to provide a basis for judging task performance: they accordingly tend to place the emphasis in their assessments on attitudes and general behaviour rather than on skills or knowledge. A further issue is whether the assessment should be used essentially for formative purposes — providing feedback to the students and then being 'filed in the bin' — or whether they should be used for summative purposes and made available to other parties like possible future employers. Some employers are likely to pay more attention to such assessments than to the school report, because they attach greater trust to the judgment of a fellow-employer and have more confidence that it will be based on relevant criteria; they may also feel more able to ring up and ask 'what is he/she really like?'. These and other issues related to assessment will be discussed in more detail in Chapter 13.

The eighth and final role is that of *debriefer*. Employers may provide periodic opportunities within the work-place for students to review their progress, to consider how their activities are contributing to the operations of the organization, and to reflect on what they are learning from the experience. In a particularly interesting experimental project, 'working coaches' met work-experience students on a weekly basis before, during and after their placements, on neutral ground away both from school and from the students' workplaces (Grubb Institute, 1986). In addition, some employers may take part in debriefing sessions back at the school. While teachers usually have the main responsibility for debriefing (see Chapter 12), employers have a distinctive contribution to make, partly because of their more detailed knowledge of the nature of the student's experience. Such involvement can also act as a valuable form of feedback to the employer on the satisfactoriness of the placement and how it might be improved for the future.

Conclusion

In this chapter we have explored the motivations of employers for taking part in work-experience schemes and the roles they may play in such schemes. It is worth noting, however, that work experience can act as a modest agent of organizational change for employers themselves. A good example relates to equal opportunities. Because work experience is only for a limited period, employers may be more willing than usual to experiment with a non-traditional placement: for instance, placing a girl in a traditionally male area of work, or a boy in a traditionally female one. A good experience may then encourage them to rethink their employment policies (Watts and Kant, 1986, p. 14).

A further example relates to understanding between schools and employers. In one of our employer workshops, part of the discussion concerned employers' reservations about making summative assessments of student performance based on limited evidence. They pointed out, for example, that students' behaviour might be related to transitional problems or to their reactions to the specific place of work rather than providing a basis for valid generalizations to be drawn — especially negative ones. They noted that such judgments might not be comparable across students: punctuality, for example, might be affected by the distance the students had to travel to the work-place, and by the extent to which the journey was familiar; again, attitudes and behaviour might be affected by the extent to which the placement was one which the student wanted. They also agreed that students should not be judged on the basis of what had been designed as a learning experience. Not the least fascinating part of this discussion was to hear employers in their 'curricular' role voicing so many of the reservations which teachers tend to raise when placed under pressure from employers in their 'selection' role — and from governments — to supply summative assessments. Because work experience brings together the two employer roles, it might be a powerful way of 'unscrambling the messages' which employers tend to pass to schools regarding assessment (Marsden, 1983).

In short, work experience can in some respects loosen the structures of the work-place and of the employer–education interface, in ways which

A.G. Watts

allow new forms and new understandings to emerge. The potential for such effects should not be exaggerated. But it is important to recognize that while work experience can provide opportunities for ideological penetration of employer concerns and values into schools, it can also provide opportunities for ideological penetration of educational concerns and values into the workplace.

148

Part III

Curricular Issues

Chapter 9

Integration

Andrew Miller

The aim of this chapter is to consider the linkages between student learning, work experience, and the school curriculum. Integration is at the heart of the relationship between the three corners of the work-experience triangle (see Chapter 2): the student, the world of work, and the school. Schools that have integrated work experience into their curricula have found ways of making links between students' prior learning, students' work placements, and teaching programmes within the school. Integration concerns both teaching and learning. In terms of *teaching*, integration means building a work-experience programme into the curriculum. This entails locating work experience within a curricular frame and planning each phase of the programme: preparation, briefing, the experience, debriefing, and follow-up (see Chapter 12). The prime object of these teaching strategies, however, is to promote the *learning* of individual students. In these terms, integration refers to how schools help students to relate learning from work experience to prior learning.

We begin this chapter by exploring the concept of integration from the perspective of learners and learning. Four different forms of integration are introduced: experiential integration; personal integration; world-of-work-learning integration; and subject integration. Next we contrast so-called 'bolt-on' work-experience programmes with programmes that have been integrated across the curriculum. Case-studies of schemes are then used to provide an overview of integration within each of the five curricular frames we have identified: academic subjects; personal and social education; world-of-work-learning; careers education; and vocational courses. The final part examines different approaches to managing the change towards greater integration and a whole-school approach through the use of case-study examples.

Integration and Learning

Integration means literally the bringing together of parts to make a coherent whole which functions as one. The concept of *experiential integration* can be used to describe the ways in which students are helped to make sense of their placement experience. This occurs when students are able to see the relationships between different aspects of their experience, and thus to gain new insights and understanding. If, for example, a student can relate an accident observed on the shop-floor to information given during the employer's health and safety briefing, then he or she can understand why particular rules are important, and can give an example of what can happen if such rules are not followed. Schools which have successfully built the experiential learning cycle into their work-experience programme generally attempt to bring about experiential integration through the debriefing phase (see pp. 225–30), where the processes of reflection and analysis can be designed to help students understand the links between the diverse experiences during the placement. In addition, employers sometimes include a time for debriefing either at the end of the placement or at regular intervals during the placement (see pp. 200–1). Accordingly, both teachers and employers can promote experiential integration.

Viewed from the perspective of the individual learner, however, the issue of integration is also concerned with how individual fragments of learning can be related to the student's prior learning. In order to identify different forms of such learning integration, we return to the work-experience triangle. In terms of learning, each point of the triangle can be held to represent a particular 'map' of students' knowledge, understanding, skills and attitudes. Box 9.1 illustrates three forms of learning integration linking work experience to these mental maps: personal integration; world-of-work-learning integration; and subject integration.

The first map is the student's existing stage of personal and social development, which includes her or his range and level of social skills, and self-awareness. When there is a planned attempt to relate personal and social learning from work experience to students' existing development, this can be termed *personal integration*. The personal and social education curricular frame for work experience aims to promote personal integration through a number of teaching strategies, including personal development plans (see p. 213) and personal reflection upon experience (see pp. 226–8).

The second map is the student's map of the world of work, which includes knowledge and understanding of work roles, work tasks, work processes and work environments. This map is acquired in part through work-related activities. It is also likely, however, to be heavily influenced through the other agencies of social learning: the family; the community; the peer group; and the mass media. When there is a planned attempt to relate learning about the world of work acquired from work experience to a student's existing map of the world of work, this can be described as *world-of-work-learning integration*. The world-of-work-learning curricular frame aims to promote world-of-work-learning integration through a range of teaching strategies, including comparing and contrasting work experience with students' experience of part-time jobs and work in the home (see p. 214).

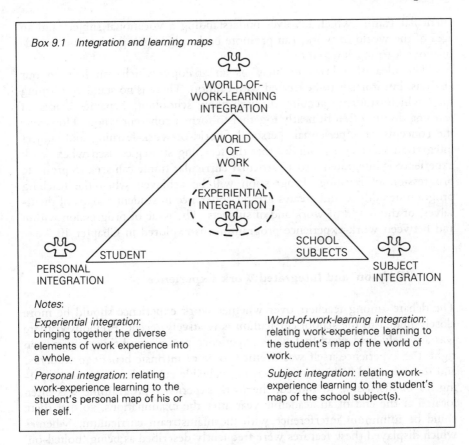

Box 9.1   *Integration and learning maps*

WORLD-OF-
WORK-LEARNING
INTEGRATION

WORLD
OF
WORK

EXPERIENTIAL
INTEGRATION

SCHOOL
SUBJECTS

STUDENT

PERSONAL
INTEGRATION

SUBJECT
INTEGRATION

Notes:

Experiential integration:
bringing together the diverse
elements of work experience into
a whole.

Personal integration: relating
work-experience learning to the
student's personal map of his or
her self.

World-of-work-learning integration:
relating work-experience learning to
the student's map of the world of
work.

Subject integration: relating work-
experience learning to the student's
map of the school subject(s).

The third map, or rather collection of maps, is the student's understanding of school subjects. Knowledge, understanding and skills acquired during a particular placement may be relevant to a range of subjects. For example, the division of labour in a factory could be used within Economics; different styles and forms of work-place writing could be used in English; different numerical operations might involve extending skills learned in Mathematics; information acquired during the work-place health and safety briefing could extend learning within Technology. When there is a planned attempt to relate learning from work experience to students' subject knowledge, understanding and skills, this can be described as *subject integration*. The academic-subject(s) curricular frame seeks to promote subject integration through teaching strategies that either provide students with subject-specific concepts with which to interpret their placement experience, or draw upon students' experiences as a resource to enhance subject learning in follow-up.

The careers-education curricular frame is concerned with the personal and social development of students as well as their understanding of the world of work. Accordingly, both personal integration and world-of-work-learning integration are relevant to such programmes. The vocational-courses curricular frame, which involves understanding a vocational subject and an area of the world of work, can promote both subject integration and world-of-work-learning integration.

The idea of a learning 'map' is an analogy which can help in our analysis, but it needs to be treated with caution. There is no standard learning map which students acquire through their schooling. Separate pieces of learning do not often fit neatly together to form a coherent whole. However, the concepts of experiential, personal, world-of-work-learning and subject integration serve as a reminder that the teaching strategies used when work experience is integrated into a particular curricular frame can seek to promote progression in learning. Progression will be achieved when the teaching programme adds to and creates greater coherence in students' maps of themselves, of the world of work and of subjects. The issue of progression within and between work-experience programmes is explored in Chapter 10.

'Bolt-on' and Integrated Work Experience

The debate among teachers over whether work experience should be more closely linked to the school curriculum is relatively recent. Previously, there was a widely-held view that work experience was a 'good thing' in its own right: the experience itself was deemed to be of intrinsic benefit to students, and there seemed little point in wasting valuable curriculum time in preparing for or discussing it. Indeed, the work-experience programme was often located at the end of an academic year after the examinations, so that there could be minimum interference with the mainstream curriculum. Schemes which displayed these features were frequently described as being 'bolted-on' to the curriculum.

Although work-experience schemes in many schools still exhibit some of the characteristics of being 'bolted-on' in this way, during the 1980s the perceptions of work experience held by teachers began to shift. More began to see its potential as a vehicle for curriculum enhancement. Thus work-experience programmes began to enter the mainstream curriculum as linkages were sought between learning at the work-place and learning in the classroom. In terms of teaching, the integration of work experience concerns the questions of what, where, when, by whom, and how such linkages are made between the work-experience programme and the school curriculum.

Box 9.2 contrasts some of the most important differences between ideal-typical 'bolt-on' and 'integrated' work-experience schemes. The main distinguishing feature of bolt-on schemes is that their development and operation are largely independent of the curriculum. In contrast, an integrated scheme with the characteristics shown in Box 9.2 is an integral part of the mainstream curriculum: the aims, objectives, processes and outcomes of the scheme promote the broader aims, objectives, processes and outcomes of

Box 9.2   *'Bolt-on' and 'integrated' work-experience schemes: a comparison*

Aspect	Bolt-on	Integrated
Policy	No policy statement for work experience. Work experience not part of school policy statement.	Agreed policy for work experience as part of overall school policy statement.
Aims	Broad aims not linked to other aspects of the curriculum.	Clear aims linked to other aspects of the curriculum.
Learning objectives	Unstated.	Stated objectives for each phase of the programme.
Preparation and briefing	Little time allocated; restricted to administrative concerns.	Long-, medium- and short-term preparation encompassing pastoral, academic and administrative concerns.
Experience	Experience regarded as an end in itself.	Experience regarded as a means to an end — student learning and curriculum enhancement.
Debriefing and follow-up	Short debrief and no follow-up.	Lengthy debrief and systematic follow-up using students' experience as a resource in a number of curricular areas.
Assessment	Focuses on student behaviour; unrelated to other school assessment	Related to other school assessment, e.g. records of achievement, subject assessments.
Staff involvement	One or two scheme organizers monitor students at their placements.	Many staff visit students; subject staff audit work-places for curricular linkages.
INSET	No INSET for staff.	INSET focuses on using work experience as a curricular resource.
Employers	Seen as deliverers of the experience only.	Seen as partners in the delivery of the whole programme.

the curriculum as a whole. The characteristics of whole–curriculum integration described in Box 9.2 assume an ideal-typical whole-school approach to integration which involves linkages made across the curriculum in a number of curricular frames. This, however, represents an extreme form of integration. In practice, it is more usual to find work experience at least initially being integrated primarily into one of the five main frames we have noted. It is to such examples that we now turn.

Curricular Frames and Integration

The main difference between schools which have integrated work experience into their curriculum is the choice of curricular frame. In Chapter 12, we will discuss the learning objectives and teaching strategies which can be found within the five frames identified in Chapter 2. In the present section, case-studies of schemes will be presented to illustrate integration within each of the five frames, and so to demonstrate the richness of work experience as a vehicle for learning.

A summary of the case-studies is shown in Box 9.3. Although many of these schemes use more than one frame, one frame tends to be more important than the others: for example, programmes which are predominantly within a careers-education or a personal and social education frame may have some follow-up work within academic subjects. The most important frame can be defined as the one in which the bulk of the preparation, briefing, debriefing and follow-up occurs.

Academic Subjects

Until the advent of the General Certificate of Secondary Education (GCSE), it was rare for traditional academic subjects to provide a curricular frame for work experience. But the search for suitable course-work assignments, and the greater stress on the application of knowledge and skills in the GCSE, has contributed to an increased interest among subject teachers in using work experience as a resource (see p. 9). It has therefore become more common for a subject area such as Integrated Humanities or (particularly) English to provide the frame for work experience. As the case-study of Testwood School in Box 9.4 illustrates, successful integration in a single academic subject often arises from the enthusiasm and energy of individual teachers.

A possible growth area in terms of single-subject integration is Modern Languages. TVEI, the Channel Tunnel development, the advent of the Single European Market in 1992, and the work of the European Work Experience Project (1989), have all provided an impetus for work experience in Europe. The second case-study (Box 9.5) illustrates how world-of-work learning and subject-specific learning can be combined in a work-experience programme in a foreign country. Further examples of different academic subjects which have linked their teaching to work-experience programmes are given in Chapter 12.

At post-16 level, traditional A-level courses do not include work experience as part of the course. Where A-level students do go on work experience as part of their total programme, it is usually justified in two ways (Fuller, 1987; Miller, Jamieson and Watts, 1989). First, as part of a programme of career choice, students may be encouraged to engage in job sampling. For example, students studying English who are interested in a journalistic career

Box 9.3   *Case-studies of curricular integration: a summary*

School	Curricular frame	Description
Testwood School	Academic subject	A one-term module for year-11 students of GCSE English; follow-up in several subjects.
Dormers Wells High School	Academic subject	Work placements in France as part of a GCSE course for year-11 students.
Weatherhead High School for Girls	Academic subject	A two-year programme of work placements in the UK and Europe for A-level language students.
Sharples School	Personal and social education	A ten-week module within a PSE programme for year-11 students.
TVEI pilot school	World-of-work learning	A five-week module using a student-centred approach and leading to a focus on world-of-work learning with cross-curricular follow-up.
Deeside High School	Careers education	A ten-week careers module as part of a GCSE in Community Studies.
William Gladstone High School	Vocational course	A two-week placement as part of a CPVE in Art and Design for year-12 students.
Palmer's Sixth Form College	Vocational course	A scheme of community-based placements on a day-release basis as part of an Alternative Studies programme.
Garth High School	Careers education; personal and social education	A careers-education frame which has developed to include PSE, with some follow-up in academic subjects for year-11 students.
Ifield Community College	Academic subjects; personal and social education; careers education; world-of-work learning	A whole-school approach to integration involving a de-timetabled Industry Month.

Box 9.4   *An English frame: Testwood School, Hampshire*

The Head of English at the school was linked to the National Writing Project and developed a world-of-work module for the GCSE. The one week of experience provided the focus for a term's work in English lessons.

The aims of the scheme were: to investigate the world of work and to widen students' experiences of it; to compare aspects of school and work, particularly with respect to writing; and to produce work-experience information guides for future students. The departmental team designed a booklet to help students to make observations and carry out research, and to give them opportunities for writing about aspects of work, in both an informational and a perceptual way.

Preparation included making initial contact with employers, thus providing scope for letter writing and telephone calls to glean information about the company and the placement. Personal Work Record Sheets enabled students to compare the purposes and types of writing at their school with writing which they would later observe, and engage in, at their placement.

During the experience students interviewed two people about writing at work, asking questions like: 'What kinds of writing do you use in your job?' 'Are any of the writing skills required those learned at school?' 'Are there any specialist requirements for writing on the job?' 'How much time in your working day is spent writing?'. In addition, the daily journal was an opportunity for students to reflect upon each day, and to record what they wanted to write: feelings, facts, and findings.

In debriefing, students analyzed their Personal Work Records, which raised many issues about the purpose of much school writing. They compiled a list of twenty-one writing activities that they had observed or engaged in. The journals enabled the students to reflect upon the whole experience, and teachers to share in those experiences. The material assembled by the students became their personal resource for further writing and learning about the world of work. For many of the group, the journal provided their best written course-work for GCSE English.

Follow-up work included examining some of the 'literature of work', encompassing a range of poetry, drama and prose from traditional sources, as well as much written material drawn from the work placements. The latter formed an important component in the 'wider reading' requirement of the examination.

Further developments at the school have included the use of students' researched material in Integrated Humanities, Business and Information Studies, Applied Biology, and Child Development, as a basis for course-work assignments. The developing coordinated model has allowed departments to cooperate in submitting researched information for GCSE English and Integrated Humanities. The main benefit of the cross-curricular links has been to raise the status of work experience in the eyes of staff and students. This has led to the establishment of a team of teachers working cooperatively to find placements and to share the preparatory work. Staff and students have become more aware of the links between different areas of the curriculum and the relevance of writing to all of them.

Source: Adapted from Vicary (1987; 1988).

might spend time in a local newspaper, economists might go to an accountancy firm, while physicists interested in reading engineering at university might seek a placement at an engineering firm. Second, a work-experience placement may be included as part of general, liberal, or alternative-studies programmes to widen students' horizons beyond their usual three A-level subjects.

The development of TVEI, however, has encouraged some schools to

---

Box 9.5   A Modern Languages frame: Dormers Wells High School, Ealing

The Modern Languages department at a West London school arranged for a group of twelve 15-year-olds taking GCSE French to live with French families and undertake a period of work experience.

The aims of the programme were: to increase the students' knowledge and understanding of the French language and culture; to enhance work-related social skills; and to promote world-of-work learning. The work placements were arranged mainly in hotels and catering establishments which met the teachers' criteria: the tasks were uncomplicated; there was team-working; and the obligation to talk would initially not be too great.

Preparation was divided between the work-experience preparation, during which a dossier on each student was compiled for the 'host' families and employers, and the linguistic preparation, which dovetailed with GCSE topic work. The students were taught language-related social skills, 'survival' skills, and work-related vocabulary. During extra French lessons there was much pair and small-group role-play and simulation to prepare them to cope with a range of possible situations while on their work experience.

During the experience, the students worked mostly on basic catering chores, and some were asked to write out the daily 'menu boards'. They kept a daily diary, and investigated health and safety at their work-places. For the majority of the students the first few days were the worst, when their lack of confidence about being able to do the job was compounded by their shyness about working with a team of total strangers, who were not only adult but also French.

Debriefing occurred informally when the teacher picked students up from work in a mini-bus, and formally in French lessons when the experience was reviewed.

Follow-up included a simulation at an international hotel in London, when students took on the roles of receptionists and waiters receiving guests from France. The role of guests was taken by the LEA French *assistants* who proceeded to introduce a range of problems for the students to deal with. Later the students prepared French food for a parents' evening about the work experience. The teacher organizer felt that the work-experience programme had longer-term pay-offs in improved GCSE results and increased numbers enrolling for A-level French.

Source: Adapted from Holbecke (1989).

---

seek to integrate work experience into A-level courses in a more systematic way. The example of A-level Modern Languages in Box 9.6 is an interesting if rare example of such integration. This case-study illustrates some progression from the pre-16 Modern Languages case-study described in Box 9.5. In general, it is more common to find A-level students undertaking specially constructed work-based projects than conventional work experience. For example, in Gloucestershire TVEI, students following A-level courses undertook the equivalent of five weeks' work experience over two years. The aims of the work experience were to challenge their intellect, to develop personal qualities, and to help them see some of the mores and moral and social values characteristic of industry. Under the 'industrial sponsorship' scheme, students investigated and presented solutions to two 'real and urgent problems'. Progression was built in, because the second problem was designed to be more complex and demanding than the first. Elsewhere, work-shadowing schemes are proving a popular alternative to work experience for A-level students (Watts, 1986; 1988).

---

*Box 9.6   An A-level Modern Languages frame: Weatherhead High School for Girls,
Wirral*

Since 1986, the Modern Languages Department at Weatherhead High School for Girls has
organized work experience in the UK, and in either Austria, the Federal Republic of
Germany, France or Spain. Twenty-two students of A-level French, German and Spanish
have participated in all stages of the programme. Although the work-experience programme
enables students to sample jobs in a European environment, the main aim is to enhance
students' performance in language use.

The preparation programme is based upon the principle of 'parallel experiences', which
allows students to undertake similar tasks at their UK and their European placements. To
date, these have been arranged in fields as diverse as banking, the chemical industry,
engineering, hotel management, journalism, law, local government, and publishing. During
year 12, students spend at least one week with a British company, or often with a British
subsidiary of a foreign company, where they become familiar with appropriate technical
knowledge relating to their chosen sphere of work, and if possible acquire knowledge of
the technical terms in the foreign language.

In the 1987 programme, three students engaged in a three-stage preparation programme
designed to equip them with a knowledge of business German, and to familiarize them with
working in an industrial environment. The first stage in February consisted of one week's
study in an Austrian vocational school specializing in Business Studies. The second stage
in March involved one week at a branch of an international pump manufacturer in Cheshire.
Students gained an insight into the administration and organization of the company, and
became aware of the interaction between departments following the product cycle from
start to finish. The third stage in July involved a return visit to the pump company to
concentrate on language-specific tasks, such as commercial and technical translation, and
sending telexes to Germany. These periods of work experience were not assessed,
although the students were entered for a GCE examination in German for Business
Studies.

The ten-day work experience in Germany took place in October of the second year of their
A-level course. The students spent their time at the German branch of the pump company,
gaining insights into the organization of the company and its role in the international group.
In addition, the students carried out tasks of commercial and technical translation. On
return to England, they completed a dissertation upon the company, which was assessed
as part of the course-work option of the Joint Matriculation Board's A-level Modern
Languages syllabus.

The programme had a significant effect on the students who participated in it. All spoke of
greater self-confidence, increased motivation for their studies, greater respect for the
world of work, and a clearer perception of their career aspirations. The success of the
scheme inspired a dramatic rise in the take-up for A-level languages, from only two
students of German and three of French in 1986, to fourteen of both languages in 1989.

Source: Adapted from Lupson (1989).

Personal and Social Education

Personal and social education (PSE) is concerned with the development of
the student as a whole, through the acquisition of a range of personal and
interpersonal skills. It has traditionally followed closely behind careers education as the most popular curricular frame for work experience. PSE can
embrace a range of cross–curricular themes: for example, sex and health

education, environmental education, political education or citizenship, economic and industrial understanding, and often careers education itself.

PSE programmes in schools have tended to fall within two distinct paradigms, which can be termed the social-and-life-skills model and the social-studies model (Barnes *et al.*, 1988; Hargreaves *et al.*, 1988). The social-and-life-skills model tends to stress the importance of teaching and learning processes and highlights the needs of individual students. It is concerned with the acquisition of skills and attitudes rather than knowledge. This approach to PSE has been criticized for being uncritical and focusing on interpersonal problems, while ignoring the broader social, economic and political context within which these problems arise (Fiehn, 1989). Within this paradigm, work experience is used to help students develop desirable personal qualities, skills and attitudes. By contrast, the social-studies model is characterized by an emphasis upon acquiring knowledge about society and the world of work. Work experience is seen as a vehicle for gathering knowledge, often in workbooks, which can be drawn upon by teachers to reinforce social-science concepts such as the division of labour and occupational gender segregation.

The organizational arrangements for PSE have important implications for its role as a frame for work experience (Barnes *et al.*, 1987; Barnes, Johnson and Jordan, 1988). Within TVEI projects it was found that where PSE was 'encapsulated' in an identifiable timetable slot, it tended to have a low status in the eyes of staff and students; whereas in 'diffused' models of organization where PSE was infused across the curriculum in different subjects and modules, its status was usually much higher. However, this dichotomy sometimes starts to break down when work experience is integrated into a PSE frame. The school described in Box 9.7 has a separately timetabled or 'encapsulated' PSE programme, but work experience has been given a broader place in the school's curriculum. The whole-school approach to industry links, including work experience, has involved whole-staff INSET and whole-staff participation in monitoring visits. In this way, this element of the PSE programme has become more 'diffused'.

World-of-work Learning

In a world-of-work-learning frame, work experience can be viewed as an important element of the work-related curriculum, which includes all those activities and experiences that are designed to increase students' understanding of the world of work (see DES, 1989; Miller, 1990). Work experience can enable students to build up a detailed picture of the structure and systems of a work organization through taking on a work role, performing work tasks, and observing and participating in work processes, within a real work environment. World-of-work learning is an important frame for many work-experience modules which have been developed within TVEI and/or for the

---

Box 9.7   A personal and social education frame: Sharples School, Bolton

Sharples School is an 11–16 comprehensive in the Metropolitan Borough of Bolton. Work experience forms part of a ten-week module for the 350 students in year 11. The school has developed, through discussions with local employers, the following main aim for work experience: 'to learn, appreciate or demonstrate a number of skills and attitudes in a working environment'. The objectives derived from this aim include helping students to develop: initiative; cooperation; self-confidence; responsibility; motivation; communication; problem-solving; teamwork and leadership; and obeying rules. In addition, students are encouraged to think through their personal aims and objectives, and to record these in their 'Record of Achievement'.

Preparation occurs within the PSE programme, within tutorial time, through year assemblies, and through counselling sessions for students who need extra support. Preparation tasks involve negotiating what will be learned, and how this learning might take place. Students are asked to find their own placements, using documentation provided by the school. This process is intended to promote the main objectives of the programme, while creating students' ownership of the experience. The use of deadlines and contracts aims to encourage responsibility.

During their two-week placement, students are encouraged to reflect upon their experiences through open-ended questions in the booklet. For each day, there is a different set of questions to consider. Each morning in the staffroom, teachers are invited to meet with visiting employers and the work-experience coordinators to discuss any problems encountered during the monitoring visit.

Debriefing occurs within PSE time immediately after the placement. Students complete: a 'before-and-after' self-assessment profile; an assessment of their placement performance; responses to open-ended questions; and an analysis of the effect of the placement upon their school work. The English department helps students to produce written statements for their Record of Achievement, and an assignment for the GCSE coursework. The school has decided not to have too much work-experience-related coursework, as this 'could detract from the value of the experience, lessen their enjoyment, and reduce the opportunity to reflect on the learning objectives'.

Source: Adapted from Berkeley, Braham and Miller (1990).

---

purposes of unit accreditation. In particular, there is a range of relatively new pre-vocational courses which make considerable use of work experience and view it primarily as a source of world-of-work learning. These include Business and Information Studies, as well as some technologically-oriented courses. TVEI has encouraged this development by insisting that all TVEI students undertake work experience pre-16, and by stimulating the growth of industry- and business-related courses.

In spite of this, as HMI observe, 'rarely is work experience seen as an opportunity to explore a wider industrial or economic brief ... many students gain little understanding of the structure and organization of business or of the nature of the local economy' (HMI, 1990, p. 20). However, the case-study in Box 9.8 shows how in one TVEI pilot school, world-of-work learning became an important strand running throughout the work-experience programme. In particular, it illustrates the use of students' experience and knowledge about the world of work as a resource. The learning potential to be gained from the pooling of experience to reveal the shape and

---

Box 9.8   A world-of-work-learning frame in a TVEI pilot school

The presence of the five-week module contributed to raising the status of work experience in the eyes of the teachers in a TVEI pilot school. It had originally been presented as an opportunity to integrate work experience into traditional subject areas. Although the module was timetabled for only one-and-a-half hours per week, the flexible organization of the school enabled those students who so wished to spend much longer on this aspect of their work.

The work placement occurred during the module, which had four stated aims: placement preparation, including for example health and safety at work; developing self-awareness; analyzing the skills associated with particular jobs; and developing job-search skills. The school-based coordinator suggested that there was also a broader goal of empowering students 'to analyse and take control or affect their environment'.

There were a wide range of preparatory activities, including: understanding and reflecting upon their own priorities; developing relationships with adults; and topics relating to industry and employment. Apart from familiar lessons on using the telephone, writing letters of application and *curricula vitae*, and managing interviews, there were less common sessions on gender roles at work, relationships between management and the community, the value of work, and the disposal of industrial waste.

The collection of information during the placement was used to furnish materials for a series of reports from students on the characteristics of the company during debriefing. This led, in turn, to discussions intended to give them 'greater understanding of the variety of management styles, working conditions, and so on'. A student-centred approach resulted in discussions of why people work, an evaluation of solitary and communal jobs, and students' conceptions of 'interesting' and 'boring' work. The overall purpose appeared to be to help students to think about job choice in a better-informed way, and to place these discussions in a wider context.

Follow-up work extended beyond the end of the module, as work experience was used as a resource for a range of individual and group projects, including: redesigning one company's job application form; design and technology projects on briefs set by employers; writing software for administrative applications in one company; developing designs for a fashion retailer; and designing for industrial safety.

Source: Adapted from Barnes, Johnson and Jordan (1988, pp. 75–8).

---

nature of the world of work and the economy is widely under-used in work-experience debriefing and follow-up (HMI, 1990, p. 12). The dissemination of a national framework for knowledge, understanding, skills and attitudes in relation to the world of work should help schools integrate work experience more effectively into this curricular frame in future. Thus the NCC (1990b) guidelines on Education for Economic and Industrial Understanding contain a set of learning objectives which could be developed through a school's pre-16 work-experience programme (see e.g. Box 9.9).

Careers Education

Careers education is the most common curricular frame for work experience. The frame is often tacit rather than overt: that is, it is assumed that the purpose of work experience is to assist the process of vocational choices and

---

Box 9.9:   *Some learning objectives for a school's pre-16 work-experience programme*

9. Industry involves the effective management of people and other resources, and industrial organisations have different ways of maximising efficiency, output and job satisfaction.

e.g. Understand that team work involving specialist tasks is an important part of the world of work.	WORK EXPERIENCE Observe specialist work roles in different contexts.

10. The part played by design and technology in industrial production.

e.g. Use knowledge and understanding gained from work-experience placements to investigate artefacts, systems or environments in industry and how these can be extended to meet human need.	WORK EXPERIENCE Develop knowledge and understanding of the organisation of industry and the nature of the local economy, through discussion, projects and written work based on work-experience placements.

Source: NCC (1990, p. 41).

---

transitions. There appear to be two main approaches to using work experience as a vehicle for career decision-making: the 'narrow' model and the 'broad' model. The 'narrow' model seeks to crystallize vocational choice through work sampling (see p. 20). Where schools encourage work sampling, there are clear implications for the selection of preparatory activities (see Chapter 12) and for the matching of students to placements (see Chapter 11). It has been argued that in the absence of counselling, or of a strong curricular frame provided by the school, the majority of students will use work experience to aid vocational choices in an ill-formed and incoherent manner (Fortune, Jamieson and Street, 1983). The 'broad' model, by contrast, stresses the expansive aim of work experience (see pp. 19–20). Students are encouraged to develop their decision-making capabilities, and careers education in this paradigm facilitates self-awareness, opportunity awareness, decision learning and transition learning (Law and Watts, 1977). Such an approach may imply a very different strategy for preparation and for matching of students to placements. In both of these models, the entire careers programme is sometimes perceived as a preparation for and a follow-up of the work–experience programme.

The case-study in Box 9.10 offers a strong careers–education frame for work experience. Although work experience is located within a subject module, it is organized and taught by the careers department. The preparation programme and the use of the Jobcentre are designed to mirror the processes of 'real' job application. The strong involvement of local employers

---

Box 9.10:   A careers-education frame: Deeside High School, Clwyd

Deeside High School is an 11–18 comprehensive of 500 students in Clwyd, North Wales. Work experience is a feature of a ten-week module which forms part of the GCSE Community Studies course taken by all students. The most important aim of the 'Work Appreciation Scheme' is 'to bring about a flexibility of attitude and a willingness to learn, sufficient to manage future changes in technology and career'.

The school in collaboration with the local Jobcentre has established a school Jobcentre where employers advertise placements or 'vacancies'. During preparation students are introduced to the Jobcentre, make at least two selections and compose *curricula vitae*. They write letters of application to the employers and, after a mock interview, have formal interviews for their chosen placement, often conducted by the employer in the work-place. If they are successful, they receive letters of acceptance; if not, the process is repeated with the second-choice placement. Local industrialists offer sessions on particular aspects of preparation: for example, on health and safety at work.

During the two-week placement, students complete a log-book which requires a consideration of the working environment, and an analysis of the skills and qualities required for the job. There is also a diary in which students record their responses to a different aspect of the work or working environment each day.

In debriefing, students are grouped together according to the occupational category of their placement, and each group is addressed by an employer representing the category. The employers encourage the reflection and sharing of experiences, as well as mutual constructive criticism. Students have access to their log-books when completing a written test, which contributes 10 per cent of the marks to their Community Studies GCSE.

Source: Adapted from Berkeley, Braham and Miller (1990).

---

in preparation, briefing and debriefing strengthens the careers–education flavour of this particular scheme.

Vocational Courses

Work experience is rarely used to develop specific vocational knowledge and skills below the age of 16. However, because the curricular frame is often blurred, and free choice remains the most popular form of matching students to placements, some students view work experience as an opportunity to develop specific vocational skills. Such skills may have been developed embryonically at school, in the home, or in a part-time job — for example, keyboarding skills and the skills associated with motor-vehicle maintenance. When viewed from the perspective of the student, it is often difficult to see the difference between vocational and pre-vocational work experience. This point is illustrated by the case-study of work experience within a CPVE Art and Design course in Box 9.11. In this case, the students had a clear idea of their future career and the educational route they wished to follow. The form of the work experience — the completion of specially-constructed tasks — enabled them to apply classroom skills in real-work contexts. Thus although

---

Box 9.11:   *A (pre-)vocational frame: William Gladstone High School, Brent*

Students studying the CPVE in Art and Design at William Gladstone High School in the London Borough of Brent undertook a two-week placement in design studios. The Head of Creative Design found and negotiated placements with a number of design companies.

All the students on the course had already decided to seek places in further education colleges, mainly on BTEC Art and Design courses. The work experience was designed as part of their career progression, as well as providing progression in terms of content, process and context.

The students learned from observing designers at work, and from using the facilities of the placement in terms of specialist materials, equipment, and advice, to complete specially-constructed projects negotiated between the teacher and designer. These projects meant that students always had something to do while at the placement. Some examples of projects completed were: designing their own letterheads and business cards; setting up and running a computer-aided design programme; designing and building a simple lighting device; and designing and making a mock-up record sleeve. The students were able to obtain useful career information and guidance from talking to the different specialists in the companies about their own college and professional training and career progression routes, and what they hoped to achieve in the future.

---

the work experience was located within a pre-vocational course, from the perspective of both the students and the teacher it was used to develop specific vocational skills in the students' chosen career area.

In contrast, Box 9.12 presents a case-study of a community-based work-experience scheme linked to 'caring' occupations within a course which is defined by the school as vocational in nature but which has strong features of a pre-vocational programme. Students undertaking the course as part of their Alternative Studies programme are by no means all committed to careers within the field of community care. Nevertheless, the rigour involved in assessing the developing skills of the students shares many of the hallmarks of vocational training.

Integration: Towards a Whole-school Approach

A feature of the case-studies of integration in different curricular frames considered in the previous section is their hybrid nature. Although many of the pre-16 work-experience schemes outlined began with a clear careers or personal and social education frame, this has tended to change over time so that a mixture of aims and frames has become evident. For example, the strong English frame at Testwood School (Box 9.4) has developed some emphasis on world-of-work learning, and follow-up now occurs in a number of different subjects. The personal and social education frame at Sharples School (Box 9.7) includes a requirement for students to find their own placements, thus mirroring the job-search process which is a common strategy within a careers-education frame. The world-of-work learning frame in the TVEI pilot school (Box 9.8) includes many elements of a

---

Box 9.12: A vocational frame: Palmer's Sixth Form College, Essex

Palmer's Sixth Form College offers an Alternative Studies programme, which provides an extensive range of subjects including a community-based work-experience scheme that comprises three linked modules. The course, for approximately twenty-five students per group, is timetabled for one afternoon per week for a year. It aims to provide a vocational opportunity, to illustrate a variety of local services, and to broaden the basis of experience and career choice. The programme was designed by college staff in association with community-service agencies, such as MIND, Open Door, Befrienders, and the local-authority Social Services department.

Preparation takes the form of an induction module, during which students either visit, or discuss with visiting adults-other-than-teachers, the five main placement areas: primary schools; hospitals; working with the elderly; working with the disabled; and pre-school playgroups, nurseries and crèches. This 'pre-vocational introduction' aims to help students to choose the placement most likely to interest and stimulate them.

The second module, which lasts for the remainder of the year, includes the placement. Students are encouraged to broaden their experience when making their choice of placement. Thus although girls are often keen to work with children, those who have already had such experience are advised to work with the elderly or the handicapped. Staff visits play an important role in the programme, because of their role in the third assessment module.

The teacher supervisor and the placement supervisor monitor the students' progress on a weekly basis. The placement supervisor records evidence of the development of skills or achievements, and this assists the students — with help from their tutor — to create a formative profile. Review sheets are an important feature of the analysis, facilitating both student recording and tutor monitoring. The formative profile is incorporated in the record of achievement, and the significance of the experience is formally discussed with teaching colleagues to facilitate cross-curricular follow-up. Placement tutors recommend students for the award of the Palmer's Vocational Certificate, which is endorsed by a range of companies and community organizations.

Source: Adapted from the Palmer's Sixth Form College entry for the Rover Award, 1989.

---

careers-education frame, as well as the academic-subjects frame in the follow-up technology projects. In practice, therefore, it is hard to find schemes with one precisely defined curricular frame providing a sharp focus for integration.

In some schools, the development of the work-experience programme over time has led to more than one frame and/or the involvement of a number of academic subjects. Such developments can occur in an uncoordinated way. For example, one school-based work-experience coordinator we interviewed described how various subject departments set course-work on work experience, but said that he had neither been consulted about this, nor was aware of the nature of the projects and assignments set. The autonomy of subject departments in some schools can lead to what has been described as 'fragmented assimilation' (Barnes, Johnson and Jordan, 1988): that is, the atomizing of learning experiences as teachers focus on one aspect of the experience, but lose sight of the relationship between the whole learner and the whole experience. The coordination of the cross-curricular integration of work experience can avoid the risk of such fragmentation.

The planned coordination of cross-curricular integration allows different teachers and subject specialists to build upon and/or extend learning derived from other curricular areas. It can lead to the harmonization of teaching strategies across curricular frames in a way that minimizes repetition, prevents overloading students with too many assignments, and avoids students being asked to talk about their work-experience placement in every classroom in their first week back at school. Coordination is made easier when there is a clear policy statement setting out the most important aspects of the work-experience programme and its relationship with the whole curriculum.

The role of the curriculum coordinator for work experience could involve a number of tasks. The first task might be to ensure that subject departments schedule lessons linked to work-experience preparation in the most appropriate sequence for the students. For example, they might check that lessons on interview techniques held by the English department occur before mock interviews with employers planned by the Careers department. The second task might be to collate ideas for assignments, projects and placement tasks from different departments, and critically to review them in the light of the aims of the scheme, the demands upon students, and the need for coherence. The end result could be a student workbook and/or diary which reflects the cross-curricular integration of the scheme. The third task might be to coordinate the visits of subject teachers to students on work experience in a way that furthers the teachers' awareness of the potential for linking their teaching to the placement experience. The final task could be to coordinate cross-curricular follow-up so that teachers are helped to view the students as a resource which can enrich the curriculum, while at the same time avoiding overload and repetition.

There are two main approaches to developing cross-curricular integration: the incremental approach and the radical approach. In the *incremental* approach, the work-experience coordinator gradually involves other teachers and subject departments in the work-experience programme. This can occur over a number of years as part of a planned expansion across the curriculum. For example, from an initial careers-education frame in the first year, the personal and social education team and form tutors might be brought into the preparation, the monitoring visits, and the debriefing. In the second year, the Humanities department could be invited to join the planning team, and to set assignments linked to the placements. In the third year, the English department might be persuaded to undertake a module on 'work', and to link it to work experience. And so on. In the *radical* approach there is a clear decision to break with previous practice and to plan the links which optimize students' learning from and through work experience. This can be accompanied by a whole-school approach to the curricular integration of work experience whereby multiple curricular frames and many subjects are linked to the work-experience programme.

The case-study of Garth High School (Box 9.13) offers an example of the incremental approach to curricular integration. The scheme was initially

---

Box 9.13   An 'incremental' approach to cross-curricular integration: Garth High School, London Borough of Merton

In 1985, work experience was located within a careers frame, and was available for some students only. In 1986, blocked work experience for the whole of year 11 was introduced for the first time. Since then the core preparation and follow-up programme has continued within timetabled careers lessons, amounting to some forty hours of tuition in years 10 and 11. The sampling and anticipatory aims of the scheme are indicative of its careers origins.

Since 1988, the personal and social education frame has become an important feature of the programme. Thus the maturational aim has been added to the original aims, and the head of year and form tutors have become closely involved. Work experience forms an important element of the school's record-of-achievement programme. Tutors and subject teachers are allocated groups of between four and six students. In special briefing and debriefing sessions, these teachers help students to identify potential areas of achievement during their work placement, and to clarify and record actual achievements for inclusion — along with the employers' reports — in the school's record of achievement. Students are encouraged during the preparatory phase to make preliminary visits in order to investigate possible learning opportunities, and to negotiate with employers about suitable placement tasks which will help them to realize their learning opportunities. During the experience, students are visited by their tutors, and a formative profile is completed, recording tasks undertaken and achievements, which is validated by the employer. They also complete a work-experience workbook, which comprises careers-related and subject-specific work, and is used as a basis for debriefing and follow-up.

As a result of school-focused INSET, academic subjects have become involved in follow-up. The English department is using the experience as a resource for extended GCSE written work. The Modern Languages department have used work experience as a focus for oral topic work for GCSE. Students research vocabulary used at their placements, and teacher assessments are made of their ability to relate their experiences in French, German or Spanish. In their final oral examination, 'work and the future' is a theme which is popular with students, and attainment has risen as a result. In addition, students in Integrated Humanities complete a project on the theme of conflict, drawing upon data collected in their work-experience record book.

---

set within a strong careers–education frame. The development of the school's pastoral programme, the introduction of TVEI, and the advent of records of achievement, provided the scope and the impetus to introduce a personal and social education frame. The use of staff INSET days on the teacher visit and on integrating work experience into subjects then led to the emergence of an academic-subjects frame — in particular, through Modern Languages.

In contrast, the case-study of Ifield Community College in West Sussex provides an unusual example of the radical approach to curricular integration (Box 9.14). The whole-school approach was introduced with the support of the LEA and the school's senior management team, and this meant a fundamental break with previous practice. The school–industry policy statement including work experience set out a number of principles which placed the scheme firmly within the curriculum (see Box 5.1). Again, INSET was important in developing cross-curricular integration (cf. p. 98). The work-experience scheme became the winning entry of the Rover Group Award for 'Quality in Work Experience' in 1989 (Berkeley, Braham, and Miller, 1990).

*Box 9.14   A 'radical' approach to cross-curricular integration: Ifield Community College,
West Sussex LEA*

Ifield Community College is a 12–19 comprehensive school with 950 students. In 1988, the school adopted a radical strategy to make a break from the traditional 'bolt-on' work-experience model which had previously operated for year-10 students. A plethora of externally-imposed initiatives provided the impetus for change: GCSE and CPVE increased demands for course-work; records of achievement stimulated a search for suitable experiences to record; equal-opportunities policies encouraged a review of the hidden curriculum, including the effects of cultural and gender pressures upon vocational choices; and the call for a local industry–education partnership encouraged the involvement of employers in the scheme.

The programme that emerged, 'Industry Month', provides work-related experiences as a central focus for the curriculum during four weeks in the summer term. Year-8 students have an 'Introduction to the World of Work' course and go on industrial visits. Year-9 students take part in workshops with apprentices from local companies. Year-12 students carry out industrial problem-solving exercises as part of their A-level studies. And the majority of year-10 students undertake a period of two weeks' work experience on employers' premises. The aims of the latter scheme are to address the initiatives referred to above and to integrate work experience into a range of GCSE subjects through course-work assignments.

In order to promote these aims, INSET sessions were held for twelve interested heads of department. All participating employers were contacted, and a committed group of them became involved in the professional development sessions with the teachers. As a result, the English department devised a module on 'Communications at Work' as a major theme for its GCSE course. ESL support teachers created suitable materials so that all students could become fully involved in the programme. In all, fourteen subject areas developed assignments. Twenty-five teachers have completed a basic training course in careers guidance to prepare them for interviewing students. The pastoral staff were encouraged to become involved at all stages, and profiling tutors were prepared for assisting students with placement selection, and for acting as catalysts in the process of reflection afterwards.

Preparation is carried out in English and PSE lessons. GCSE coursework preparation is undertaken in subject lessons. The first week of Industry Month is devoted to briefings, a preliminary visit to the placement, and a workshop with local employers on equal opportunities at work. A special parents' evening is held to inform and involve parents. Employers welcomed the link with GCSE as it enabled them to gain insights into this 'new' qualification.

During the two-week placements, students undertake — in addition to conventional work experience — a variety of other work-related activities. For example, a group of sports enthusiasts spent a week coaching PE in local primary schools. This was followed up by a second week in placements at the local leisure centre. In place of a workbook, students have three assignments to complete during their placement. The GCSE-linked English assignment concerns defining and evaluating their practical experience, and either carrying out an interview or completing a diary. The GCSE Mathematics assignment involves the collection of statistical data. In addition, all students carry out a health-and-safety assign-ment which is used for the evaluation of the placements and of the programme as a whole.

The fourth week of Industry Month is devoted to debriefing and follow-up. The first debriefing day is set aside for exercises designed to assess personal and social skills developed during the placement. English teachers require all students to evaluate their use of language while on work experience. Other staff follow up the placements through GCSE subject-specific assignments. Profiling tutors use the employer's report and a student self-assessment, for a major joint review of progress at the end of year 10. Careers teachers and careers officers follow up the vocational value of the work experience. All employers are invited to a series of 'open mornings', and a joint teacher–employer evaluation takes place during one afternoon. Throughout the week, there are presentations on students' projects and displays of work.

Source: Adapted from Allen (1988).

Conclusion

The diversity of the case-studies in this chapter illustrates the range of the choices facing schools which wish to integrate work experience into the curriculum. The preliminary step for most schools wishing to move away from a 'bolt-on' relationship to the curriculum is likely to be the creation of a stronger curricular frame surrounding the placement phase. This will entail securing time for adequate preparation, briefing, debriefing and follow-up, but also reviewing learning objectives and teaching strategies in the light of a clearer set of aims.

Schools which already have a strong curricular frame tend to have an integrated programme of teaching in that there is a logical relationship between the learning objectives and teaching strategies adopted in each phase of the programme. In this case, however, it may be useful to review the programme from the perspective of the individual learner. The concepts of personal integration, world-of-work-learning integration, and subject integration provide one way of seeing to what extent the programme helps learners to make links between work experience and their maps of themselves, of the world of work, and of subjects respectively. This poses the question of the extent to which the work-experience programme can be modified to promote integration in learning.

Cross-curricular integration offers another option for development of a school's work-experience scheme. The case-studies highlight the importance of planned INSET in developing such links, and the need for management and coordination if 'fragmented assimilation' is to be avoided. The incremental approach to cross-curricular integration involves strategic planning. Over a period of years, additional curricular areas can be invited to participate in the work-experience programme. The role of the work-experience coordinator can be to persuade a head of department that linking subject teaching to work experience is both feasible and desirable. Experience suggests that once one major department has been signed up, and the benefits to teachers and students become clear, then it is easier to involve other departments subsequently.

The radical approach to cross-curricular integration involves a review of the whole work-experience programme and a consideration of how it could contribute to the whole curriculum. This might involve the whole staff, and/or a cross-curricular or whole-curriculum working group. The first task in integrating work experience into the whole curriculum is to decide how work experience can promote the aims and learning objectives of the whole curriculum. The second task is to decide where work experience should be located in the curriculum — that is, which curricular frame(s) would best promote the aims. This could be followed by a decision about the type of teaching strategies which should be included in the programme, which teachers should be involved, and when. However, there are two important factors to consider in moving towards a whole-school, whole-curriculum approach. The first is the INSET and support needs of the teachers involved. The second is the issue of whether or not the new work-experience programme will promote coherence in learning without overburdening both individual students and the experience with too many linkages into the curriculum.

Chapter 10

Progression

Andrew Miller

Progression in learning concerns the extent to which there is 'value added' at each stage of a young person's education. In work-experience programmes, 'value added' will exist when there is a planned attempt to build upon or to extend the range and/or depth of students' knowledge, understanding, skills and attitudes. At the heart of the notion of progression lies the relationship between teaching and learning. Teachers plan the curriculum in order to promote student learning. Generally this involves deciding upon aims, learning objectives, teaching strategies, and appropriate forms of assessment. But there is often a gap between teachers' intentions and the learning outcomes for individual students. This is particularly true in the case of experience-based learning programmes, and especially so with work experience where the teacher has little control over the experience itself. Ensuring progression in work experience, therefore, poses a major challenge for work-experience coordinators.

This chapter explores the idea of progression in learning through work experience. We begin with a discussion of why progression is currently regarded as an important issue. This is followed by an analysis of two forms of progression: progression *within* a school-based work-experience programme; and progression *between* different work-experience placements. The ensuing section considers the place of work experience within a sequence of work-related activities. The conclusion identifies some of the main questions which schools need to address when introducing planned progression into their work-experience programmes.

Why Progression?

In the past, progression has seldom been a major concern for work-experience coordinators. When work experience was usually 'bolted-on' to the curriculum (see pp. 154–5), learning from work experience and learning from the school curriculum tended to be viewed quite separately. The current interest in progression in work experience derives mainly from the increasing integration of work experience into the curriculum. Unless such integration takes place, progression is unlikely to be a meaningful issue to address. Three main developments have focused attention on curricular progression in relation to work experience: HMI reports, TVEI and its extension, and the National Curriculum.

Over a number of years, HMI have stressed the importance of planned progression as an important principle of curriculum planning:

> Children's development is a continuous process and schools have to provide conditions and experiences which sustain and encourage that process while recognising that it does not proceed uniformly or at an even pace. If this progression is to be maintained there is a need to build systematically on the children's existing knowledge, concepts, skills and attitudes, so as to ensure an orderly advance in their capabilities over a period of time. Teaching and learning experiences should be ordered so as to facilitate pupils' progress, with each successive element making appropriate demands and leading to better performance (HMI, 1989a, p. 48).

This quotation illustrates how the notion of progression is linked to that of continuity. The idea of curricular continuity is concerned with helping teachers to perceive, plan and deliver the curriculum from years 1 to 13 as an entity. Curricular continuity can be achieved when 'the experiences provided by a school ease the social, emotional and cognitive adjustments that pupils have to make when transferring from one class to another or from one school to another' (SCDC, 1988).

HMI suggest that few schools have addressed the issue of progression in work-experience programmes, and that post-16 work-experience schemes are likely to stress discontinuity rather than continuity of curricular experience (HMI, 1990). This is particularly likely to occur when the transition to post-compulsory education is coupled with transfer to a different institution: 'Few colleges made effective use of the experience gained by students before coming to college. . . . Some students expressed frustration at the failure to take full account of their previous experience when planning the learning programme' (HMI, 1989b, p. 11). The tendency to begin a new school year by wiping the slate clean — the *tabula rasa* approach, as Blyth *et al.* (1976) call it — makes planning the work-experience programme easier, as individual differences between learners based upon prior learning can be ignored. This may appear efficient in terms of teaching, but it is inefficient in terms of learning.

The prime inefficiency of the *tabula rasa* approach is that there is likely to be repetition, which may involve a waste of scarce and valuable curriculum time. There are two main forms of repetition: planned and unplanned. *Planned* repetition can be successfully used when the intention is to consolidate learning. *Unplanned* repetition can occur in a number of ways in work-experience programmes. First, the preparation programme might repeat teaching strategies used on previous preparation programmes. Second, students might be allocated a work placement in a field in which they have already gained considerable experience — for example, through a part-time job. Third, students might be given tasks by the school — or by the employer — which repeat tasks completed, and involve skills acquired, on previous work placements. Some unplanned repetition may serve to consolidate learning and/or to give students new insights, but it may also reduce student motivation. In general, it could be argued that teaching strategies and placement tasks which aim to help students learn things which they already know, understand or are able to do, constitute a form of curriculum 'clutter' (DES, 1985, p. 18), which in the interests of ensuring progression should be swept away.

A further factor which has focused attention on progression has been the development and extension of TVEI (p. 7). This has led to the spread of work experience across the 14–18 curriculum, and in particular to a rapid growth in the number and range of courses incorporating a compulsory work-experience placement. When students were likely to have only one work placement during their 14–18 education, the issue of progression between different periods of work experience was unimportant. Increasingly, however, many students undertake work experience in their last year of compulsory schooling, followed by another placement usually in year 12. In some schools, students have a number of placements either within one academic year or in successive years. These trends draw attention to the need for planned progression between the work-experience placements.

In addition, the introduction of the National Curriculum is designed to introduce stronger planned progression into the 5–16 curriculum as a whole. At a general level, the accumulated evidence of unplanned repetition, the widespread *tabula rasa* approach (both within and between institutions), and the lack of whole-curriculum planning, with the resulting absence of continuity and progression, have all provided strong arguments for the introduction of the National Curriculum. The identification of programmes of study, attainment targets and other elements of the whole curriculum offers for the first time an 'agreed' framework for the pre-16 school curriculum (NCC, 1990a). The ten levels of attainment identified by the TGAT report (DES, 1988c) and enshrined in the foundation subjects provide a framework for progression in curriculum content, covering the knowledge, understanding, skills and attitudes that schools should teach. The curriculum review which schools are having to undertake in response to the National Curriculum could include a consideration, not only of what aspects of the curriculum are being delivered through the work-experience programme, but also of how the programme ensures progression in student learning.

Progression within a Work-experience Programme

How can work-experience coordinators ensure progression within a work-experience programme? As we have noted, the term 'progression' can be applied to learning programmes which add to or extend students' knowledge, understanding, skills and attitudes. It highlights the importance of identifying prior learning as a starting point. As we have seen in Chapter 9 (pp. 152–3), the concepts of personal, world-of-work-learning and subject integration refer to the process of relating aspects of work experience to students' existing mental maps. Teaching strategies used during each phase of the work-experience programme can then be planned in order to make increasing demands upon students. The details of such teaching strategies will be discussed in Chapter 12; here we will examine briefly how the promotion of progression can guide the choice of such strategies in each of the five curricular frames identified in Chapter 2.

Progression can be achieved within a personal and social education frame through the process of personal review and goal setting with the record-of-achievement tutor. Such processes are designed to help students identify personal and social skills which can be developed through work experience. Similar methods can be used within a careers-education frame when the guidance tutor helps students to establish targets that can be met through the work-experience programme.

Students' existing experience and understanding of the world of work could be built upon in preparation within a world-of-work-learning frame. HMI argue that work experience could become 'the jewel in the crown of a programme of industrial and economic understanding' (HMI, 1990, p. 20) for 14–19-year-olds, but this 'depended upon the school knowing or being able to determine the existing levels of economic and industrial understanding on the part of the students. Very few schools had ... successfully determined existing knowledge or understanding' (ibid, p. 10). Students within a particular group or class are likely to have a range of knowledge and experience of the world of work, gained from part-time work and family work, as well as from different areas of the curriculum. Whole-group and small-group discussion can often draw out such knowledge and understanding, which can then be used as a resource in the preparation programme.

Within a vocational-course frame, progression tends to be less problematic than for other curricular frames, because the main aim of the placement phase is to allow students to apply skills acquired in the classroom setting. Nevertheless, during the placement, progression in vocational skills can be achieved in various ways: through increasing the range of students' techniques and levels of competence; through an increased speed of working, reflecting greater confidence; and through increased levels of responsibility for their own work (Evans, Brown and Bates, 1987).

Within an academic-subjects frame, a major aim is to deepen students' understanding of concepts. Progression can occur through three main stages of the work-experience programme. In preparation, students can be introduced to or reminded of the concept: for example, in Technology the concept might be that of a system within the context of business and industry (DES, 1990a). At the placement, students can then use this concept in order to make sense of the placement. For instance, they might construct a systems diagram showing the main parts of the work organization, and the interrelationships between them. The students might also attempt to evaluate the system, through observation and interviews with key personnel, in order to identify its main strengths and weaknesses. During follow-up, the findings can be shared with other students who have engaged in parallel tasks at other work-places. This can promote a deeper understanding of the concept through the examination of a range of examples drawn from contrasting work contexts.

One strategy for promoting progression in learning both within and between work-experience programmes is the idea of the *learning agreement* (Berkeley, Braham and Miller, 1990). Learning agreements require all parties — students, teachers and employers — to think hard about individual learning through work experience. An example is shown in Box 10.1. The basic format of a learning agreement includes three main elements. First, 'what is to be learned' through the work-experience programme must be identified. This might include the development of new — or the deepening of existing — knowledge, understanding, skills and attitudes, and involves the identification of prior learning. Second, 'how is it to be learned' needs to be clarified. This part of the learning agreement links phases of the work-experience programme to intended learning outcomes. Third, 'how will the learning be presented' for assessment should be specified. This indicates the evidence which will demonstrate the extent to which the learning goals have been achieved. The evidence of student learning contained in this third element could form part of the record of achievement (this is discussed further in Chapter 13). The record from one period of work experience could constitute an essential document for ensuring planned progression in a subsequent period of work experience. It is to progression between different work-experience programmes that we now turn.

Progression between Work-experience Programmes

When progression is discussed by work-experience coordinators, it is usually progression between work-experience programmes that is debated. Sometimes the focus is upon the need to differentiate between the year-10 and year-11 programmes, but more often the issue is the distinction between pre- and post-16 programmes. Planned differentiation between two periods of work experience can facilitate progression in learning through helping students to acquire 'new' knowledge, understanding, skills and attitudes. Box 10.2 illustrates some dimensions and examples of differentiation between

---

Box 10.1   A learning agreement pro-forma

Name of Pupil ....

Name of School ....

School Work Experience ....
Co-ordinator

Rover Work Experience ....
Co-ordinator

Workplace Supervisor ....

Dates of Placement:

From: .... To: .... 199.

What is to be learned?

Knowledge:

Understanding:

Skills:

How will it be learned?

Programme of activities:

What evidence of learning will be offered and how will it be assessed?

Written evidence:	How assessed:
Oral presentation:	
Other evidence:	

Source: Prepared by the Learning from Experience Trust for the Rover Group (1990).

---

work–experience programmes. A prerequisite for differentiation between programmes is a clear set of aims and objectives. Many of the dimensions shown in Box 10.2 — for example, the matching strategy, the forms, the school-related tasks and the assessment — can be derived from the overall aims and objectives of each programme. The determination of different aims for successive placements may be promulgated by the school or by the LEA

Box 10.2 Progression between work-experience programmes: some possible dimensions with examples

Dimension	First placement	Second placement
Curricular frame	— personal and social education/world-of-work learning	— careers education
	— personal and social education/academic subjects	— world-of-work learning
Aims (within a curricular frame)	— expansive/anticipatory	— sampling
(between frames)	— maturational	— investigative
Matching strategy	— directed/guided choice	— free choice
	— counselled choice	— guided choice
Work context	— local company	— company elsewhere in UK/Europe
	— manufacturing	— services
Placement objectives	— teacher-determined/student-teacher-negotiated	— student-determined/student-employer-negotiated
Forms	— rotating around different departments	— doing an actual job
	— helping someone in an actual job/doing an actual job	— carrying out specifically constructed tasks
School-related tasks	— diary/workbook of teacher-devised tasks	— student-devised workbook/negotiated assignments
Assessment	— record of achievement	— employer-based assessment/assessment of assignments

work-experience unit, but such educational distinctions may not be at all clear to students. Some of the students we talked to in our fieldwork were unable to distinguish between the aims of different periods of work experience they had undertaken. On the other hand, HMI report that:

A school where two periods of placement were organised, one during Year 10 and one in Year 11, was successful in persuading a proportion of its students to concentrate on 'the demands, values and relationships in the world of employment' in the first and saving the career orientation to the second (HMI, 1990, p. 4).

Students are more likely to be able to distinguish between different aims of successive work-experience placements when coordinators vary a number of

---

Box 10.3   Progression through a three-year work-experience programme in Denmark

Year 8 (aged 14) 'Local work experience'

1. Duration: 5 days
2. Matching strategy: directed
3. Learning objectives: — to gain a broad understanding of being at work (anticipatory aim)
   — to relate the work-place to the local context (investigative aim)

Year 9 (aged 15) 'Limited choice work experience'

1. Duration: 10 days
2. Matching strategy: restricted choice/guided choice
3. Learning objectives: — to gain experience of conditions at a work-place (anticipatory aim)
   — to acquire knowledge of different branches of trade and industry: a class is spread over a range of placements and pools knowledge in follow-up (investigative aim)

Year 10 (aged 16) 'Work experience of one's own choice'

1. Duration: 10 days
2. Matching strategy: free choice/counselled choice
3. Learning objectives: — to test out a chosen occupation (sampling aim)

Source: Adapted from Aalborg Kommune, Denmark.

---

the dimensions shown in Box 10.2, so that the programmes involve not only distinctive objectives, but also different teaching and learning strategies.

A scheme for progression between work placements developed by the Aalborg Kommune in Denmark is shown in Box 10.3 (see also IFAPLAN, 1987). There are four main points about this programme. First, it shows how progression can occur within a curricular frame, that of careers education, culminating in job sampling in the final placement. Second, the scheme recognizes the class, as well as the individual, as the unit of learning, through the emphasis during the second placement on the class experiencing the full range of work available locally, and pooling this information in follow-up lessons. Third, it acknowledges the growing maturity of students through allowing them a greater say over their choice of placement by moving from 'directed "choice"' through to 'free choice' as matching strategies (see Chapter 11). Finally, the duration of the placement phase is increased to allow for a broader range of objectives to be met in the second and third placements.

Some aspects of a scheme for progression developed by the Yorkshire Martyrs Collegiate School in Bradford are illustrated in Box 10.4. This scheme shares some of the features of the Aalborg model: for example, the variations in the duration of the placement phase. There are three main points of interest in this example. First, there is a mix of aims drawn from different curricular frames in the pre-16 placements, whereas the post-16 placement focuses specifically upon curricular enhancement. Second, different teachers

---

Box 10.4   Progression through a three-year work-experience programme in Bradford

Year 10 (aged 15)

Duration: 5 days
Aims: — to facilitate the experience of work on employers' premises (anticipatory aim)
Preparation: — in core curriculum and tutorial time
School-devised tasks: a 'world-of-work-based' workbook (investigative aim)

Year 11 (aged 16)

Duration: 10 days
Aims: — to help students appreciate links between the school curriculum and the world
            of work (enhancing aim)
         — to help students in making a career choice post-16 (sampling aim)
Preparation: — in core curriculum and tutorial time, plus in subjects (English, Mathe-
                  matics, Information Technology)
               — a formal interview with the employer
School-devised tasks: a 'subject-based' workbook, including assignment prepared by
                           subject teachers

Year 12 (aged 17)

Duration: 15 days spread in blocks throughout the year
Aims: — to apply the curriculum to the world of work, e.g. through completing an
            integrated assignment for CPVE (enhancing aim)
Preparation: — individual counselling to identify needs
               — student visit to the employer to plan aims, objectives and tasks
School-devised tasks: an 'individually-prepared' workbook comprising negotiated tasks
                           and assignments, review and diary sheets

Source: Adapted from Yorkshire Martyrs Collegiate School, Bradford.

---

are involved in preparing students each time. The varied subject backgrounds of the staff involved, and the variations in teaching strategies used by these different teachers, are likely to lead to distinctive preparation programmes. Third, the main strategy for structuring learning during the placement — the workbook — has a different style and focus in each year. Both the Aalborg and the Bradford examples show how differentiation between work-experience placements can promote progression through broadening the range of students' knowledge, understanding, skills and attitudes.

Another strategy for broadening students' experience and learning is to require them to undertake successive placements in varying work contexts. As we have noted earlier (pp. 39–40), in Sweden the PRAO system requires all students to undertake one-week placements in three contrasting contexts between the ages of 12 and 16: manufacturing, commerce, and social services. Some schools in the United Kingdom encourage students to attend two one-week placements in contrasting contexts within a single work-experience programme. Hope High School in Salford LEA has used this approach in order to broaden students' horizons, and to throw up similarities and differences between the two work-places which can be analyzed in debriefing and follow-up. HMI (1990, p. 4) note an example of a school

Andrew Miller

Box 10.5` Monitoring progression in work contexts: sample computer records

Record 166 on screen   Record found
Surname Jones   Forenames 1. Andrew   2. John
Preferred 1   Date of Birth 19741119   Date of entry 198609   Date of leaving
Sex Male   Registration Group P   Previous School Swanwick Primary
Address Derby Road   Swanwick
         Derby   Postcode
Parent/Guardian Mr & Mrs Jones   Home tel. 111111
Options: English, Mathematics

SCIP Placement 1 Albion Travel, Ripley
SCIP Placement 2 Alfreton Leisure Centre
SCIP Placement 3 Albion Travel, Ripley
SCIP Placement 4
SCIP Placement 5
SCIP Placement 6
Career Interest Pharmacy

Destination —

Record 181 on screen   Record found
Surname Smith   Forenames 1. Sonja   2. Marie
Preferred 1   Date of Birth 19750811   Date of entry 198609   Date of leaving
Sex Female   Registration Group P   Previous School Riddings
Address Cottage Estate   Riddings
         Derby   Postcode
Parent/Guardian Mr & Mrs Smith   Home tel. 222222
Options: English, Mathematics

SCIP Placement 1 Farm, Long Eaton
SCIP Placement 2 Video shop
SCIP Placement 3 Oldroyds Architects, Alfreton
SCIP Placement 4
SCIP Placement 5
SCIP Placement 6
Career Interest —

Destination —

Source: Swanwick Hall School, Derbyshire.

---

which has community service placements in year 10, followed by a free choice of placements in year 11.

When schools aim to broaden students' experience by requiring them to undertake placements in different work contexts over a number of years, adequate record-keeping becomes particularly important. Swanwick Hall School in Derbyshire have had an annual 'Experience of Work Week' in which students from years 7, 8 and 9 have engaged in work observation and work shadowing on employers' premises, and students in years 10 and 12 have had work experience. The school has placed each student's experiences of work on a database so that a record can be kept as they progress through the school. An example of the computer record of two students is shown in Box 10.5.

Progression in Work-related Activities

The proliferation of work-related activities such as work visits, work shadowing and mini-enterprises (see pp. 24–5) — not only in the 14–19 curriculum, but also in the curriculum of younger students (Smith, 1988) — has led to demands for progression in work-related activities. The spread of work-related activities has largely been a product of the attempt to relate the 14–19 curriculum to the world of work through TVEI. The Education Reform Act 1988 placed a duty on schools to offer a 'relevant' curriculum, and work-related activities provide one way of achieving this. In addition, the efforts of the school–industry movement (Jamieson, 1985) have served to popularize work-related activities as useful devices for delivering a range of cross-curricular issues, and for motivating students of all abilities. This has led — as noted earlier (p. 161) — to the notion of the 'work-related curriculum', which includes all aspects of the school curriculum that are deliberately linked to the world of work. The most easily identifiable aspect of the work-related curriculum is work-related activities, including work experience.

As HMI have observed, one of the most important elements in a successful work-experience programme is 'a policy for all work-related activity in which work experience is part of a progression of linked experiences' (HMI, 1990, p. 19). Although few schools have attempted to set work experience within the context of a progression of work-related experiences, those that have done so have reaped benefits in terms of student learning:

> Those who had previously been involved in a progression of work-related experiences in school — previous 'placement' experience, simulations, industry-related projects and problem-solving, mini-enterprise, or visits to industrial and commercial premises where 'general awareness' had been encouraged — often felt that they had settled in more quickly. They were able to relate learning from these previous experiences to the work placement (HMI, 1990, p. 5).

This evidence suggests that there are two main benefits from progression in work-related activities leading to work experience. First, in terms of personal and social development, students are able to 'settle in' more quickly. Student learning will be enhanced when they have overcome feelings of nervousness at the start of the placement, and can more rapidly take advantage of the learning opportunities offered. Second, the progression facilitates world-of-work-learning integration by enabling students to establish links between their work placement and other aspects of the work-related curriculum.

How can work-experience coordinators involved in curriculum planning sequence work-related activities in order to optimize learning from work experience? In Chapter 2 we discussed various forms of work-related activity, including work shadowing, work visits and work simulations, and drew parallels and contrasts between work experience and these other methods.

Box 10.6   A sequence of work-related activities

Year   Work-related activity

1   Visits or fieldwork as a basis for project and topic work.

3   Enterprises, e.g. small-scale, occasional enterprise activities for younger pupils; longer mini-enterprises for older pupils.

7   Suspended-timetable work-related modules, e.g. one-day work simulations either self-contained or linked to subjects. Activities days or weeks; careers conventions, including simulation games, role-plays and mock interviews.

8   Work-based projects set by clients, e.g. problem-solving activities set by local industry; task-focused projects set by the local community; 'taskweeks' when students in teams tackle specially constructed tasks on employers' premises; community enterprise schemes or enterprise ventures.

9   Work simulations, e.g. business games; production-line simulations; design-and-make simulations; mini-enterprises.
     Voluntary community service, e.g. for half a day per week for one term.

10   Work practice in a simulated environment either on or off the school site.
     In-school work experience, e.g. undertaking the role of receptionist or working in the school office or as a laboratory assistant.
     Work experience on employers' premises.
     Work visits, e.g. one-day visits linked to a specific curriculum area.

12   Work shadowing, e.g. shadowing a manager in a local company.
     (Pre-)vocational work experience, e.g. students undertaking a CPVE course.
     Industrially-based project work, e.g. carrying out specially-designed assignments on employers' premises.

Source: Adapted from DES (1989).

The proliferation of these and other work-related activities in the curriculum of primary and secondary schools has made it possible to construct models of different types of activity. Box 10.6 offers a descriptive sequence of work-related activities, based upon an analysis of current practice and showing the school year in which the activities are usually first encountered. Each activity promotes all or some aspects of world-of-work learning: that is, understanding and/or experience of work tasks, work roles, work processes and work environments or contexts. The optimum solution to the question of sequencing will depend upon the curricular framing of the programme of work-related activities. The literature on curriculum sequencing tends to be 'full of dogma, rhetoric, personal creeds and rule-of-thumb suggestions' (Blyth et al., 1976, pp. 125–6). It is not surprising, therefore, that schools have chosen various ways of sequencing work-related activities based upon the aims of the particular schemes (Jamieson, Miller and Watts, 1988, pp. 214–17).

Some LEAs have undertaken a curriculum mapping exercise to find out at what ages different work-related activities have been introduced into schools. An example of a map of work-related activities in Ealing LEA is shown in Box 10.7. The model also provides some over-reaching aims for each phase of the curriculum 5–19, using the categories of education 'through', 'about' and 'for' the world of work. As work experience occurs towards the end of this sequence, other work-related activities can be viewed as part of the long-term preparation for work experience, in the same way as work experience is seen as the preparation for subsequent experiences of work.

Work-related activities can also be linked to work experience within a particular scheme of work:

> Not infrequently, forms of work simulation are used as a means of preparation for 'real' work experience: a Sheffield school's use of school work tasks for this purpose ... is an example; another is the Bradford work practice unit, which one headmaster saw as 'a very useful intermediary step between school-based work and work experience'.... Again, in a Tameside school, a mini-enterprise project was followed by work shadowing as a way of introducing students to the 'real-life' counterpart of their school-based experience, and this was then followed in turn by work experience (Jamieson, Miller and Watts, 1988, p. 216).

In one Doncaster school, students attended for a one-day work visit followed by a one-day work-shadowing scheme prior to their work-experience placement. This preparation enabled students to 'settle in' immediately and therefore gain more from the placement experience. Work-related activities can be sequenced within a work-experience programme, between work-experience programmes, and throughout the curriculum 5–19, in order to promote progression in student learning.

Conclusion

There are four circumstances which tend to assist the process of building progression into school-based work-experience programmes. The first is when there is a whole-school approach to curriculum planning, including a policy for work experience stating how it fits into the whole curriculum. Such a policy might spell out students' entitlement to a series of work-related activities or experiences culminating in work experience in years 11 and 12. The second is when there is a team approach to work-experience planning and preparation: this can help the process of identifying prior student learning, which is an essential aspect of progression. The third is when student learning is assessed — for example, through a record of achievement, and other assessments using different forms of evidence of learning. The records of learning can then be used by teachers planning subsequent periods of work

Box 10.7 Map of school-industry practice in one LEA

AIMS & RESPONSIBILITIES OF SCHOOL	5–7	7–12	12–14	14–16	16+	WORK
	FIRST, COMBINED, MIDDLE SCHOOLS		HIGH SCHOOLS		SIXTH FORM/ COLLEGE	
PRIMARY						
• Development of interpersonal and basic skills education	• Work observation • Work games/ role plays					
Through 'World of Work'	• School work tasks • Work trails					
• High degree of teacher supervision		• Work shadowing • Industry visits • Industry simulations (i) short, e.g. production line, design & make, problem solving (ii) long, e.g. mini-companies, mini-enterprises				
• Informal assessment						

SECONDARY	Industry days	Community placements; Work experience (generic) 1–2 weeks; Task weeks; Career preparation	Work experience (vocational)
• More complex & alternative forms of organization & interaction education *About 'World of Work'* • Less teacher supervision • Formal assessment	• Industry days	• Community placements • Work experience (generic) 1–2 weeks • Task weeks • Career preparation	• Work experience (vocational)
SIXTH/COLLEGE • Vocational orientation education *For 'World of Work'* • Flexible programmes			

Source: London Borough of Ealing, 1989.

Box 10.8   Progression: some key questions

* Do the aims and learning objectives of the work-experience programme build upon students' prior experiences of work-related activities (e.g. mock interviews, work practice unit, work simulations)?

* What methods can be used to identify prior student learning (e.g. group discussion, one-to-one counselling)?

* How will students be encouraged to identify personal learning goals (e.g. learning contracts, peer-group discussion, student–tutor negotiation, student–employer negotiation)?

* In what ways will the preparation programme be differentiated to make varying demands on students with different levels of knowledge, understanding and skills (e.g. negotiated preparation programme, self-supported study units, learning tasks which allow for differentiation by outcome)?

* What aspects of the work-experience programme will be assessed and what form will the assessment take? What information about students could help in the planning of subsequent periods of work experience?

* In what ways will the curricular aspects of subsequent programmes of work experience be differentiated from the current work-experience programme (e.g. curricular frame, aims, learning objectives, forms of work experience, school-designed tasks, work contexts)?

* In what ways will the organizational aspects of subsequent programmes of work experience be differentiated from the current work-experience programme (e.g. more detailed application forms, different matching strategy, different timing and duration of placement, different purposes of the teacher monitoring visit)?

---

experience. The fourth is when the same teachers are responsible for work-experience organization and curricular integration for different year-groups. This tends to reduce the effect of the '*tabula rasa*' approach which we have noted is common when students move between phases of their education.

In rethinking a work-experience programme, there are a number of questions that need to be addressed if there is an intention to build in progression in student learning. These key questions are summarized in Box 10.8. Curriculum progression is an ideal which is difficult to achieve, because it is concerned with the progress of learning among a diverse range of individuals. Probably the first practical step which schools can take towards progression is to view work experience as an integral part of the whole curriculum. Once this perspective is adopted, it should be easier to see how the content and process of teaching and learning in each phase of the work-experience programme can be modified to reflect what has come before and what will follow in students' educational careers.

Chapter 11

Matching Students to Placements

Andrew Miller

The matching of students to placements is a central process in all work-experience programmes. To many work-experience organizers, the process is unproblematic: it is a task undertaken by the teacher or work-experience coordinator in order to fit 'round pegs into round holes' (Sutton, 1989, p. 48). A snapshot of a typical matching process is illustrated by the following hypothetical example:

> Sonia is about to go on two weeks' work experience during the autumn term of the fifth year. Preparation has been undertaken in PSE lessons with her form tutor, and the main aims of the scheme are to promote broad careers education, in addition to personal and social development. She works on the check-out of a supermarket on Saturdays, but has aspirations to work for a bank after leaving school. On her work-experience application form, she has chosen the following work areas, in rank order: bank; building society; retail. The competition for bank and building-society placements results in the work-experience coordinator selecting students on the basis of their attainment in Mathematics and English; even then, some students have to attend interviews for the employer to make a final choice. Sonia is allocated a placement in a fashion boutique.

The three prime actors in matching, particularly in school-organized work-experience schemes, are the student, the teacher and the employer. Each may have different perceptions of the aims and desired outcomes of a work-experience placement. In the example above, the *student* wished to job sample an area of work in which she was interested as a career; while the *teachers* sought to promote personal and social skills, and a greater understanding of the world of work. On the other hand, the student's first choice of *employer* — the bank — was concerned that the student would have not only an interest in banking as a career but also a minimum level of task and social competence. The effect of applying this criterion was to exclude the student from this particular placement.

This example raises a number of issues about matching. Who should be involved? How important is it to involve someone who knows the student well, such as the form tutor? To what extent should the stated aims of the work-experience scheme influence the matching process? What are the implications of allowing 'job sampling' to become the main criterion for matching students to placements? How should scarce placements be allocated? To what extent should academic ability or competence be used as a criterion for access to certain types of placement? Should stereotyped student choices, and gender segregation in work-experience placements, be tackled; and if so, how? Should particular attention be paid to students with special educational needs? How can the matching process be evaluated?

This chapter examines these and other issues. It begins by discussing the general limitations upon the matching process, and the effects of different organizational models. It then examines possible matching criteria and how they relate to the various possible aims of work experience. This is followed by an analysis of matching strategies and matching techniques, by an extended discussion of equal opportunities in relation to matching, and by an exploration of provision for students with special needs. The final issue examined is evaluation: how can work-experience organizers measure the success of the matching process?

Matching Limitations

In the matching process, students generally choose or are allocated placements from a pool. The nature of the pool may impose limitations upon student choices in a number of ways. First, the local economic base is likely to restrict the range of possible placements, so that students in certain parts of the country may not have access to certain types of placements. Second, the total number of placements will vary. School-organized schemes are likely to have fewer placements than centralized schemes. Third, the development of local Compacts and partnerships that cut across traditional LEA boundaries can reduce the available pool of placements to a particular school, as employers grant exclusive rights to work experience to the schools in the partnership which they have joined. Fourth, the timing of the scheme in the school year can limit the available placements. In particular, the popular end-of-the-summer-term slot often involves excess demand for placements as schools compete for the available supply, and the number of students obtaining first choices is reduced. For all these reasons, many schemes allow students to name placements which are not on the databank, for the work-experience coordinator to try to find. Alternatively, students may be encouraged to find their own placements, if none of those on the databank are suitable.

A further set of limitations on the choices of particular groups of students may be introduced by teachers because of the aims and nature of the scheme. There are a range of examples of matching limitations of this kind. First, in vocational courses, students will generally have to choose a placement from within a particular vocational area. Second, in work experience related to an academic-subjects curricular frame, the placement may have to be related to the subject in question: thus within GCSE Business and Information Studies, students may have to choose an office placement. Third, where they can go on more than one placement, students will usually have to choose a different work area from previous placements. Fourth, students with special needs will generally have to select from a smaller range of placements, often those where employers have expressed a willingness to take such students (cf. pp. 205–7). Finally, in some schemes, popular but scarce placements are allocated to post-16 students before pre-16 students.

Organizational Models and Matching

The organization of a work-experience scheme can have an important influence upon the matching process. There are a variety of ways of organizing school-based work experience (see Chapter 5), but there is a tendency for such schemes to be under-resourced. Thus when a work-experience coordinator has to process — say — whole-year, blocked work experience in years 11 and 12, there is a tendency to use a simple, standardized matching formula. If, however, a team approach to matching is adopted with tutors actively involved, this can considerably enhance the process by adding the crucial ingredients of face-to-face contact, so making possible the identification of individual needs, counselling, and the negotiation of learning contracts.

In principle, these supporting factors can also be used in conjunction with 'self-seek' work experience, but this is less common. School-organized, self-seek schemes, in which students find their own placements, have some drawbacks in terms of matching. They have the potential to reinforce stereotyping, and narrow career horizons. Students with two parents in white-collar occupations will often have an advantage over students whose parents are unemployed. Students without a network among the employed and self-employed work community will be disadvantaged: this may apply in particular to certain ethnic groups (Eggleston, Dunn and Anjali, 1986). These problems should be taken into account by work-experience coordinators when planning the guidance programme to accompany self-seek programmes.

In LEA-organized schemes (see Chapter 6), there are often four main actors involved in matching: the student, the form tutor, the school-based link teacher, and the central coordinator. The Coventry scheme (see pp. 116–18) also involved school-based careers officers and parents in the application process. It should be noted that parents are likely in any case to have an important influence on placement choices, especially where students are given a 'free choice' by the school, or where students are asked to find their own placements in self-seek schemes.

In general, the form tutor is likely to be best placed to understand the needs and interests of the student, but less well placed in terms of understanding the experience offered by particular placements. On the other hand, a central work-experience coordinator is likely to be familiar with the placement experiences, but unlikely to encounter individual students. The school-based work-experience coordinator or link teacher is in a mid-way position between these two poles, probably knowing a certain amount about both the student and the placement, but having detailed knowledge of neither. There are therefore advantages in involving all three roles in the matching process. Hence the development of systems for matching which follow a set of rules, stating who will undertake which tasks in the matching process.

The major external organizers of work experience in the UK, Project Trident, offer a good example of such a system (for an account of the Project Trident LEA-based organization, see pp. 111–4). In Trident schemes, students select three jobs in rank order from a job-description manual, which is supplied to participating schools. The application form has space for students to record the subjects they are studying, and for teachers to make comments. The teachers' comments are intended to inform the Trident Director of any problems which may be relevant: for example, spasmodic attendance, emotional difficulties, learning difficulties, special needs or behaviour problems. These applications are sent to the Trident Director, who checks all first choices against availability. Students can indicate on their forms other choices which are not in the job index. An attempt is made to give all students their first-choice placement.

There are three main points to be made about this and similar matching models. First, when large numbers of applications have to be processed centrally, with a number of different schools sending students on work experience at the same time, there will tend to be a premium upon efficiency. This means that the range of criteria that can be taken into account in matching will be limited, especially when the process is manual rather than computerized. Second, the model does not take into account the different aims of work experience in participating schools. The literature of Project Trident suggests that the aims of their schemes are basically — in our terms (see Chapter 2) — maturational and anticipatory, and schools which have different aims that require different matching principles may find that these cannot be accommodated in the matching process. Third, there is unlikely to be any face-to-face contact between the central coordinator who is carrying out the matching, and the student. This can lead to difficulties: as one local evaluator points out, 'where matching is a paper exercise carried out by someone with no knowledge of the students a close match will be difficult to obtain' (Sandford, 1989).

These difficulties can be overcome, in part, through modifications to the matching process. In the Swindon work-experience scheme, for example, each placement is classified according to the 'aims' which can be met at that placement. Each placement falls into one or more of the following categories: social and life skills; careers; pre-vocational; vocational; and subject-based. These categories have been defined by the central coordinator, and the placements are classified into them by the employers. The computerization of the placement bank enables large numbers to be handled more easily than in manual systems. The school-based link teachers identify the aims of their scheme, together with the occupational areas requested by their students. The database is then interrogated in order to produce a ratio of three placements for every two students. This allows some flexibility for tutors when negotiating the final placement allocation with students.

Work-experience Aims and Matching

The need for work-experience organizers to take into account the aims of the work-experience scheme when implementing the matching process raises the question of which matching criteria are pertinent to each of the possible aims (see pp. 17–21). In order to achieve any particular aim satisfactorily, certain information is likely to be needed on the student and/or the placement. This information is examined in Box 11.1 in the form of key matching questions.

Four main points arise from the identification of these questions and the matching criteria they contain. First, there are a large number of potentially relevant criteria. It seems unlikely that a manual matching process will be able to take into account more than a small number of them. Second, there is not much overlap between the aims in terms of the matching questions associated with them. This means that in schemes with a number of aims, the number of potentially relevant criteria will multiply. Third, some of the criteria are conflicting. Aims need to be prioritized so that clear decisions can be made about the relative weight to be attached to the different criteria in such cases. Without attention to such matters, there is a tendency for a 'careers pull' (Watts, 1986) to be exerted, with the career aspirations of students as registered through their placement preferences becoming the dominant matching criterion. Fourth, although many of the questions require information which is objective and publicly available, there are a number which demand information that is more subjective and private in nature.

Box 11.2 uses this distinction between public/private and objective/subjective information to categorize matching criteria relating to the student. *Public information* is commonly recorded in written form in school reports and records, and on work-experience application forms; it relates largely to the student's life within the school, and is likely to be readily accessible to teachers. *Private information* is often not recorded in written form; it relates, in part, to the student's life outside the school, and includes information which

Box 11.1 *Work-experience aims and some possible matching questions*

	Student	Placement
1. Enhancing	What subjects is the student taking? What are the knowledge and skills acquired in the subject(s) which can be applied in work experience?	Does this placement allow this set of knowledge and skills to be applied?
2. Motivational	What is the student's current level of academic attainment? What kind of placement will most motivate the student?	Does this placement demonstrate the relevance of school to the world of work?
3. Maturational	What is the student's current level of maturity and social competence? What are the personal and social development needs of the student?	What level of social competence is required by the employer and by the demands of the job? Are there structures at the work-place to support the personal and social development of the student?
4. Investigative	What is the student's existing knowledge and understanding of the world of work? What aspects of the world of work does the student need to experience in order to extend this knowledge and understanding?	Does the employer tolerate/ welcome investigative work by students? Are the relevant aspects of the world of work present and accessible?
5. Expansive	What is the student's prior experience of work? What are the student's present career aspirations? What is the occupational background of the student's family? What is the student's gender? What are the attitudes of the student and the parents to a 'non-traditional' placement?	What is the attitude of the employer to students who do not have a prior interest in their area of work? What is the attitude of the employer to 'non-traditional' placements? What structures exist to support students undertaking 'non-traditional' work placements?
6. Sampling	What are the career aspirations of the student?	Does the placement enable the student to gain a fair picture of the career or job in question?
7. Preparatory	What vocational or pre-vocational course is being studied? What vocational knowledge and skills does the student already possess?	Does the placement include tasks related to the vocational area? What induction and training is given to promote vocational competencies?
8. Anticipatory	How well can the student cope with the demands of work?	What special demands are placed upon work-experience students,

		e.g. behaviour, appearance, hours of work?
9. Placing	Does the student have a part-time job already? What are the student's career aspirations?	Does the employer sometimes recruit students following satisfactory work experience? Does the employer offer jobs with training for school-leavers?
10. Custodial	What behavioural, emotional and/or learning difficulties does the student have? What are the possible benefits to the student (and the school) from work experience?	Does the employer understand the problems of the student?

Box 11.2   *Some matching criteria relating to the student*

	Public	Private
O B J E C T I V E	* Age * Gender * Ethnicity * Home address * Medical conditions, e.g. asthma, colour-blindness * Previous school work experience * Attainment in school subjects * Learning difficulties	* Student's out-of-school leisure activities * Previous family-based and part-time work experience * Parental/guardians' occupations
S U B J E C T I V E	* Student's vocational aspirations * Student's placement preferences * Teacher's perceptions of student's developmental needs * Teacher's perceptions of student's task and social competence	* Student's perceptions of own developmental needs * Student's perceptions of own task and social competence

may not be generally known by the teachers. On the other dimension, *objective information* is factual in nature, whereas *subjective information* includes preferences, perceptions and opinions. This classification creates four categories of matching criteria: public/objective; public/subjective; private/objective; and private/subjective.

Public/objective information includes basic factual information about the student, such as age, gender, and subjects studied. From a matching viewpoint, previous school work experience is relevant if repetition is to be avoided. Gender and ethnicity are important where the school has chosen as a matter of policy to undertake gender and ethnic monitoring. School attainment in academic subjects can be pertinent when employers lay down minimum levels of performance: for example, in literacy and numeracy.

Public/subjective information includes the student's preferences for the placement, and a number of criteria based upon the perceptions of teachers about the student. Teachers' perceptions of the student's developmental needs, and of the student's levels of task and social competence, may all be relevant criteria, but they are subjective, difficult to record, and open to challenge. Nonetheless, teachers often use such criteria when appraising students' work-experience application forms. In LEA-organized schemes, there is frequently room on the form for the teacher to make a statement about the student and his/her choices. Such statements are usually based upon public/subjective information.

Private/objective information comprises background facts relating to the student that may be particularly relevant when the aim is to broaden the student's career horizons. Knowledge of the student's previous experiences of work outside school, for example, can help to ensure that school-organized work experience extends rather than repeats such experiences. Awareness of parental occupations may also be relevant in some circumstances, such as in self-seek schemes, where parents provide a main source of placements. Private/objective information can be garnered through the application form, but it may be important to explain the reasons for wanting this information to students and to their parents.

Private/subjective information includes the student's perceptions of himself or herself. Often these perceptions will be unstated, but they sometimes can be found embedded in students' supporting statements on application forms. However, such information as the student's preception of his/her developmental needs is most likely to be obtained through some form of one-to-one counselling.

An adequate assessment of a student's needs is likely to mean considering a broad range of public/private and objective/subjective information. Such a needs assessment would probably have to be carried out by someone with a pastoral responsibility for the student, in close association with the student him/herself.

The other half of the match is the bank or database of work-experience placements. Placement details usually include information about the *workplace*, and about the specific *job* and the tasks it involves. Often this information is collected at the time when the work-experience coordinator negotiates the initial agreement with the employer. Some of these data are then recorded for use by students, teachers and others who are involved in the matching process. Such data tend to be descriptive and relatively stable. This *formal information* can be distinguished from *informal information*, which is more evaluative in nature and subject to change. Matching criteria relating to the placement are analyzed in Box 11.3, using these categories of work-place/job and formal/informal information.

	Formal information	Informal information
W O R K P L A C E	* Sector: private/public/ voluntary * Size: number in work-force * Male/female ratio * Location * Induction: health and safety/ training * Employer rules: dress/hours * Working environment	* Employer attitudes towards girls/boys in non-traditional roles * Perks offered by employer * Status of employer in the local community * Potential for part-time/ full-time employment
J O B	* Occupational classification * Job title * Job description/task description * Requirements: level of competence/skill * Outcomes: skills/competencies acquired/practised * Support: nature of supervision	* Flexibility in nature of place- ment tasks * Degree of autonomy given to students

Box 11.3   Some matching criteria relating to the placement

The basic information about the work-place and the job includes matters which are particularly important in relation to legal issues like health and safety (see Chapter 7). The job titles and descriptions are also important, if students are selecting placements from them: gender-typed names and language can be off-putting for students who might otherwise have considered non-stereotyped choices. In vocational courses, it is important that placement information records the level of skills and competencies required for the placement, as well as the skills and competencies to be developed through the placement.

The informal information can generally only be obtained from a careful investigation of a placement. For example, employer attitudes to girls and boys undertaking non-traditional work roles are more likely to be ascertained from direct discussion with an employer, and from observation of working practices, than from expressed views on a standard form. The degree of flexibility in the nature of tasks allocated may be important, in particular, where there is an academic-subjects curricular frame. The potential for student autonomy and enterprise may be especially important for the achievement of the maturational aim.

Matching Strategies and Techniques

As we have seen, various constraints are placed upon the matching process by limitations on the pool of placements, by the nature of the organizational model, by the aims of the work-experience programme, and by the quantity

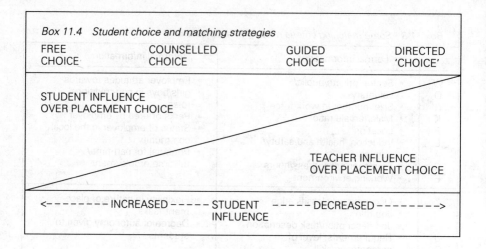

Box 11.4   *Student choice and matching strategies*

| FREE CHOICE | COUNSELLED CHOICE | GUIDED CHOICE | DIRECTED 'CHOICE' |

STUDENT INFLUENCE
OVER PLACEMENT CHOICE

TEACHER INFLUENCE
OVER PLACEMENT CHOICE

<------- INCREASED ----- STUDENT   ----- DECREASED --------->
                         INFLUENCE

and quality of information available about the students and the placements. Within these constraints, schools adopt a range of matching strategies to effect the final distribution of students to placements. Matching strategies define how the decision over placement distribution is taken. The main variable is the degree of influence over this decision that is exerted by the student and the teacher respectively.

Box 11.4 illustrates the spectrum of matching strategies. At one extreme, complete 'free choice' would permit the student to select the placement without influence by the teacher. 'Counselled choice' occurs when the teacher seeks to influence the student's choice in a non–directive way. 'Guided' choice' involves the teacher in advising the student in a more directive way either to choose or reject particular placements. 'Directed "choice"' is operative when the teacher prescribes either the type of placement or the specific placement that a student will be allocated.

Many work-experience coordinators advocate *free choice* as a matching strategy on the grounds that it is likely to increase student motivation and, therefore, increase the chance of a successful placement. When students have freely chosen their placement, the responsibility for the success or failure of the placement can be more clearly laid at the student's door. If, on the other hand, the teacher has allocated the placement to the student, then the teacher could be blamed by student, parent, and employer, if the placement proved unsuccessful. The other common argument for 'free choice' is that employers want a student who is interested in their line of work, and who is motivated by the placement. This seems more likely to happen when the student has chosen the placement. Reluctant students tend to be the work-experience coordinator's nightmare, with the threat they carry of damaging the carefully constructed relationship with an employer. Allowing 'free choice' thus seems a safer option than the alternatives, since it is more likely to find support among students (and their parents) and among employers.

There are, however, two main reasons for questioning the primacy of the 'free choice' matching strategy. The first is the recognition that stereotyping exerts limitations on this 'freedom'. Students' 'free' choices are likely in practice to be constrained by such factors as social class, ethnicity, and gender. True 'freedom' needs to include measures to remove these constraints. This may be done in part through the preparation for work-experience choices, which can endeavour to make students aware of the constraints. Efforts to counteract stereotyping in work-experience choices may also, however, result in greater teacher influence over matching decisions.

Second, 'free choice' may not always be an appropriate matching strategy for schemes which have particular curricular aims and objectives. We examined a number of instances earlier in this chapter (p. 191). In general, if students' learning needs are identified prior to matching, it is likely that counselled or guided choice may be necessary in order to find a suitable placement. For example, a student who wants to investigate the use of information technology in production will by choice be limiting the pool of placements, and will then generally depend upon the specialist knowledge of the work-experience coordinator to guide the choice of the most suitable placement.

In some schemes, students' freedom of choice may be more rhetoric than reality. Pseudo-free choice occurs when students believe that they have an equal chance of obtaining their first choice of placement, but in fact either have a less-than-even chance or no chance at all. Such a situation can result from the work-experience coordinator applying some covert matching criteria, which discriminate against certain categories of student for certain types of placement. These decisions are frequently based upon subjective criteria, such as the teachers' perceptions of the student's task and social competence.

An example of pseudo-free choice occurred in one centrally-organized scheme where the coordinator ensured that students in lower 'bands' would not obtain 'white-collar' placements in banks and building societies. This covert practice was endorsed by the school-based link teacher and justified on the grounds that these employers favoured more literate and numerate students, and that the academically less-able students would be unable to cope. The problem of pseudo-free choice can be avoided if all parties — including the students themselves — are clear about the use of selection criteria for particular placements. Such clarity is evident, for instance, when employers insist on selecting a student from a field at a formal interview. It is less evident when the selecting is done by the teacher on 'subjective' grounds that are not open to scrutiny. It seems reasonable that some employers should insist on minimum levels of task and social competence for their work-experience students, but it is equally reasonable that students be made aware of this further limitation on their freedom of choice.

Counselled choice is a matching strategy which involves the teacher helping students to determine their choice of placement. This occurs most commonly where work experience falls within a careers-education frame, and where the teacher has undergone some training in counselling techniques. Without this training, it is easy for teachers — because of their adult role, greater knowledge and experience — to override student autonomy by becoming directive (Clarke, 1985, pp. 27–8). The role of the teacher/counsellor in this matching strategy would be to highlight all the relevant considerations that the student might wish to consider before making a choice. This is likely to involve exploring some of the subjective as well as the objective matching information included in Box 11.2. The result could be to bring to the surface the underlying needs, as distinct from the immediately expressed wants, of the student as the basis for decision-making. The focus of the teacher's role is upon ensuring that the students go through a particular *process*, rather than attempting to influence the *content* of the students' choices.

A related example is where the teacher permits a group of students to operate a process of peer negotiation. In this model, a group of students such as a tutor-group of twenty-five students might be allocated, say, thirty placements. The students will then discuss, negotiate and agree who will go to which placement. Such a student-centred approach to matching might also involve learning contracts, in which students agree to collect information on common themes to provide the basis for a joint analysis and investigative project during debriefing and follow-up. The role of the teacher here is to act as a facilitator, using student-centred learning techniques (Brandes and Ginnis, 1986).

In the East Sussex LEA scheme, the structure adopted at LEA level lends itself well to the peer-negotiation model. Schools are allocated enough placements for a year-group — say, 210 placements for 180 students. Each tutor-group is allocated a proportion of these placements, so that in a class of twenty-five there will be only five unfilled placements. The form tutor and the students must negotiate the matching strategy, and make the matching decisions.

Guided choice can be intentional or unintentional, and positive or negative. 'Unintentional guided choice' can result from teacher interventions in what are supposedly free-choice or counselled-choice strategies: for example, 'I know just the placement for you!' (positive) or 'I don't think you would like it there!' (negative). Positive interventions encourage, and negative interventions discourage, students from choosing a particular occupational area or placement. Such interventions can easily reinforce existing stereotypes. 'Intentional guided choice' occurs when guidance is a planned part of the programme. 'Guided choice' may be favoured as a matching strategy when there are conflicting aims for work experience, and the organizers have given a particular aim priority. Thus, for example, the maturational and sampling aims are congruent with a 'free choice' matching strategy, but if the expansive aim was given priority in the scheme, this might require recourse to 'guided choice'.

Matching techniques may be used in association with 'guided choice'. Many of these techniques are derived broadly from careers guidance, such as those cited by Law (1986):

> 'Matching' techniques seek key features in the personality of the person, compare them with key features in the opportunities being considered, so that a match can be made.... There are aptitude tests, career-interview schedules, paper-and-pencil interest question-naires, self-assessment schedules, computer programmes and forma-tive profiling techniques designed to bring this person to the point where he or she might be able to say 'that's for me!' (p. 117).

A matching technique of particular interest is the competence-based approach advocated by the Rover Group (Berkeley, 1988). A small-scale project at the company's Coventry car plant involved students from a TVEI pilot school undertaking work-experience placements based around existing YTS jobs. The placements fell into two broad categories — clerical and engineering — and these titles tended to encourage gender-typed choices among students. In an attempt to avoid this, each placement was analyzed and described in terms of competence statements, based upon what students could expect to know, understand and be able to do as a result of the placement. The role of the teacher was to help students to identify their existing competencies, and those which could be developed. Students then selected a placement which matched their particular needs. In this matching technique, the placements were classified according to experiential learning outcomes rather than job categories, as a way of guiding choice.

Another interesting matching technique to guide student choices was used by a TVEI pilot school in the London Borough of Sutton. Work experience in Sutton TVEI is based upon a progression in the aims of the scheme through the four years of the 14–18 curriculum. In order to promote the expansive aim of the first placement at the end of year 10, students completed the JIIG–CAL programme. JIIG–CAL (Closs, 1986) is a computer-aided careers guidance system which is used to generate possible career areas, based upon students' interests, likes and dislikes. It provides each student with a rank-ordered list of twenty possible jobs which might suit them. In the Sutton scheme, the students' choices of placement were confined to those near the bottom of the list. This was on the understanding that in subsequent placements they would be able to choose from jobs towards the top of the list.

In *directed 'choice'*, the placement decision is made by the teacher with little or no participation on the part of the student. The term 'directed "choice"' is a paradoxical one, 'choice' being the antithesis of 'direction'. Such a strategy may be favoured when the primary aims of the scheme are likely to conflict with the 'free choices' made by the students. The most common example is when the scheme aims to broaden students' horizons by tackling the issue of stereotyping. Some TVEI work-experience coordinators have seen teacher allocation of work placements as the way to break the mould of stereotyped selections: 'compulsion is the best, if flawed, guarantee of progress and paradoxically, genuine long-term freedom of choice' (Luxton, 1987, p. 59). Directed 'choice' may also be appropriate in subject-related work experience or in a world-of-work-learning frame where a group of students are to experience a particular work area such as clerical duties or retailing. In this case, placements may be broadly similar to one another, and therefore the need to involve the student in a matching process may be reduced.

Matching and Equal Opportunities

Whenever criteria are applied in matching that involve abilities and attitudes which are unevenly distributed between individuals and groups, this can give rise to inequalities in access to particular types of placement. How, therefore, can teachers and coordinators undertaking matching of students to work placements ensure equal opportunities?

The answer will depend, in part, on the definition of equal opportunities found in LEA and school policy statements, and their interpretation in practice. Such policy documents do not, in general, guarantee equal opportunity in the sense of an equal chance to secure a particular type of placement. Equal opportunity tends to be used in the sense of 'open competition for scarce opportunities' (Lloyd-Thomas, 1977). For practitioners, this means making it clear to students that certain types of placement are scarce, and ensuring that placements are allocated in an open way according to fair and relevant criteria.

Within a school, the work-experience programme may include specific objectives relating to equal opportunities, particularly in relation to the 'expansive' aim (see pp. 19–20). Sometimes these objectives have been derived from guidance emanating from HMI or central-government sources. For example, HMI (1988a) suggests the broad aim of 'the erasure of stereotyping'. TVEI statements on equal opportunities tend to focus on gender: for instance, their criteria state that 'care should be taken to avoid sex-stereotyping' (MSC, 1984). DES guidelines develop this aim to include an explanation of why this is desirable:

> It is the school's job to promote realistic but positive and challenging aspirations, and work-related activities present an important opportunity to pursue this. It is however easy, in the search for placements, to take up ones which reinforce narrow conceptions about what a pupil is fitted for, through gender, ethnic background or other factors such as disability. Stereotyping not only prejudices self-fulfilment, it represents a substantial waste of skills and talent to the economy as a whole (DES, 1988a, p. 6)

Four main approaches to equal opportunities, within and through work experience, can be identified (Fonda, quoted in Chambers, 1987, pp. 5–9):

- *The unlocked door*. In this approach all students are treated as if they had the same background. There is equality of access, in the sense that all students are able to apply for any placement in the 'pool'. Students wishing to undertake work experience in a non-traditional area of work (i.e. an area not traditionally associated with their gender) would have to take the initiative to apply — they must push the 'unlocked door'.

- *The open door*. In this approach the school has checked, reviewed and revised teaching materials, and teaching and learning styles, to appeal to all groups. Students are encouraged and supported in choosing non-traditional work placements, but they must decide to walk through the 'open door'.

- *The special escalator*. In this approach the school aims to compensate students for any deficiencies in knowledge, skills and experiences so that they can begin adult and working life on an equal, or potentially equal, footing. Special programmes might include: non-traditional schemes for some or all students; the entitlement to more than one placement in order to sample a range of traditionally male or female, white-collar or blue-collar, work environments; and single-sex groupings for skill enhancement. All students would have the same entitlement, but some would need the 'special escalator' in order to 'catch up' with others.

- *Equal outcomes*. In this approach the aim is to break down job segregation in the labour market. The long-term end would be to have patterns of employment in particular jobs which reflected the distribution of any particular group in the local labour force as a whole. Work-experience schemes are judged by the extent to which they contribute to this goal.

These approaches differ in terms of their intended impact upon the attitudes of individual students towards their choice of work-experience placement, and ultimately upon their choice of career. It is possible to identify six stages of individual response to particular jobs or work placements. These are shown in Box 11.5. The 'unlocked-door' approach would be of help to those students who have reached stage 5 and want to go on a non-traditional placement: it does nothing, however, to help students who are still at stage 1 to proceed beyond that stage. In the 'open-door' approach, the focus is on helping such students to reach stage 2, where their awareness is raised, and they understand aspects of stereotyping in the labour market and the world of work. The 'special-escalator' approach aims to help them reach stage 3, by equipping them with the necessary knowledge and skills to undertake a range of jobs, including non-traditional ones. Schools adopting

---

Box 11.5   *Students' attitudes to particular jobs or work placements*

Stage 1   'That job is suitable only for a girl/boy/black/white/able-bodied/disabled person'.

Stage 2   'That job could be done by anyone'.

Stage 3   'I could do that job'.

Stage 4   'I would not object to trying that job'.

Stage 5   'I want to try that job'.

Stage 6   'I am interested in that job as a career'.

---

this approach would usually want students to undertake non-traditional work experience: they would therefore usually try to ensure that the students reach at least stage 4, where they are not actively opposed to trying out a non-traditional placement. The goal of the 'equal-outcomes' approach would be to help a substantial proportion of students to reach stage 6, where they change their plans and decide to choose a non-traditional career.

The four approaches also have different implications for the matching strategies adopted by schools. The 'unlocked-door' approach is consistent with a 'free choice' matching strategy, with its inherent dangers of reinforcing the *status quo* of stereotyped choices. The 'open-door' approach is congruent with 'counselled choice', which would work with students whose needs and interests are such as to suggest that a non-traditional placement might be appropriate, and would offer them help and support in making their decision. The 'special escalator' approach suggests 'guided choice' or 'directed "choice"' strategies, in order to guarantee the entitlement to a particular set of knowledge, skills and experiences.

Although many schools have promoted non-traditional work experience, the success of these schemes has often been limited (Millman and Weiner, 1987). Some of the guidance issued to schools recognizes the problems associated with such schemes. For example, the National Union of Teachers (1989) draws attention to the risks of an unsatisfactory period of work experience, which could permanently discourage a student from pursuing a particular career. The NUT also quotes Cockburn's (1986) warning about non-traditional work experience: 'All the evidence shows that young people are acutely perceptive of the potential rewards but also the serious difficulties and discomforts that ensue from entering work or training in occupations that are gender contrary'.

The difficulties likely to be encountered by work-experience coordinators embarking on non-traditional programmes were illustrated in a project involving five schools (Agnew, 1985). The evaluation of the project showed how the attitudes and behaviour of students, teachers, parents and employers all contributed to maintaining the *status quo* of stereotyped choices. Students who opted for non-traditional placements were the objects of ridicule from their peers, and several succumbed and changed their work-experience choices. Parents, in several cases, played an important role in determining students' choices of work placement. For example, one boy who wanted a hairdressing placement was discouraged by his parents, who wanted a more traditionally-male placement. Teachers were reluctant to interfere with the convention of 'free choice' as a matching strategy, and some teachers allowed their own sex-stereotyped attitudes to influence students in their choices. Sometimes this took the form of a 'joke' or teasing directed at particular students; at other times, it took the form of well-intentioned words of advice. Some employers specified the sex of students required for particular placements, and work-experience coordinators seemed reluctant to challenge these requirements, as they feared the withdrawal of the placements.

This example highlights the powerful range of forces which serve to maintain the *status quo*, and to subvert attempts to counter stereotyping in matching. Work-experience coordinators who want to tackle this issue need to be aware of all the factors which impinge upon matching decisions before deciding what action to take. One method for doing this is the use of 'force-field' analysis. This particular tool for the management of change suggests that in any situation there are a number of forces promoting change (facilitators), and a countervailing set of forces resisting change (inhibitors). The change can be managed, according to the analysis, by reducing the inhibitors, by enhancing the facilitators, or by a combination of both processes. The force-field analysis for non-traditional work experience in Box 11.6 suggests that schemes which focus solely on changing the attitudes of the students are unlikely to make much impact upon stereotyping.

Matching of Students with Special Needs

Another aspect of equal opportunities in work experience concerns students with special educational needs. These include students with a broad range of different learning difficulties, who can be found both in special schools and in ordinary secondary schools. In LEA-organized schemes, there appear to be two main approaches to catering for such students. Some central work-experience organizers have a pool of 'sheltered' placements which are allocated to students with special needs. In contrast, some LEAs have a policy of equality of access, which aims to give all students the same range of choices from the placement pool, and then to provide extra support for those that need it. In school-based organization, it is usual for special schools in particular to build close relationships with a restricted set of sympathetic employers who are used regularly as a source of work placements.

Particular care is generally taken when matching students with special needs to placements. Staff involved in matching tend to know the students concerned very well and therefore are able to relate the capabilities and level of readiness of individual students to the challenges of particular placements.

Box 11.6   Non-traditional work experience: a force-field analysis

Facilitators	Inhibitors
Environment	
Government guidelines and criteria — — — —>	
LEA equal-opportunities policy — — — —>	
Demographic trends leading to labour/skill shortages — — — —>	Youth unemployment leading to 'safe' traditional choices <— — — —
Employer policies — — — —>	Lack of policies in many <— — — — businesses
Adult role models — — — —>	Absence of adult role <— — — — models
Parental attitudes — — — —>	<— — — — Parental attitudes
School	
	Lack of implementation strategy for school
School equal-opportunities policy — — — —>	equal-opportunities <— — — — policy
Teacher attitudes — — — —>	<— — — — Teacher attitudes
'Expansive' aim of work-experience scheme given priority — — — —>	'Sampling' aim of work experience has <— — — — priority
'Counselled', 'guided', or 'directed choice' matching strategies — — — —>	'Free choice' <— — — — matching strategy
Peer-group attitudes — — — —>	Peer-group <— — — — attitudes
	Student attitudes towards <— — — — work experience
Student role models, i.e. students who have undertaken non-traditional placements — — — —>	
Opportunity for more than one placement — — — —>	Opportunity for only <— — — — one placement

The small pool of placements allows in–depth knowledge of the range of jobs on offer and strong links with the work-place supervisors.

As an example, Broughton Park School in Salford is a school for students with moderate learning difficulties. It has close links with about twenty employers. Students are matched by the work-experience coordinator according to their capabilities and readiness for particular experiences, with an emphasis on enhancing social skills. The work-experience programme is designed to provide progressive challenges for students during years 10 and 11. Typically, students' confidence is increased through one-day work visits which lead to three-day placements in the summer of year 10. This creates the foundation for two, two-week blocks of work experience in the autumn and spring terms of year 11. Whereas in the earlier placements choices are 'guided' or 'directed', in the final placement students have a 'free choice' from the pool. Students are accompanied on their initial visit to the workplace, and their progress is closely monitored through regular contact with the supervisor.

Burleigh Community College, by contrast, is a 14–19 secondary school in Leicestershire. In the initial planning stage of the work-experience programme, form tutors are asked to identify students with special educational needs. These include students with basic learning difficulties, with language or communications problems, and with behavioural, attitude or attendance problems. Interviews are arranged with specialist staff to match students to placements, and additional or alternative briefing is given. In addition, staff help these students to contact employers, and if necessary take them to the pre-placement interview. During the placement, students with special needs are visited and supported by specialist staff.

These two case-studies illustrate the importance of full information about individuals and particular placements in matching students with special needs. They also demonstrate the need for additional support from the school for such students, although the progressive reduction of staff support during placements can help students to become more independent (HMI, 1990, p. 6).

Evaluating the Quality of Matching

Work-experience organizers vary in their perceptions of the matching process. Most organizers, however, can give examples of 'good matches' and 'mismatches'. How do they make judgments about the relative success of matching?

Most schemes evaluate matching in terms of outcomes. One obvious indicator of 'good' matches is the proportion of students expressing satisfaction with their placements. The proportion of students demanding to be rematched, or leaving their placements before the end of the work experience, is a behavioural indication of 'mismatches'. However, these measures are likely to be flawed, because a number of factors will influence students' feelings about their placements. For example, interpersonal relationships at the placement are often influential upon student perceptions of the match.

A distinction can be drawn between a 'good match' in theory, based on a sound fit between criteria relating to the student and criteria relating to the placement, and a 'good match' in practice, based upon student, teacher and employer perceptions at the end of a placement. In theory, a 'good match' occurs when the student's interests are congruent with the teacher's curricular aims, and the student's task and social competence meet the levels required by the employer. The central work-experience coordinator in Coventry (see pp. 116–8) argued to us that most of the LEA's placements were 'good matches'

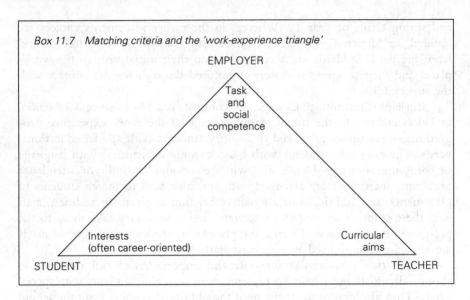

Box 11.7 *Matching criteria and the 'work-experience triangle'*

EMPLOYER

Task
and
social
competence

Interests
(often career-oriented)

Curricular
aims

STUDENT

TEACHER

in these terms, but that during the course of the placements it became clear in about 5 per cent of cases that, in practice, the match was not a 'good' one. According to the coordinator, the main reason for this discrepancy was that certain relevant information about the students was not evident on the work-experience application form. Students had a tendency to 'oversell' themselves on the form, and this was not always picked up by the careers officer and the form tutor, whose comments could serve to reinforce the students' perceptions of their own abilities.

Project Trident schemes tend to take a different view of matching, and of its evaluation. As we noted earlier (p. 192), the 'free choice' matching strategy favoured by Trident is congruent with its expressed aims for work experience. Thus a 'good match' occurs when an individual student is allocated a first-choice placement. Consequently, the matching task can be evaluated in terms of the percentage of students obtaining first, second, third, and other choices from year to year. Expanding the number and range of available placements, and spreading the demand from participating schools over the school year, help more students to obtain their first choice. The annual publication of these statistics accordingly provides one measure for judging the success of matching in Trident schemes.

A number of factors will tend to make it easier for work-experience coordinators to increase the proportion of 'good matches'. The first is when there is an increased number and range of placements, offering more scope for the matching process. The second is when the matching process generates accurate information about the student and the placement. The third is when all parties accept and understand the aims of the work-experience programme and appreciate that the matching strategy is congruent with these aims. The fourth is when the person undertaking the matching — whether the teacher/coordinator and/or the student — knows the student and understands the learning potential of each placement. The fifth is when there is a facility for 'rematching', if a mismatch seems likely to occur. The absence of these factors will increase the likelihood of 'poor matches', or matches which leave one or more of the parties dissatisfied.

Conclusion

We began this chapter by arguing that for many work-experience coordinators, matching is a straightforward if time-consuming business, which attempts to give as many students as possible their first choice of work placement. We have noted, however, that there potentially are some tensions between the concerns of key parties in any work-experience programme: the students, the employers, and the teachers. These are demonstrated in Box 11.7 in an adapted form of our 'work-experience triangle' (cf. Box 2.3 on p. 23). The process of rethinking work experience at the level of the school means that a number of key questions need to be addressed:

- What are the most important aims of the work-experience programme?
- What matching criteria concerning the student and the placement are relevant to achieving these aims?
- How can the relevant information about students and placements be assembled?
- What is the school's approach to equal opportunities, and what implications does this have for matching?
- Who should be involved in the matching process, and what role should each party play?
- What matching strategies are consistent with the aims of the scheme, and the school's 'approach' to equal opportunities?
- When introducing a revised matching process, what are the factors which will tend to inhibit or promote change, and how can these be managed?

Chapter 12

Teaching Strategies

Andrew Miller

This chapter is concerned with the ways in which schools help students to learn from their work experience. Teaching strategies are used during each of the five phases of a work-experience programme: preparation, briefing, placement, debriefing, and follow-up. *Preparation* refers to teaching and learning activities which occur prior to students being allocated a particular placement, and which aim to prepare all students in a general way for the experience. *Briefing* occurs after students have been allocated their particular placements, and is focused primarily on operational issues. The *placement* phase is when the students are on employers' premises. As noted in Chapter 7 (p. 124), one of the significant features of work experience is that this central phase occurs out of sight of the teacher in the work-place; however, teachers may endeavour to guide student learning at the work-place through structured tasks, often in the form of workbooks and diaries, and through visits by teachers. The school *debriefing* occurs immediately after the placement and aims to encourage reflection and analysis in order to identify what has been learned. *Follow-up* refers to subsequent learning experiences which draw upon and/or extend learning from work experience. The chapter provides an overview of issues and current practice related to each of these phases.

Aims and Objectives

Curriculum-related work-experience programmes have a general goal of promoting student learning. In Chapter 2 we introduced ten possible aims for work experience, seven of which were linked to a curricular frame. Such learning aims provide a broad guide for teachers planning work-experience programmes. But in order to make decisions about, for example, what kinds of preparation and follow-up are required, it is important to be more precise than this. One approach to this problem is for teachers to seek to specify learning objectives or desired outcomes in some detail, and then to base their teaching strategies on these objectives. An alternative approach starts from the premise that the outcomes from a diverse, experience-based programme are impossible to specify in advance, particularly where the school has very little control over the learning experiences at the placement; it accordingly suggests that the focus of preparation should be upon 'learning to learn' strategies which include helping students to identify their own learning objectives. Perhaps the optimum approach to maximizing learning from work experience is to acknowledge that there are likely to be both intended and unintended learning outcomes from experience-based programmes. Teaching strategies, according to this view, could both support school-defined learning objectives, and help students to define personal objectives and to learn from experience.

Although most schools have identified general aims for work experience, few in the past have produced lists of related learning objectives. Such objectives specify what students should know, understand, and be able to do as a result of a planned learning experience. One implication of linking work experience more closely to the curriculum is the need to be more specific about the knowledge, understanding and skills that will be developed as a result of the programme. Without a clear set of objectives, it is difficult to assess student learning and evaluate schemes (HMI, 1990, p. 9) (though cf. the concept of goal-free evaluation — see p. 275). Whereas aims are usually described as intentions for the work-experience programme as a whole, it may be easier to define objectives for each phase of the programme.

The identification of learning objectives may also need to differentiate between students. This makes it possible to acknowledge the fact that many students have different prior experiences of work and different levels of prior knowledge, understanding and skills; and also that each placement provides unique learning opportunities. For effective differentiation to take place, it is important that there should be opportunities for negotiation of individual learning objectives between three main parties: teachers, students, and employers. The development of records of achievement, personal and career action plans, and learning agreements/contracts, can encourage students to identify additional learning goals which can be achieved through the experience. Form tutors and record-of-achievement tutors can negotiate these personal learning objectives with the students as a part of the process of personal development, through one-to-one counselling. Personal learning objectives can also be identified through discussion with peers. Learning objectives linked to a particular placement can develop from negotiation between the teacher and the employer and/or between the student and the employer. In some cases, in particular with special-needs students, the teacher, the employer and the student may meet to identify specific learning objectives in a pre-placement visit: this is in many respects ideal, since it can enable all three parties to confirm their common understanding of the agreed objectives, though it may not always be feasible in practice. Whatever model is used, the determination of basic learning objectives by the school and of additional personal learning objectives by students can itself form an important part of the preparation programme.

Preparation

What other forms of preparation should students have before undertaking a period of work experience? Schools respond in different ways to this question when planning their work-experience programmes. There are three main reasons why preparation programmes vary considerably. First, as already noted, work experience can be located in a number of different curricular frames, with different associated aims (see Chapter 2), each of which has different implications for preparation (see Boxes 12.1–12.5 below). Second, the range of teaching strategies which are employed in preparation will depend, in part, on the subject backgrounds and favoured teaching styles of the teachers involved. Third, the length of the preparation period is a prime determinant of its content, and this is related to the length of the work-experience programme as a whole: it may be compressed into one short block of time, during which all five phases must be completed, or it may be spread out over a year or more.

When planning a preparation programme, it is important to identify the knowledge, understanding and skills that students must have in order to gain access to, cope with, and benefit from, their work experience. Teaching strategies which seek to develop these form a core part of the preparation programme. For example, unless the student is properly prepared in the sense of having the personal and social skills to cope with working with adults for an extended period in a strange environment, it is unlikely that additional learning goals will be achieved. It can be argued, therefore, that there is always a role for personal and social education in the preparation phase, whatever the aims of the programme; though it will clearly be given greater prominence and attention if a PSE frame is being adopted for the programme as a whole.

Once students have gone beyond the threshold represented by such core elements, the nature of the preparation programme will be determined by the nature of the curricular frame(s) that have been chosen. As we have noted (p. 163), the most common curricular frame for pre-16 work experience has tended to be *careers education*: some typical learning objectives and teaching strategies associated with this frame appear in Box 12.1. The second most popular frame is provided by *personal and social education*: Box 12.2 illustrates some typical learning objectives and teaching strategies linked to this frame.

An interesting feature of the learning objectives identified in Boxes 12.1 and Box 12.2 is the extent to which they are concerned with the development of skills and capabilities. This emphasis upon helping students to *do* things is reflected in the kinds of teaching strategies which are suggested. For example, role-plays and mock interviews are aimed at providing students

---

Box 12.1   *Some typical learning objectives and teaching strategies associated with the careers-education frame for work-experience preparation*

CAREERS EDUCATION	
Learning Objectives	*Teaching Strategies*
Students should:	
• develop their vocational interests, e.g. identify their working preferences	— job-interest inventories; JIIG–CAL/CASCAID
• develop job-search skills, e.g. be able to write a *curriculum vitae*/letter of application	— completing pro-formas; simulated Jobcentres; 'self-seek' placements
• develop interviewee skills, e.g. know how to prepare for and create a good impression in an interview	— mock interviews with employers; video feedback
• understand the reasons for job segregation and sex-stereotyping, e.g. know the benefits and problems of choosing a non-traditional career	— studying employment statistics; providing access to positive role models

---

Box 12.2   *Some typical learning objectives and teaching strategies associated with the personal and social education frame for work-experience preparation*

PERSONAL AND SOCIAL EDUCATION	
Learning Objectives	*Teaching Strategies*
Students should:	
• develop self-awareness, e.g. understand their own strengths and weaknesses	— self-assessment checklists; one-to-one counselling
• develop interpersonal skills, e.g. deal confidently with a range of situations involving adults	— assertiveness role-plays; role-play of social encounters
• develop personal goals, e.g. identify competencies that could be developed through work experience	— individual reflection on needs; peer/tutor counselling
• develop teamwork skills, e.g. be able to listen to others and contribute own ideas when solving problems	— group problem-solving/team-building exercises

---

Box 12.3   *Some typical learning objectives and teaching strategies associated with the world-of-work-learning frame for work-experience preparation*

WORLD-OF-WORK LEARNING	
Learning Objectives	*Teaching Strategies*
Students should:	
• understand the meaning of 'work', e.g.	
— know the reasons why people work	— interviewing family members and people during work visits
— know the main differences between school and work	— brainstorm; drawing on students' experiences of part-time/holiday work
— understand the range of meanings of the term 'work'	— undertaking 'home' work; investigating voluntary work/informal economy
• understand business/industrial organization, e.g.	
— know that organizations are made up of parts which contribute to the whole	— constructing organization charts; business simulations/case-studies
— know the main roles of people at work	— interviewing visiting managers/supervisors
• understand that business/industrial organizations are economic units, e.g.	
— be able to identify their main resources	— identifying resources from photographs
— understand the need for efficiency	— production-line simulations
• understand industrial relations, e.g.	
— know the rights and responsibilities of people at work	— case-studies of situations at work; equal-opportunities role-plays
— understand the role of trade unions	— trade-union visitors; trade-union role-plays

---

with vicarious experiences which mirror situations they may later face in the work-place. These and other activities are designed to provide a basis for individual and group reflection.

The *world-of-work learning* frame for work experience is concerned with increasing students' understanding of the world of work. Some typical learning objectives and teaching strategies associated with this frame are shown in Box 12.3. Three main points arise from this list. First, drawing contrasts and similarities between the school and the work-place is a standard feature of most pre-16 preparation programmes. This teaching strategy has traditionally been associated with aiding the transition from school to work (i.e. with the anticipatory aim within the careers-education frame), but now tends also to be used to promote economic awareness. Second, there is a distinction between education for economic understanding, and education for industrial understanding. The former is generally designed to enable students to recognize the usefulness of economic concepts within the work-place — or, as one trade unionist put it, 'to make the invisible, visible'; the latter includes other non-economic issues, such as human relations at work, and health-and-safety considerations. Third, schools need to clarify the meaning which is attached to the word 'work' in learning materials, and by teachers in preparation lessons (cf. pp. 36–7). Most work-experience programmes provide students with experience of jobs in the paid-employment sector of the world of work. In order to define work more widely, one school included within its work-experience preparation programme a module on work in the home, which involved students in undertaking a six-hour task which they would not normally have considered doing: for example, boys might prepare meals for a number of evenings; girls might tackle a painting and decorating task.

The *vocational-course frame* tends to use the preparation phase to practise skills which will be applied during the work placement. As we have noted (p. 20), the vocational frame is unusual in school-based work-experience. Nonetheless, pre-vocational rhetoric is often used to argue that work experience helps prepare students in a broad way for the world of work by helping students acquire core skills, and beyond this it is clear that a few programmes are 'unambiguously vocational in intention' (Barnes, Johnson and Jordan, 1989, p. 11). Some typical learning objectives and teaching strategies associated with this frame are shown in Box 12.4.

The *academic-subjects* frame is largely concerned with enhancing students' subject-based knowledge, understanding and skills through involvement in the work-experience programme. Some learning objectives and teaching strategies used in academic-subject preparation are shown in Box 12.5. Academic-subject teachers who want to draw upon work experience as a resource often seek to provide students with concepts which they hope will act as 'cognitive spectacles' through which the placement experience can be perceived and interpreted. When subject departments are involved in preparation, the most usual purpose is to clarify theoretical principles for which practical examples might be found in the work-place. Typically the preparation aims to equip students to collect relevant data during the placement for later use in follow-up lessons. English tends to be a particularly common vehicle for work-experience preparation, because essential tasks which students must undertake involve written and oral communication: for example, writing letters to employers, using the telephone, and attending 'mock' and 'real' interviews.

Briefing

Briefing is the second part of the work-experience programme. It occurs after students have been allocated to their placements. School briefing deals

---

Box 12.4 Some typical learning objectives and teaching strategies associated with the vocational-course frame for work-experience preparation

VOCATIONAL COURSE	
Learning Objectives	
Students should:	*Teaching Strategies*
Motor engineering	
• understand the principles of a car exhaust system	— textbooks; formal inputs
• be able to dismantle, repair and replace standard exhaust systems	— practice in dismantling, repairing, replacing exhaust systems in the school workshop/garage
Graphic design	
• understand the basic principles of calligraphy	— textbooks; formal inputs; critical review of examples
• be able to select suitable typefaces for advertising copy	— practice in a range of design briefs; critical study of examples
Management skills	
• understand the role of manager	— interviewing visiting manager(s); writing a *curriculum vitae*/job description for a manager
• be able to problem-solve in conditions of ambiguity	— business games and simulations

---

with the organizational aspects of work experience: for example, the best way to travel, how long it will take, and who to report to on the first morning. While some of this can be covered on a group basis, it is most effective when these points are clarified in one-to-one discussion with the teacher who will subsequently make the monitoring visit (HMI, 1990, p. 10). Some typical learning objectives and teaching strategies used in briefing are shown in Box 12.6. The primary concern of the briefing stage is often with operational tasks necessary for the effective execution of the programme: the learning objectives indicate, however, that wider learning yields can be sought and achieved.

During the briefing period, some schools place considerable emphasis upon influencing students' attitudes and behaviour whilst on work experience. Students are often perceived by the school as fulfilling an ambassadorial role on its behalf, representing it to local employers. The students' behaviour whilst on work experience is seen as influencing the opinion of an important section of the local community about education in general, and about the school in particular. Strategies to encourage 'good behaviour' might include lectures from senior staff, and the introduction of disciplinary codes of practice. One school developed a system of 'yellow cards' for disciplinary warnings, followed by 'red cards' for dismissal from work experience. These

---

Box 12.5   Some typical learning objectives and teaching strategies associated with the academic-subjects frame for work-experience preparation

ACADEMIC SUBJECTS	
Learning Objectives	*Teaching Strategies*
Science	
Students should:	
• understand the sources of power and control technology used by machinery in local industry, e.g. in installed machinery, transport devices	— group work on identification of possible sources of power and technology for using power at work
	— work visit to identify sources of power and control technology
• understand the properties of materials, e.g. composition, characteristics, sources, costs	— exercises in investigating the composition, choice and use of materials in the school environment
	— compiling checklist for use in investigating the use of materials in industry
English	
• understand the range of communications used in business, e.g. memoranda, business letters, notices, meeting agendas	— business simulations; communications' exercises; work sampling; sample documents
• develop communication skills	— simulated telephone calls to employers using an internal telephone system
Technology	
• understand some of the applications of information technology in the world of work	— videos; software packages; reviewing company in-house journals
• understand the criteria that can be used when appraising a working environment	— appraisal of the school as a working environment; appraisal during work visits

cards were to be signed by the employer, the student, the tutor and the parents, the aim being to deter 'problem' behaviour. Another school invited the local police in to lecture students on the perils of being caught stealing while in the work-place. A further technique is to invite students into school wearing their 'working clothes' on the final briefing day before the work placement, so as to identify those students who are inappropriately dressed. Such methods reflect the widespread use of 'employability criteria' such as appearance and demeanour in employers' assessment forms (see Chapter 13).

Another feature of briefing in some schemes is the use made of pre-placement visits to the work-place by students. Many work-experience coordinators regard such visits as an important aspect of briefing and

---

Box 12.6 *Some typical learning objectives and teaching strategies for work-experience briefing*

Learning Objectives Students should:	Teaching Strategies
• develop self-awareness, e.g.	
— be aware of their own and others' expectations	— identifying their 'hopes' and 'fears'
	— talking to visiting employers
	— clarifying the main tasks which the school expects them to carry out, e.g. diary, recording
• develop communication skills, e.g.	
— be able to communicate with employers, by telephone/in writing	— writing letter to employer
	— contacting work-place by telephone
• develop personal decision-making skills, e.g.	
— plan the route to work	— using maps/timetable to plan journey to work
— manage time	— using a 'time-planner' to plan use of time during the work-placement period
• develop personal action plan, e.g.	
— be able to explain own needs/goals to an employer	— negotiating placement tasks/learning opportunities in a pre-placement interview

---

induction, for several reasons. First, they give students a *trial run* at planning their journey, finding the work-place, and identifying their contact person. Second, they permit *negotiation*: they allow the employer in a short interview to talk to the student in order to explain what is possible and what is not, and for the student to describe her/his background and particular learning goals for the placement. This aspect of the pre-placement visit is particularly important when students are being asked to carry out assignments during their work placement (HMI, 1990, p. 10). A mutual exploration of this kind can in principle enable the employer to tailor the placement tasks to suit the expressed needs and interests of the student, while at the same time checking that the student has sufficient confidence in her/his social and task competencies to carry out the range of planned tasks. Allowing some time between the pre-placement visit and the start of the placement permits the standard placement programme to be modified where this is appropriate. Third, the visit enables some *pre-induction* to take place: if accompanied by a tour of the work-place, it allows the students to begin forming an overview of the work organization, and of how the work they will be doing fits into the overall framework.

The Placement

There are two main strategies which are used by schools to structure and focus student learning during the placement. The first involves setting school-devised tasks for the students to undertake: this commonly takes the form of workbooks, diaries and/or projects. The second involves a visit or visits by a teacher to the student. In general, however, as noted on p. 124, work-experience programmes mean franchising employers to deliver part of the school curriculum. In this sense we can in principle adopt the notion of the 'curriculum-related work-place', which entails viewing the world of work as a learning resource for students. Some employers are concerned to activate this notion and to review work-experience placements in the light of the learning goals they can promote. Where this is the case, both teachers and employers can be viewed as being involved in 'teaching strategies' during the placement phase. There are four variables which influence the degree of student learning from work experience, so constituting the 'learning-from-work-experience system': the individual learner; formal learning structures; opportunities; and the ethos or learning culture of the work-place (Boydell, 1976).

The first and most important is the *individual learner*. Different students will vary in their capacity to learn from the same placement. Apart from obvious individual differences, such as age and intelligence, important variables here include students' prior experiences of work, and their existing 'map' of the world of work. It seems likely that the degree of confidence shown by students has an influence over the opportunities which employers offer them (Fiehn and Miller, 1989). Thus more confident students may be allowed more autonomy, and may be given access to a wider range of tasks, than less confident students. The extent of a student's task and social competence as perceived by the employer or the supervisor can, therefore, narrow or broaden opportunities for learning. Students will also differ in their ability to learn from reflection upon their own experience. This is one reason for schools to try to improve students' reflective abilities through 'learning to learn' activities during preparation, and through devices such as a daily diary in which students can record their experiences. The diary — which can be divided into separate sections on actions, thoughts and feelings — encourages reflective observation on a regular basis. Sometimes such diaries include key questions to aid the process of reflection and recording.

The diary may form one element of the second part of the 'learning-from-work-experience system': that is, the *formal learning structures* established by the school and the employer to aid learning. The most common strategy used by schools is the workbook which contains tasks to be undertaken during the placement. Work-experience workbooks have been critically reviewed elsewhere (Jamieson, Newman and Peffers, 1986). They generally ask students to collect information about the work placement based on observations and on interviews with work colleagues. The main problem with such tasks is that they take the student out of the role of worker:

> They will have to depart from the normal working pattern to complete these tasks, and so set themselves apart from other employees. Because of their additional tasks they may seem to their fellow workers to be preoccupied and not fully immersed in the job. In the workplace, other people's moment-by-moment perceptions of individual students are important in influencing the amount of information and personal attention they provide, the work opportunities they offer, and the degree to which they admit their temporary colleague into the working group (*ibid*, p. 2).

These difficulties can be overcome if students are permitted some space within their programme, but away from their work station, to undertake such investigative work. Alternatively, some tasks can be written up in the evening, although such a strategy is unlikely to prove popular with tired students. A further possible strategy is for students to carry out such investigative tasks during a later follow-up visit: this has the benefit of clearly separating the student role from the worker role in temporal terms.

A development which has coincided with the introduction of the GCSE examination with its emphasis upon course-work assignments has been the trend towards setting projects for students to undertake while on work experience (see pp. 28–9). As with workbooks, it is important that schools review the unintended consequences of such projects upon the placement experience as a whole:

> Projects set by subject teachers of students in Years 10 and 11 designed to be completed during the work experience and later assessed were generally disliked by the students because they felt there were pressures enough associated with a set of new experiences without taking on additional burdens (HMI, 1990, p. 9).

Work-based projects seem to fit better with programmes which do not involve taking on the role of a worker and performing work tasks. For example, in post-16 placements where there is a work-shadowing element, and time to write up observations, projects can more easily be built into the placement programme.

Other aspects of the formal learning structures at the work placement may be provided by the employer. Many employers have an induction programme (see p. 145). Many also have a final debriefing session with the student: this provides an opportunity for formative assessment and feedback to the student, as well as for joint evaluation of the placement experience. Some employers are building in a more formal and systematic programme of learning sessions into the placement period. Thus, for example, the Rover Group have established 'partnership centres' which students attend for induction, for mid-placement debriefing and for end-of-placement debriefing.

The third variable which influences the extent of learning from work experience is the *opportunities* offered by the placement. There is no doubt that work-places and specific placements vary enormously in the learning opportunities which they provide. These opportunities can be identified by the student, by the work-experience coordinator, or by the employer prior to the placement. Some employers in longer placements try to build in opportunities for greater autonomy, and a more flexible range of tasks, towards the end of the experience. The opportunities offered by the placement are also likely to vary with the forms of the work experience (see pp. 26–30). For example, it is probable that 'rotating around different departments' will provide more opportunities for meeting a wider range of adults, and for observing a wider variety of work tasks, than, say, providing an 'extra pair of hands' in one department.

The fourth variable in the learning-from-work-experience system is the extent to which the work organization endorses a *'learning culture'*. Some employers have an ethos of promoting staff development through training, and work experience may be viewed as part of the training programme. A number of factors contribute to work experience being perceived in this way as an opportunity to promote student learning, including: endorsement by senior management of closer links with education; high priority being attached to training; and responsibility for work experience being located with the personnel, training, or human resources development department. The effect may be to drive the programme to some extent towards a 'preparatory' aim (see p. 20), regardless of the view held by the school.

The Teacher Visit

Although a teacher visit to each student on work experience is widely recognized as highly desirable, the majority of schools have found such a commitment difficult to fulfil (HMI, 1990, p. 18). A few years ago it was common for such visiting to be undertaken by the school-based work-experience organizer (often the careers teacher) working alone. Some schools still cling to this model on the grounds that such a task cannot be efficiently delegated (*ibid*, p. 18). In recent years, however, LEAs in their work-experience guidelines have stressed not only the essential nature of the teacher visit, but also the desirability of involving more staff in it. What then are the main purposes of a teacher visit?

The first purpose is to *monitor the student*. In many schemes, indeed, the term 'monitoring visit' is used. The concern here is to check on the student's behaviour and welfare. Frequently this involves asking the student and the employer if there are any problems regarding the student's experience and progress, and then trying to sort them out if this is feasible. Monitoring may also include ensuring that students are acting as positive 'ambassadors' for the school. Thus guidelines issued to visiting teachers in one LEA state: 'Please remind pupils that *a good attitude and appropriate dress is very important*'.

Second, teachers are commonly asked to *monitor the placement*. In such cases, a pro-forma and key questions are sometimes provided to act as prompts for teachers when talking to the student and the employer (an example is shown in Box 12.7). For example, students and employers might be asked about the health-and-safety induction provided. Another important area is the extent to which the placement programme matches or diverges from the job description. Ensuring that the same opportunities are available to girls and boys may be a further focus of the monitoring process. The main purpose of this aspect of monitoring is to improve the placement experience of the student. In order to be effective in achieving this aim, such monitoring visits have to occur at an early stage of the placement.

Third, teachers can be asked to *evaluate the placement and the work-place* for use by future students. Such evaluation may require judgments to be made on the basis of observations and of discussions with the employer, the supervisor and the student. The information collected, together with the teacher's comments on the suitability of the placement, can provide useful information for work-experience coordinators who are trying to improve the quality of placements for the future. The placement assessment in Box 12.7 incorporates a means through which work placements can be evaluated according to performance indicators which are felt to be important by the LEA concerned. Teachers are asked to rate the placement according to six criteria. Placements which have a score of six meet all the criteria; those with a lower score may require an intervention by the work-experience coordinator before being used again.

Fourth, the teacher visit can be part of the process designed to *assess student learning* (see Chapter 13). The precise role of the visiting teacher here will depend upon the nature of the assessment used by the school. In many cases, teachers are asked simply to explain to the employer the student assessment form, and to request that the employer provides some feedback to the student at the end of the placement. If, however, work-experience assessment is closely linked to the record of achievement, the visiting tutor might help the student to begin to formulate formative, positive statements about what has been achieved during the placement: this can then be built upon during debriefing. Another more specific example is visits by English teachers to tape-record students talking with the employer for GCSE oral assessment.

Fifth, teachers can *investigate resources* during the visit. This can be particularly fruitful if subject teachers visit work placements which have a

---

Box 12.7   A teacher visit report form

Student name   School/college

Employer

Contact   Telephone

Period from   to

PLEASE TELEPHONE THE EMPLOYER CONTACT BEFORE YOUR VISIT.
TRY TO VISIT THE STUDENT IN HIS/HER WORK-PLACE.

Some suggested questions to ask students

Are you enjoying the placement?   Do you have plenty to do?
What have you been doing?   Who have you worked with?
What equipment have you used?   Have you asked for advice?
What Health and Safety instructions have   What have you learned about working
  you been given?   conditions?
What does this section do?   What have you found out about the
How is your day planned?   company's organization?

PLACEMENT ASSESSMENT   Yes (1)   No (0)

1. The employer/employees were aware of the aims of
   Vocational Experience

2. The student was inducted to the placement (which
   included health and safety training)

3. There was a planned programme providing a variety
   of experience

4. The student was adequately supervised

5. The student was meaningfully occupied most of the time

6. Similar opportunities were offered to boys and girls
                                                  _ _ _ _ _ _ _ _ _
                                    TOTAL =
                                                  _ _ _ _ _ _ _ _ _

     Comment (if any) on health and safety

PLACEMENT SUITABILITY

GENERAL COMMENTS

Signed (tutor) _____ Date _____
               Please return to Vocational Experience Unit

Source: East Sussex LEA.

---

close association with their subject area. For example, Home Economics teachers might visit hotels and restaurants, Business Studies teachers might visit banks and offices, and Art and Design teachers might visit design studios. This can offer opportunities for building links with particular employers which may lead to other joint activities, such as students visiting the work-place or adults-other-than-teachers visiting the school. It can also help subject teachers to be in a better position to design assignments linked to the specific work placement, or to similar categories of placement.

Finally, there are three main 'hidden' purposes of the teacher visit. The first is to show the students that the school is interested in them and their work experience, and is concerned to make sure that their experience is of high quality. Secondly, the teacher visit can demonstrate to the employer the commitment of the school to work experience, and its desire to form closer relationships with employers. Thirdly, visits by a broad range of staff can lead to their personal and professional development, as they take on an ambassadorial role for the school, and meet people from different areas of the world of work.

Some of the students we interviewed in the course of our fieldwork complained about the perfunctory nature of the visit and/or about their impression that the visit was mainly concerned with monitoring good behaviour. Such feelings were reinforced when the bulk of the visit comprised a private chat with the employer. Clearly, there are practical difficulties in organizing a large number of visits; nevertheless, some of these problems can be overcome by making the purpose of the visits clear both to the staff involved and to the students.

How should visiting teachers be allocated to work-experience students? Schools which attempt to involve many staff in the visits often place a list of students, placements and contacts on the noticeboard and request teachers to sign up for the visits. The main problem with this and similar arbitrary methods is that many students are then visited by teachers who they do not know. A number of the students we interviewed complained about visits by teachers who they barely recognized and who they felt had little interest in them. Some schools seek to surmount this difficulty by ensuring that all visiting teachers at least make contact with their students during the briefing period.

There is, however, a strong case for considering the appropriateness of particular teachers in relation to the key purposes of the visits and/or the curricular frame adopted for the programme as a whole. For example, a random allocation of teachers to students may be appropriate if the main purpose of the visit is to monitor the student's behaviour, and to explain the employer assessment form to the employer. If, however, the key purpose is to monitor and evaluate the placement, in particular in relation to health-and-safety and equal-opportunities considerations, it is important that the visiting staff should have been adequately trained to carry out this task. Within a personal and social education frame, if the visit is linked to completing the record of achievement, a visit by the form tutor or pastoral staff is likely to be the most appropriate. If the purpose is resource-investigation within an academic-subjects frame, it is subject teachers who are best placed to identify the potential for curricular links with the work-places being visited.

It is also important to consider the process of the visit, and the effect this might have on students and on employers. The shortest teacher visit reported to us involved a student working in the local careers office: the teacher put his head around the door and called to the student across the room

> *Box 12.8   A possible process for the teacher visit*
>
> Stage 1   Teacher discusses progress with the employer and identifies any problems.
>
> Stage 2   Employer fetches student from the work station.
>
> Stage 3   Teacher discusses progress with the student in private and identifies any problems.
>
> Stage 4   Student shows teacher to work station to meet work colleagues, if the student so wishes.
>
> Stage 5   Teacher, employer and student meet to sort out problems, if necessary.
>
> *Source:* SCIP, (1988).

'OK?', the student nodded, and the teacher left! Some students experience problems on work experience which they may want to discuss with the teacher out of earshot of the employer. The most difficult of these involve racial and sexual harassment. An employer in a small company who has given a great deal of thought to the best process for the teacher visit has recommended the pattern outlined in Box 12.8. He argues that such a process enables any problems to come to light, and allows the student to remain in the role of young worker with work colleagues, rather than being thrust back into the role of student as can result from an insensitive teacher visiting the work station itself.

Debriefing

Debriefing is a vital stage in the integration of work experience into the school curriculum. Students return to school with a wealth of anecdotes, ideas, impressions, feelings, thoughts, knowledge, skills and insights. They have forged new relationships, and taken on adult roles in a working environment. The school has stressed the importance of work experience, and many hours have been spent in preparation sessions, and in the careful completion of diaries and workbooks. What lies in store for them as they walk through the school gates on the first day back at school? In the past, sadly, debriefing for many of them has taken place informally in the playground in discussions with friends, but not in the classroom where it has often been 'business as usual' as subject teachers have urged them to press on with their course-work in order to make up for the time lost to the work-experience programme. Fortunately, the lack of curricular integration which led to this all-too-familiar scenario is gradually being eroded.

There are four main purposes which can be tackled during the debriefing period. First, there is a need to help students make sense of their experience through *reflection*. Second, after the students have described, discussed and shared what happened, there is a need to draw out the main learning points through *analysis* and forming *generalizations*. Third, debriefing affords an opportunity for the *assessment* of student learning, and for the *evaluation* of the placement and the work-experience programme. Finally, the debriefing offers a chance to round off some *administrative* aspects of the placement phase, through the completion of school-assigned tasks and writing the thank-you letter to the employer. Box 12.9 summarizes some typical purposes and associated teaching strategies used by schools for debriefing work experience. Much of the published material on debriefing of other experiential learning activities, such as work simulations, is of relevance to teachers planning work-experience debriefing (Boud, Keogh and Walker, 1985; Jamieson, Miller and Watts, 1988; Jones, 1988; Miller, 1988; van Ments, 1983).

The first part of the debriefing stage is *reflection*. Work experience is above all a learning experience for students who acquire knowledge, skills and understanding of a particular work-place. The notion of experiential integration (pp. 151–2) involves reconstructing different aspects of the experience, in order to add meaning by examining the links between them. In terms of the experiential learning cycle (pp. 22–3), this is the stage of reflective observation when students attempt to describe their experience. Such a description can focus upon what they did (actions), what they perceived (observations), what they thought (cognitions), and what they felt (feelings). The reflection process often takes two forms: individual reflection, and reflection in small groups.

Reflection upon work experience enables students to identify what they have experienced. The idea of the work-experience triangle (p. 23) provides a useful framework for identifying the focus of this learning, which could be the student and/or the world of work and/or academic subjects. For each focus, a number of questions are pertinent. With the *student* as the learning focus, questions might include: 'What skills have I practised?' 'What did I do to improve upon my weaknesses?' 'How did I overcome my feelings of nervousness?' 'What feedback did I receive from my supervisor on my social skills, reliability, and employability?'. With the *world of work* as the learning focus, the questions could include: 'What was the role of the supervisor?' 'What things motivated people at the work-place?' 'What level of skills and training were required to carry out the different jobs?'. With *academic subjects* as the learning focus, questions might include: 'What mathematical operations did I undertake?' 'What kinds of technical and specialist language were used?' 'What design opportunities existed?'. All these questions ask students to describe *what* they experienced during the placement.

Reflection often involves the sharing of experience with peers and with the teacher. The work-experience Johari window in Box 12.10 illustrates this process. At the start of the debriefing period, most of the knowledge of the experience rests with the student, although the teacher may have some information which the student does not possess — such as the employer assessment and perceptions gathered during the visit. At the close of the reflection period, much of the knowledge has been shared, although both teacher and student may retain some knowledge which they have not

Box 12.9   *Some typical purposes and teaching strategies for work-experience debriefing*

Purposes	Teaching Strategies
Students should:	
Reflection	
• reflect upon individual experience	— talk through experiences (feelings, thoughts, actions) with another student — engage in one-to-one counselling
• share experience	— discuss in small groups — discuss key questions in employment-sector groups
• derole from their role as young workers	— allow students to wear 'working' clothes on debriefing day — use students' work 'titles'
• record and disseminate reflection and analysis	— flip-chart key ideas — write accounts of experiences to be assembled in a newsletter — present experiences orally/on video to other students/employer visitors
• compare expectations to outcomes	— review 'hopes' and 'fears' in the light of the experience
Analysis	
• identify curriculum-related learning	— involve subject teachers in debriefing — share information gathered at the placement and recorded in the workbook
• analyze individual and group experiences	— identify and explain key incidents — address problems and issues
• generalize about the experience	— identify key learning points focusing on learning about the student and/or the work-place and/or academic subjects
• review personal learning goals	— discuss the extent to which goals were achieved with peers
Assessment and evaluation	
• assess learning outcomes	— consider employer assessments — complete record of achievement, moving from a formative to a summative statement
• evaluate individual placements and the work-experience scheme as a whole	— complete evaluation questionnaires — discuss placement quality and suggest improvements
General	
• complete school-set tasks	— assemble assignments — finish diaries/logs — write thank-you letter to employers

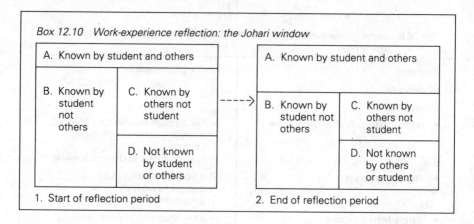

Box 12.10   Work-experience reflection: the Johari window

revealed to the other. Sharing experience with peers can also shed additional light on each student's individual experience. The greater the expanse of window representing shared knowledge, the greater is its potential use as a resource for learning by the individual and by the group.

Asking students to share their feelings in the whole group is sometimes less productive than small-group techniques. One relatively non-threatening method for enabling students to recall their feelings during the placement period is to ask them to sketch a line graph showing 'highs' and 'lows'. In small groups, students can share their graphs and discuss the factors that led to the high and low points. Such feelings might include success, praise, boredom, stress, anger, passivity, embarrassment and lack of confidence. Some students may have had particular experiences such as being bullied, sexually harassed or patronized. Teacher debriefers have to decide whether such feelings and issues are best handled in one-to-one counselling, or by discussion in the classroom. Helping students to overcome any negative feelings is an important part of the initial stage of debriefing.

Another set of feelings which can be powerful for many students is associated with re-entry into the school. Work experience can be viewed as part of the *rite de passage* from adolescence to adulthood: an important stage in the transition from school to working life. The role of adult worker involves some of the disciplines of work, such as good time-keeping, but it also means being given responsibility, wearing your own clothes, calling adults by their first names, and being talked to as an adult. It is hardly surprising, therefore, that re-donning the school uniform, being expected again to call adults 'sir' and 'miss', and being harangued in the lunch queue, can be a profound 'culture shock' (see Grubb Institute, 1986). The debriefing phase could encourage students to air their feelings about returning to school, and could identify strategies to handle the attendant problems that some may experience.

The second stage of debriefing, *analysis*, involves placing the particular knowledge, understanding, skills and experience acquired by each student in a wider context. In terms of the experiential learning cycle, this is the stage of abstract conceptualization, which involves drawing upon experience and reflection in order to make generalizations or learning points. The focus of the debriefing will depend upon the curricular frame that is being adopted. A PSE frame might involve a reassessment of strengths and weaknesses, modifications to personal development plans, enhanced self-awareness, and development of a broader range of strategies for coping with interpersonal situations. A careers-education frame might involve analyzing the knowledge, skills and training involved in performing various jobs observed during the placement, and reviewing career plans. A world-of-work-learning frame might involve a clearer understanding of the differences between school and work, greater knowledge of health-and-safety procedures, and improved economic and industrial understanding. A vocational-course frame might involve identifying skill areas which require further development. An academic-subjects frame might involve an awareness of the practical applications of, for example, Mathematics and Technology, and an enriched conceptual vocabulary.

The third aspect of debriefing involves *assessment* of student learning outcomes, and *evaluation*. Assessment is discussed in Chapter 13; evalution is discussed in Chapter 14.

The fourth and final aspect of the debriefing period is the *administrative* category. This includes completing logbooks and assembling assignments, as well as writing thank-you letters to employers.

How long should the debriefing stage last? The answer to this question depends upon the purposes which are being addressed. Debriefing sessions can last from a single period to a number of days: the most popular choice is half a day or a full day. Many schools have tended to commit limited lengths of time to debriefing: 'They found it difficult to organize the time, to determine the purpose and content, and to acquire the skills required for reflecting, reviewing and recording with students' (HMI, 1990, p. 11). Often staff not involved in the work-experience programme are resistant to the idea of yet more teaching time being allocated for debriefing and follow-up. But a strong case can be made for adjusting the balance between the placement and the debriefing phases to allow more time for the latter. For example, if a ten-day placement plus half-a-day debriefing became a nine day placement plus a one-and-a-half-day debriefing, it is probable that the gains in student learning from the extra debriefing day would more than offset the losses from the shortened placement.

Clearly, it is easier to convince colleagues of the importance of debriefing if the purposes and content are well-defined and linked to the curriculum. There is a wide range of purposes that can be met during the debriefing period, and many teaching strategies that can be employed in meeting these aims. Box 12.9 summarizes some of the teaching strategies which schools use during debriefing, and links these to related purposes. Schools could select from the purposes and teaching strategies appropriate to their work-experience programme in order to construct debriefing programmes, such as those described by HMI in their report:

> The most successful schemes for debriefing were those where there was a mixture of approaches including students working in twos and small groups in order to 'swap experiences' with their peers; course or form tutors and PSE teachers sharing with 'interest' groups and with individuals to talk through their various experiences; and 'subject' groups working with specialist staff to develop the links to the curriculum through the medium of written, graphical, numerical and oral work. Where there had been opportunities for students to 'talk through' first-hand observations, very real apprehensions, particularly concerning gender, ethical and management issues, were raised. Students appreciated the chance to raise these issues and the sessions seen resulted in heightened awareness for all involved (HMI, 1990, pp. 11–12).

This statement, it should be noted, implicitly suggests that the adoption of multiple curricular frames is preferable to the adoption of a single frame.

An example of a work-experience debriefing programme from East Sussex LEA is shown in Box 12.11. The debriefing took place over one-and-a-half days and involved eight tutor-groups. It illustrates how a longer debriefing period can be managed through variations in student groupings, teaching and learning processes, teacher facilitators and visiting employers. This example included a period of reflection at the start of day one, followed by analysis, in work-place category groups. The debriefing incorporated placement evaluation by students, as well as general 'rounding off' activities, such as the thank-you letter to employers. The final session on the preparation of an English course-work assignment signalled the end of the debriefing phase, and the beginning of follow-up.

Follow-up

The follow-up phase refers to curricular activities which occur after debriefing and draw upon individual and group learning. In this sense, the period of reflection and analysis during debriefing can provide a resource, a stimulus, and a springboard for further work. In terms of the experiential learning cycle, the follow-up phase of work experience can be equated with active experimentation. This final stage in the cycle involves students in applying knowledge, understanding and skills developed during the first four phases of the work-experience programme. Box 12.12 illustrates some of the learning objectives and teaching strategies associated with follow-up in each of the five curricular frames. Further examples of follow-up strategies can be found in the case-studies in Chapter 9.

Box 12.11   A work-experience debriefing programme

Aims:

— for students to share their experiences with other students, teachers and members of the business/industrial community;

— for the negotiated report on the student's work experience to become part of their record of achievement;

— for students to record their learning and utilize the information gathered in relevant course-work or other suitable programmes of study.

Programme

Day 1

Session 1: Feedback on work experience (1 hr. 10 mins.)

Groupings: Students in tutor groups with adult-other-than-teacher.
Process: Students in friendship groups of three share their immediate reactions/impressions/comments/observations. Students complete sentences on flipcharts placed around the walls (e.g. 'The person who was most helpful was . . .'; 'the thing that surprised me most was . . .'). Students read each others' comments, followed by whole-group discussion.

Session 2: Placement evaluation (1 hr. 10 mins.)

Part 1

Groupings: Students work individually, then form groups of four.
Process: Students complete placement review in their work-experience diaries. Students share evaluation in small groups, followed by report back to the whole group.

Part 2

Groupings: Students are placed in two circles of 15 with the tutor and an adult-other-than-teacher.
Process: Students consider their responses to a series of key questions (What aspects of my placement have things in common with other placements? Did I handle problems in the same way as others? Have I changed my views?). Experiences are shared, focusing on the key questions, with the tutor as facilitator.

Sessions 3 and 4: Areas of work on placement (2 hrs. 10 mins.)

Groupings: Students work in groups determined by work-place categories (Business and Administration; Civil Engineering; Distribution; Literacy/Creative; Agriculture/Horticulture; Transport, Mechanics, Plant; Services to People; Technical Services; Production).
Process: Students focus on learning outcomes related to different work-place categories. Adults-other-than-teachers join in group's discussion.

Day 2

Session 5: Diary completion/thank-you letters (1 hr. 5 mins.)

Groupings: Students work individually in tutor groups.
Process: Students complete diary and then draft a thank-you letter to their employer.

Session 6: Theme workshops (1 hr. 5 mins.)

Groupings: Students sign up for one workshop on a theme of particular interest.
Process: Students discuss and highlight learning on four key areas of world-of-work learning: Information Technology in the Work-Place; Health and Safety at Work; People at Work; Company Organisation.

Session 7: English assignment

Groupings: Students attend English classes.
Process: Students use information collected during the placement and the debriefing period to prepare an English course-work assignment.

Source: East Sussex LEA.

Andrew Miller

Box 12.12 Some typical learning objectives and teaching strategies during work-experience follow-up

Learning Objectives	Teaching Strategies
PERSONAL AND SOCIAL EDUCATION Students should: • develop personal and social skills • develop teamwork skills	— personal development review and action plans — working in a team to inform younger students about work experience
CAREERS EDUCATION Students should: • be aware of their own developing vocational interests • further develop interview techniques	— career development review and action plans — mock interviews with employers
WORLD-OF-WORK LEARNING Students should: • understand conflict at work • understand the nature of job segregation at work	— assignment on resolution of conflict at work placement(s) — assignment on job-segregation based on data from work placements
VOCATIONAL COURSE Students should: • further develop vocational skills	— work simulations and work practice units
ACADEMIC SUBJECTS — ENGLISH Students should: • explore literature • develop discursive writing skills	— analyzing accounts of work in novels — essays on themes related to work experience, e.g. school and work, women and work
ACADEMIC SUBJECTS — MODERN LANGUAGES Students should: • develop vocabulary • develop oral ability	— researching technical/work-related vocabulary — assessed group discussion in a foreign language based upon their work experience
ACADEMIC SUBJECTS — TECHNOLOGY Students should: • develop capability in design and realization • develop skills in appraising environments	— producing solutions to design problems identified during work experience — using photographs taken at work placement for developing critical understanding of work environments

Conclusion

The notion of teaching strategies suggests a planned approach to a programme of learning. One dimension of this involves the teacher-managers in deciding upon the curricular frame(s), the learning aims, the learning objectives, and then selecting teaching strategies accordingly. The other dimension is represented by the theory of experiential learning. This model emphasizes the importance for learning of what occurs after the experience: that is, the period of reflection, analysis, and application. When these two dimensions are brought together, a coherent programme of learning should emerge, based on clear aims and objectives, and involving the five phases of preparation, briefing, experience, debriefing, and follow-up. In our fieldwork, however, this rational and systematic approach appeared to be relatively uncommon in school-based work-experience schemes.

Many work-experience programmes resemble old hotels that have undergone periodic refurbishment of an unsympathetic kind. The resulting stylistic hotch-potch makes it difficult to distinguish the original architect's conception. Initially most work-experience programmes had an unequivocal careers-education frame, but this has been added to substantially over the years: additional aims; additional preparation sessions; additional pages in the workbook. The *ad hoc*, incremental manner in which most school work-experience schemes have developed makes it difficult to trace a clear relationship between aims on the one hand, and on the other the content and process of teaching and learning in the five phases. Perhaps the missing link hitherto has been learning objectives which can offer a guide to the selection of appropriate teaching strategies. As we have noted (p. 9), however, the pressures of the National Curriculum have led to growing demands to justify all aspects of the curriculum in terms of what students can be expected to know, understand and do as a result of planned learning experiences.

When schools begin to review the teaching strategies used in the work-experience programme, it is probable that three main points will emerge about their current arrangements. First, there tends to be an emphasis on front-loading the teaching programme. In other words, more time and effort is expended upon preparing and briefing students for work experience than upon debriefing and follow-up, though the gradual spread of a greater understanding of experiential learning principles in schools has led to some redressing of this balance.

Second, the kinds of active learning methods which are a major part of the teaching strategies in experiential-learning programmes — for example, role-play, simulation, drama — require a particular set of teaching skills. Not least are the skills involved in the teacher visit and the debriefing phase. In relation to the latter, the ability to initiate individual and group reflection through posing catalytic questions, to change class groupings in order to maintain motivation and interest, to involve adults-other-than-teachers in discussions, and to draw out key learning points from a diverse range of experiences, are all important skills that need to be developed. There is accordingly a need to provide INSET for teachers involved in work-experience programmes, particularly on the rationale for experiential learning, on active learning methods, on discussion skills, and on debriefing skills.

Third, as whole-year-group work experience spreads, more teachers from diverse backgrounds will tend to be drawn into the programme. Many teachers lack up-to-date knowledge and experience of the world of work outside the school, and this makes it more difficult for them to relate to, and to draw upon, work experience in their lessons. The teacher visit provides one means for updating staff on developments in the world of work, and for creating greater empathy with their work-experience students. This experience, combined with greater numbers of staff entering industry on short-term secondments, should help to convince teachers that work experience provides a rich resource for learning.

Chapter 13

Assessment

Ian Jamieson

It is one of the characteristic features of schooling that the work of students is assessed. In its most traditional form, we recognize this in the publication of the results of public examinations and standardized tests for individual students. In everyday language, how well children are performing at school is largely judged on the basis of such assessments.

If assessment is such a ubiquitous feature of schooling, we need to ask what functions it performs: in other words, why it is thought to be so important. Assessment has four main functions. In the first place, it provides feedback for students on their own learning, either diagnostically and/or against certain criteria (criterion-referenced assessment) or compared to the work of their peers (norm-referenced assessment). Secondly, it can be used as an indicator of how effective the learning environment is. This environment can embrace the teaching, the ethos of the school, and the physical environment. Thirdly, the process of assessment identifies those features of the curriculum which are deemed to be important (and assessable). Finally, the results of assessment are often used by a variety of 'end users' — in particular, further and higher education and employers — and used in the process of selecting students for educational courses and for jobs.

The wide variety of these functions suggests that what is to count as an assessment is likely to vary according to its purpose. For example, it is unlikely that an assessment, the prime purpose of which is to provide feedback to students on the effectiveness of their own learning, will look quite the same as an assessment the main purpose of which is to help end-users to make selection judgments. A number of different dimensions along which assessment can vary are shown in Box 13.1.

Our traditional conception of assessment, the public examination system, is clearly founded largely on the dimensions in the left-hand column of Box 13.1 (public, formal, recorded, summative and universalistic). The only difficulty is with the last dimension. The old English school-leaving examination at 16+, the General Certificate of Education (GCE), was a hybrid

---

Box 13.1   The dimensions of educational assessment

Public assessment: the results are placed in the public domain and can be used by people other than the individual who is the subject of the assessment. In this way, assessments are translated into credentials.

Private assessment: the assessment remains with the individual unless he or she wishes to release it into the public domain.

Formal assessment: usually carried out by a body which has some standing as an accrediting body — e.g. an examination board or a professional body. This almost always results in some form of certification: a document which can be used by the student as evidence of achievement.

Informal assessment: an assessment process which is *ad hoc* and carried out by individuals who have no formal position as assessors.

Recorded assessment: always results in some form of written record, which is invariably retained by the assessor though copies may be given to the student.

Unrecorded assessment: usually made verbally, leaving no recorded trace.

Summative assessment: made at the end of some learning programme.

Formative assessment: usually made at intervals during the life of a programme.

Universalistic assessment: judgments made about skills, knowledge or understanding which are context-free, i.e. are not constrained by space or time (e.g. assessments of mathematical or scientific knowledge and skills).

Particularistic assessment: constrained by the particular context in which it is made.

Criterion-referenced assessment: where the student's performance is assessed against a clear set of criteria.

Norm-referenced assessment: where students are assessed in relation to their peers.

---

of criterion- and norm-referenced assessments, whilst its replacement — GCSE — is slowly moving towards a criterion-referenced system. Although we have depicted these dimensions as dichotomies, in practice many assessments that take place in schools are hybrids.

Work-experience Assessment

It is not easy to provide a clear picture of the assessment profile of work experience in relation to the dimensions in Box 13.1 because of the way in which the curricular frame of the experience varies (see Chapter 2). In Box 13.2 we attempt to explore the relationship between these frames and the different dimensions of assessment. In this box we have added a new category of *direct* and *indirect* assessment. In direct assessment, work experience is itself being assessed; whilst in indirect assessment, the main object of the assessment is not the work experience but what that experience might have

---

Box 13.2 *Likely characteristics of assessment of work experience within different curricular frames*

Curricular frame	Likely assessment characteristics
A. Academic subjects	Public, formal, recorded, summative, universalistic, criterion-referenced, indirect.
B. Personal and social education	Private, informal, unrecorded, formative, particularistic, criterion-referenced, direct.
C. World-of-work learning	(Depends on how this frame is handled in the school).
D. Careers education	Private, informal, unrecorded, summative, universalistic (though 'sampling' aim is particularistic), criterion-referenced, direct.
E. Vocational courses	Public, formal, recorded, summative, universalistic, criterion-referenced, direct.

---

contributed to some other objective — for example, a general understanding of the world of work.

Some interesting patterns emerge from this tabulation. Where the framework is provided by an academic subject, the assessment model tends to follow the traditional public-examination pattern outlined earlier. The same is true with the vocational-courses frame, except that here work experience tends to be assessed directly rather than indirectly. Vocational courses are almost exclusively the province of post-compulsory schooling, so effectively work experience in compulsory schooling tends not to be directly assessed for use within the public domain.

Most work experience in the fourth and fifth years is undertaken within the curricular frameworks of careers education, personal and social education, or world-of-work learning, and although there are variations in assessment practices in these areas, in general — where assessment is carried out at all — it is marked by an emphasis on the private, informal, unrecorded, formative and particularistic dimensions. Work experience in these curricular areas is often assessed directly, however, and the influence of the industrial world is felt by some shift from norm-referencing to criterion-referencing. The criteria used here tend to be derived both from the nature of the work-experience tasks (can the student accomplish certain work-place tasks?) and from the individuals themselves (has the student improved her or his social and interpersonal skills?). The main exception to this general pattern is that in careers education, assessment tends to be made summatively because of the emphasis that is placed on particular decisions that are crucial in career development; and tends to adopt universalistic criteria concerned with abilities to cope with jobs and occupations.

How world-of-work learning is assessed depends on the direction in which it 'leans' in the work-experience triangle (see p. 23). Standing at the apex of the triangle, it can align itself with the AC axis of academic and vocational subjects and be assessed in a somewhat traditional mode, or it can be more closely associated with the BC axis of the triangle and follow the assessment modes that are common in careers and in personal and social education.

Issues

The first question that we need to address is *why* we should assess work experience at all. This is an important question because work experience has often been one of the few school activities that have not been systematically assessed. Yet work experience consumes a significant amount of time. We have already argued that one of the functions of assessment in schools is symbolically to underline what is regarded as important. If work experience is not assessed at all, this will tend to undermine its importance in the eyes of parents, teachers and students. Moreover, all of the aims of work experience discussed in Chapter 2, with the exception of the placing and custodial aims, assume that students will learn something from the experience (about themselves, about future careers, about the world of work, about the application of academic subjects, etc.). If this is the case, then some form of assessment is vital to check the efficiency and effectiveness of that learning. In addition, the various 'end users' — further and higher education institutions and employers — might demand or at least appreciate some evidence about student performance on work experience.

A major problem with the assessment of work experience is that it is almost certainly impossible to meet all these purposes with a single assessment: different purposes require different forms of assessment. This problem is exacerbated by some of the technical difficulties involved in assessing many work-experience objectives. Broadfoot (1982) sums up the dilemma this poses when she argues that examinations 'lead to an over-emphasis in the curriculum on that which is relatively easily measured — knowledge and intellectual ability — at the expense of that kind of educational progress which is almost impossible to measure such as attitudes, skills and personal qualities' (p. 34). This is an important issue for work experience, which tends to concentrate heavily on the development of the 'attitudes, skills and personal qualities' referred to by Broadfoot.

Writers like Raven (1980) seem to agree with Broadfoot that the problem is largely one of technique. Raven puts forward the view that 'had we had available to us objective measures of qualities like resourcefulness, initiative, leadership qualities, and ability to learn from experience, there is little doubt that these would have been included in the selection process' (p. 105). Not all of the qualities described by Raven are likely to be demonstrated on work experience, but it does provide a location where at least some of these qualities might be displayed. The major issue here is deciding what is to count as a reliable and valid assessment which serves the purpose of the particular work-experience placement. Unfortunately, the discussion of assessment in schools is unduly influenced by the practices of traditional examining, which act as a kind of gold standard. Assessment which does not measure up to this standard is thought to be literally 'sub-standard', even though it might be perfectly appropriate for the purpose it serves. Since work-experience assessment rarely measures up to the gold standard of traditional assessment, this for some confirms the dubious place of work experience on the school timetable.

Once it has been agreed that work experience should be assessed, a school is then faced with the issue of *what* should be assessed. Assessment of student performance in any situation always depends on a criterion or set of criteria, even when the assessment is norm-referenced against the comparative performance of the student group as a whole. Work-experience schemes are rich in aims and therefore in potential assessment criteria. This is particularly the case for work experience within compulsory schooling, where it is not uncommon to find schools which have encouraged a number of different curriculum areas to draw on work experience to enhance their courses. Unless this is very carefully handled, work experience can soon be effectively converted into a multi-disciplinary work-based project (see Chapter 9). We also believe that when students are given a multiplicity of objectives which are to be assessed at a later time, they tend to 'surface process' (Marton and Säljö, 1976) or skim the experience looking for 'evidence' which will allow them to fulfil the assessment criteria, at the possible expense of a deeper understanding of the work-place and their own persona.

This is linked to a major dilemma in assessing work experience in compulsory schooling, which is that where the assessment is formal, relating to the enhancing or investigative aims, it often distorts the experience and the learning. This is because it is difficult for formal and universalistic assessment criteria to cope with the unpredictable nature of work experience, which is where much of its power lies: the tendency is therefore to try to control or deny this unpredictability. On the other hand, where the work experience relates to the maturational, expansive, sampling, or anticipatory aims, and the assessment techniques are consequently more informal, these techniques may not be taken seriously by some of the parties to the assessment.

Assessment aims which are related to one subject seem the easiest for students to manage. In subject-related assessment, however, there is always a tension between the set of criteria emanating from the internal logic of the subject, and those drawn from elsewhere — either from the students and their interpretation of the experience that they have undergone, or from the work-place itself. This is why those subjects which have relatively weak classification and framing (Bernstein, 1975) often provide the curriculum framework for work experience. English is a particularly good example of this, and of all of the traditional curriculum subjects it is English which most commonly provides the curriculum framework (see p. 251).

It is significant that, in general, post-16 pre-vocational and vocational courses seem to present the fewest problems in the assessment of work experience. This is because work experience has an important, unambiguous and fully integrated role in these courses. In the case of CPVE, it might even be argued that work experience provides the framework around which the whole course revolves. With work experience in such a pivotal position, it can easily feed the assessment criteria for the whole course. Industrialists also find it easier to play some role in the assessment process here, because the assessment goals are related in one way or another to the concerns which they have as potential employers.

Another key problem in the assessment of work experience is *who* will make the assessment. Traditionally, the question of who should assess the quality of students' work has not been an issue in British schools. Until the 1960s, it was taken for granted that university-based examining boards should examine the work of students in public examinations. During the 1960s, this position began to be eroded by the development of CSE Mode 3 examinations which were set and marked at the level of the school by teachers and only moderated by examining boards. The tension between 'local' assessment by teachers and 'national' assessment by bodies like the examining boards has been a fundamental one in the recent history of assessment. Teacher assessment, it was argued, brought the curriculum and its assessment closer together, and so permitted the development of innovative and more relevant curricular activities. Certainly, some such model would have had to have been developed if work experience was to be formally assessed. Work experience raises particular difficulties for such formal assessment, first because it is transacted off the school site, and second because the experience received by the students is of its nature very varied. Teacher assessments are more likely to be able to accommodate these problems.

In contrast to these teacher assessments, the university-dominated examination boards have tended to reinforce the claims of a curriculum which Young (1971) characterized as embodying literate, abstract, differentiated and uncommonsense knowledge. Of course, not all the examining boards have traded exclusively in this currency. An important development has been the rise of examining boards that are not based around the universities, but instead are more closely associated with the interests of industry and commerce. Bodies like the Royal Society of Arts (RSA), the City and Guilds of London Institute (CGLI) and the Business and Technician Education Council (BTEC) have made considerable inroads into the world of school examining, particularly in pre-vocational education. To some extent, the university-based boards have begun to follow the lead of these bodies: the GCSE criteria, with their greater emphasis on the practical application of school subjects to the outside world, certainly make it easier to include an industrial dimension in the school curriculum.

In direct and immediate terms, there are three main parties involved in the assessment of work experience: teachers, students, and employers.

Teachers are at a disadvantage here because they are neither in control of the learning stimulus (the work-place) nor are they physically present in the work-place except for the occasional visit. The traditional response to this problem has been for students to bring back evidence of their learning from the work-place, usually in an inscripted form — a logbook, a diary, or occasionally longer pieces of work (see pp. 251–2). An equally common approach is for the teachers to cede to the employers the rights to carrying out the assessment of student performance.

This is rarely a case of merely changing assessors. Employers are in a better position to make assessments of students on work experience *per se* because they are on site (although this raises important questions about which individual[s] in the work-place make the assessment). If, however, one sees work experience as part of a learning programme which begins in school with preparation and briefing and ends in school with debriefing and follow-up, then the employers' advantage is considerably moderated. Moreover, employers often use different criteria from teachers when assessing young people on work experience. Overall, whereas teachers tend to try to assess *learning*, employers are much more likely to assess against criteria related to *employability*, although they do this with varying degrees of explicitness and formality (see pp. 244–9). Sometimes teachers try to influence employers' criteria by providing their own assessment pro-formas, though even here, the educational assessment format often mirrors what the teachers believe are employment criteria.

Students, too, are often given a significant stake in the assessment of their own learning in work experience. Experiential learning, of which work experience is an example, places most of the responsibility for learning on to the student. Students have privileged awareness of their own learning, and in work experience they are usually in a good position to judge what they can and cannot do, and what they know and do not know. It is thus now not uncommon to find 'triangulated assessments' where teachers, students and employers negotiate both the criteria for assessment and the assessments themselves: the term 'triangulation' aptly evokes our 'work-experience triangle' (p. 23).

The final issue facing the assessment of work experience is related to credentialling — how should the results of the assessment be signified and communicated to others? Traditional examinations at 16+ or 18+ result in examination certificates with national currency. The credentialling bodies, the examining boards, offer some guarantees both about reliability and validity, and about the comparability of standards. Work experience is only credentialled via this route if it can make a direct contribution to subject knowledge: its unique contribution is not separated out from knowledge acquired in other ways. The other main way in which work experience can be accredited is through pupil records of achievement. The DES (1984) statement of policy on such records stated that 'records and recording systems should recognise, acknowledge and give credit for what pupils have achieved and experienced, not just in terms of public exams but in other ways as well'. It is now common for work experience to contribute to the record of achievement, and in some cases a separate certificate of work experience is included, signed by both the school or LEA and the relevant employer. It is not as yet clear how helpful employers find records of achievement or how far the records are used in selecting students for employment (DES, 1988d).

An important issue for assessment is how universal any work-experience credential should be. Public-examination results have national and even international currency, whereas the evidence suggests that pupil profiles have much more restricted acceptance. As we have argued, many employers involved in work-experience schemes use them to assess the employability of young people. In some cases this leads to public credentials, which often are included in student records of achievement. Such credentials can then be shown to *other* employers when the young people in question apply to them for jobs, and so can have an exchange value in the labour market. Less formal assessments, too, can have an exchange value in the youth labour market, which for most young people is local in character (see p. 72). In these local labour markets, a telephone call from one manager to another within the same district will often elicit assessments as to an individual's employability based on a period of work experience. Such assessments may not even exist in a written form, and will remain in the relevant industrialist's memory for a relatively short space of time — which may, however, include the period covering the young person's crucial first formal entry into the labour market. The development of local partnership arrangements between local employers and schools, particularly where these are part of a Compact, is likely to increase pressures for more formal certification of work experience, because the judgment of employability is being made on behalf of groups of employers rather than single employers. This may lead to a more formal set of arrangements for assessment and subsequent credentialling.

Assessment in Practice

There are some fundamental questions which need to be answered when making assessments of students on work experience from an educational point of view. These relate to asking questions and setting tasks, to the nature of evidence, to making observations, to viewing products, to recording work, and to reporting assessments.

For any work experience which is to be assessed, there must — as we have seen — be some initial decisions about *what* should be assessed. The object of the assessment could be unilaterally deduced from the requirements of a particular subject syllabus set by an examination board; it could be unilaterally decided by teachers (or even, perhaps, employers); or it could be

---

Box 13.3   A workbook section related to a world-of-work-learning frame

Use this space for your answers

Take a look around the place where you are working and try to find out how many workers, foremen, supervisors, managers, directors, etc. there are.

If you can, draw up a pyramid to show how they fit in. (If where you work people have different titles to worker, foreman, etc., use their proper titles in your pyramid.)

Write about a page on the way your place of work is organised — what departments there are, how they are set out.

How does all this fit in with what is produced where you work?

Source: Spencer Park School, London; included in Jamieson, Newman and Peffers (1986).

---

the result of negotiation between students, teachers and employers, or any combination of these groups. Once the object of assessment has been decided (and it could be unique to each student), the assessment process can begin.

Asking Questions and Setting Tasks

The first assessment task is to help students prepare for the learning or performance which is to be assessed. This is most commonly accomplished by posing students a set of questions which will need to be addressed on placement. It could also involve negotiating with the employer a task or set of tasks which could test the student's capabilities.

The question–setting is often performed through the mechanism of the student workbook or log (for a critical review of work-experience workbooks, see Jamieson, Newman and Peffers, 1986). The nature of the questions posed must clearly reflect the curricular frame within which work experience is placed. Many workbooks for students of compulsory school age seem to reflect a 'world–of–work learning' frame with a strong investigative aim: an example of the sorts of questions posed within this frame is presented in Box 13.3. Other questions are likely to relate to the curricular frames provided by personal and social education and/or careers education: an example of this approach is provided in Box 13.4.

The tasks which are set for students on work experience can include tasks which are related to finding out about the work-place. Alternatively, employers may give students particular work tasks to do and then assess them on the basis of their performance.

Box 13.4   *A workbook section related to a PSE/careers-education frame*

You . . . and your future

Work Experience can help you to sort out some important questions . . .

What kind of person am I?
What am I good at? What do I like doing?
What is important to me?
What am I looking for in adult and working life?
What can I contribute (give) to the community through my work?
How can I make my plans and my dreams come true?

Looking back at your Work Experience (and your other experience of life), write down your answers to these questions. You may need help and practical advice on the last question — the careers or guidance teacher can often help you make plans, and so can other teachers, your family, and the careers office.

Source: EITB (1981).

The Nature of Evidence

Once questions and tasks have been set, the assessors — be they teachers, employers or students — have to agree about the nature of the evidence that they will accept as answers to the questions, or as representing successful completion of tasks. The major difficulty here is common to a wide variety of assessment activities: the simpler the task, or the simpler and more factual the question, the easier it is to agree on the nature of the evidence and to make an assessment. If a work-experience question asks for the total number of employees in the work-place, or whether there is union representation, these are relatively straightforward enquiries.[1] If, however, students are asked about the employer's education and training policy, or about the general attitude of the employees to the company, the question of what constitutes evidence is more difficult to answer. The same is true of work tasks: if a student has the task of riveting components on to a metal frame, performance is relatively easy to assess; but if the task is serving customers, say in a retail outlet selling goods with a high technical content (e.g. electrical goods), the nature of the evidence for successful task completion is more problematic. A further difficulty is that in some circumstances it may be relatively difficult to agree criteria for acceptable evidence in advance, particularly if the framework for the work experience is deliberately open-ended and exploratory.

Making Observations

The next stage in the assessment process involves making observations of the students whilst at the work-place and during follow-up work, and reviewing the results of their work for assessment purposes. Most observations of students on task at the work-place are made by employers (or, more

---

Box 13.5   *An employer assessment form (I)*

We would be very grateful if you could complete this section as it will help students identify their own strengths, and areas which need improving when seeking full-time work in the future. Please be as honest as possible in your appraisal within the limitations of the short period of time. Areas which could be included are punctuality, attendance, numeracy, literacy, attitude or tasks they coped with well.

STUDENT'S PARTICULAR STRENGTHS

_____

_____

_____

_____

_____

AREAS WHICH COULD BE DEVELOPED OR IMPROVED

_____

_____

_____

_____

_____

STUDENT'S COMMENTS

_____

_____

_____

_____

_____

Source: Newham LEA.

---

accurately, by the students' first-line supervisors). Employers are usually asked to make some such assessment, although it is very rare to find this a compulsory part of the scheme. The wording adopted by one LEA captures the spirit of many schemes: 'The completion of this form is not obligatory but the employer's views on each individual young person are absolutely crucial to allow teachers to follow up the experience in schools' (Bradford LEA: *Employer's Guide to Work Experience*). Occasionally, employers are left to write what they wish in the format that suits them (the employer's own appraisal instrument is sometimes used if this is appropriate). More commonly, employers are given a format by the school or LEA. Standard LEA forms are becoming more common as work experience becomes more centralized (see Chapter 6). A few LEAs use a relatively open format like the one shown in Box 13.5. More common is a structured format in which employers are asked to tick a series of options within a category, although few are as thorough as the example shown in Box 13.6. By far the most common

Box 13.6   An employer assessment form (II)

STUDENT'S NAME: _____

EMPLOYING ORGANISATION: _____

TYPE OF WORK UNDERTAKEN: _____

FIRST DAY OF ATTENDANCE: _____ LAST DAY OF ATTENDANCE: _____

TOTAL DAYS OF WORK EXPERIENCE: _____

Some of the questions outlined below will not be appropriate to every student. Please tick where the answer is positive and in other cases add comments.

1. PUNCTUALITY AND ATTENDANCE

   (a) Always in good time; full attendance ☐

   (b) Some absence but with good reason ☐

   (c) Slack timekeeping ☐

   (d) Timekeeping improved ☐

   (e) Timekeeping deteriorated ☐

   Other comments:

   _____

   _____

2. INTEREST

   (a) Continuous interest maintained in all aspects of work ☐

   (b) Reasonable interest but few questions asked ☐

   (c) Interest only in particular job ☐

   (d) Showed no interest ☐

   Other comments:

   _____

   _____

3. SPEED OF LEARNING

   (a) Quick to learn ☐

   (b) Average performance ☐

   (c) Speed increased as became familiar with surroundings ☐

   (d) Slow to learn ☐

   Other comments:

   _____

   _____

4. ATTITUDE TO WORK

   (a) Always completed tasks thoroughly, carefully and willingly ☐

   (b) Very keen but at the expense of some accuracy ☐

   (c) Painstaking and thorough but lacking in enthusiasm ☐

   (d) Did not appreciate the need for thoroughness or accuracy ☐

   Other comments:

   _____

   _____

5. INITIATIVE SHOWN

   (a) Readily took the initiative to do things on his/her own and showed good judgement in choosing when to do so ☐

   (b) Took the initiative when the opportunity was clearly offered ☐

   (c) Kept closely to allotted tasks ☐

   (d) There was little opportunity for him/her to show initiative ☐

   Other comments:

   _____

   _____

6. REACTION TO SUPERVISION

   (a) Readily accepted any instruction, criticism or correction ☐

   (b) Accepted instruction but reacted less ☐

   (c) Reluctant to accept close supervision at first but adapted to it later ☐

   (d) Tended to resent criticism or correction ☐

   Other comments:

   _____

   _____

7. RELATIONSHIP WITH OTHER EMPLOYEES

   (a) Quickly accepted as a member of the working group ☐

   (b) Established friendly relations with colleagues ☐

   (c) Tended to remain aloof and detached except when actually working in a group ☐

   (d) Did not adapt or fit in well with group ☐

   Other comments:

   _____

   _____

8. Did the student appear to benefit from the work experience?

   YES   NO

   If so, in what ways?

   _____

   _____

   _____

9. Did any administrative or disciplinary problems arise?

   YES   NO

   If yes, please explain briefly: _____

   _____

   _____

10. GENERAL COMMENTS

    _____

    _____

    _____

    DATE: _____ SIGNED: _____

    POSITION: _____

Source: Bradford LEA.

Box 13.7   An employer assessment form (III)

Name and address of firm_____

_____

Name of pupil _____

When the above pupil has completed the work-experience period, would you please fill in the following report, preferably after discussion with the pupil. This information is confidential to the pupil, employer and the school and will not be shown to any prospective employer.

	Good	Acceptable	Poor	COMMENTS
Attendance				
Time keeping				
Ability to understand written and spoken instructions				
Clear speech				
Adequate numeracy				
Accuracy of work produced				
Ability to work without constant supervision				
Relationships with other employees				
Relationship with supervisor/manager				
Adaptability				

GENERAL COMMENTS _____

_____

_____

Source: Perryfields High School, Oldbury; included in Jamieson, Newman and Peffers (1986, p. 37).

---

format is where employers are given a list of categories, like the one shown in Box 13.7, and are asked to tick an appropriate box (it is worth noting that in this particular example there is an explicit assurance that the report will *not* be shown to other employers).

As is illustrated in Box 13.6, the emphasis in most employer reports is on *attitudes* rather than *skills* or *knowledge*. There are at least two reasons for this. In the first place, because of the relative brevity of school-based work experience, it is difficult for employers to make much of a judgment about relevant skills or knowledge, which tend to be acquired only after some time in the work-place. By contrast, it might be argued that students arrive at the work-place with a set of relevant attitudes that employers can assess. The second reason is that the attitudes of young people to work have traditionally been a matter of some concern to employers (see pp. 74–5). This emphasis can shift, however, when the frame is more vocational and the curricular aim is essentially preparatory. In such cases it is often possible to specify particular skills in which students are expected to demonstrate competence. Some examples are indicated in the list of skills developed by the Core Skills Project in the context of YTS work experience (see Box 13.8).

Although it is common to involve employers in the assessment process, this does raise some important questions for education. The most important question relates to the purposes of assessment. The exact purpose of student assessment on work experience can vary with the curriculum framework adopted, but it is nearly always centred around the key concept of *learning*. This might refer to learning in subject terms, to learning about the world of work, or to learning about oneself in terms of capabilities and competencies. Theoretically at least, learning is at the heart of schooling, but it is not the pivotal concept of the majority of organizations which provide work place-ments for students. As noted earlier (p. 241), the key assessment concept for employers when they assess tends to be *employability*. Criteria relating to employability can feed into criteria relating to learning — particularly if the curricular frame is related to personal and social education, careers education or vocational courses — but there remain fundamental differences between the two sets of criteria.

Not only is there a potential clash of assessment criteria between teachers and employers, but there are differences in the importance given to assessment by the two different kinds of institution. As we have already argued, assessment is central to schooling, and as a consequence every teacher has professional training and experience in the assessment of students. The same is not true of employers, and although large employers will in all probability operate employee appraisal schemes, the skills of assessment and appraisal are often not widespread in work organizations. There is, however, some evidence to suggest that as a result of YTS, more supervisors have acquired relevant skills, and it is clear that many of the supervisors involved in assessing YTS youngsters are also responsible for supervising school students on work experience.

When employers come to make assessments of students, they usually use an assessment device like the one reproduced in Box 13.7, which has two major features. First, it is related to employment criteria, i.e. criteria which are concerned with employee performance. Second, it is relatively quick to complete. This is why the box-ticking format is so common. Whether the criteria used by employers are norm-referenced against employees or against other students on work experience, or whether they are criterion-referenced in some way, varies from case to case. Either way, teachers are inclined to accept employers' assessments of student performance in the work-place, in the same way that employers tend to accept the judgments of educationalists as manifested in examination results.

Although employers are clearly in a good position to make observations about the performance of students on work experience, because they are physically present in the work-place, so too are the students. As we have seen, it has become increasingly common for students to be involved in

Box 13.8 *Core skills keywords*

Core skill groups	Keywords
1. Operating with numbers	Count
	Work out
	Check and correct
	Compare
2. Interpreting numerical and related information	Interpret
3. Estimating	Estimate
4. Measuring and marking out	Measure
	Mark out
5. Recognising cost and value	Compare
	Recognise value
6. Finding out information and interpreting instructions	Find out
	Interpret
7. Providing information	Provide information
8. Working with people	Notice
	Ask for assistance
	Offer assistance
	React
	Discuss
	Converse
9. Planning: determining and revising courses of action	Plan
	Diagnose
10. Decision making: choosing between alternatives	Decide
11. Monitoring: keeping track of progress and checking	Check
	Monitor
	Notice
12. Preparing for a practical activity	Locate
	Identify
	Handle, lift or transport
	Adjust
	Arrange
	Carry out procedures
	Check
13. Carrying out a practical activity	Adopt safe practices
	Lift or transport
	Manipulate
	Operate
	Set up
	Assemble
	Dismantle
14. Finishing off a practical activity	Carry out procedures
	Check
	Restock

Source: Levy (1987).

assessing their own performance on work experience. One of the reasons for this is that work experience is now commonly recorded on the student's record of achievement, and much of this document is compiled by the student. Students' own assessment of their performance is thus often placed alongside that of the employer, and in some schemes a negotiation then takes place between the two parties until they agree a 'final' assessment.

It is also common for teachers to visit students on work experience, and this presents further opportunities for observations and assessment. As noted on pp. 221–5, there are several other potential aims of such visits: these include underlining symbolically the importance that schools place on work experience; forging wider links with local employers; and ensuring that the students are satisfied with the placements and that the employer is treating them appropriately. A few schemes have, however, tried to make the observations made on these visits serve assessment functions. Project Trident in Northumberland states that the aims are 'to determine whether the student's behaviour is satisfactory or not' and 'to assess the commitment of the student to the work he/she is doing'. Similar aims are illustrated in the form reproduced in Box 13.9. The form also indicates the multiple purposes of the visits, with its additional references to the assessment of the placement itself.

Viewing Products

Most assessments made by teachers of students' work experience, however, relate not to direct observations of their *work performance*, but to their *educational performance* based on that work. This is the traditional arena of educational assessment, where judgments about the extent and quality of learning are made on the basis of viewing students' 'school' work. Thus the educational tasks set in students' work-experience workbooks, or subsequent course-work based on the work experience, tend to constitute the subject-matter of the assessment. Such assessments are most readily related to a curricular frame supplied by an academic subject, where the aim of work experience is the enhancement of subject knowledge, or alternatively by a vocational course.

Assessment of 'products', as we have termed it, is nearly always based on the inscripted mode where students have to write something: much less common are presentations which are largely iconographic — pictures, drawings, etc. For many students, this is paradoxical: firstly, because they usually were not required to make heavy use of such modes whilst undertaking their work-experience tasks; secondly, because for many less-able students their weakness lies precisely in the area of writing!

Of the more traditional academic subjects, it is — as noted earlier (p. 239) — English which has drawn most heavily on work experience as a source for assessment. A good example of this is to be found in Rokeby School in the London Borough of Newham. Here a world-of-work module for GCSE English Language has been developed which draws heavily on work

Ian Jamieson

Box 13.9   Form for teacher visits to student placements

Please tick the appropriate column.

	YES	NO
(1) Has the pupil established a good relationship with employees?		
(2) Is the pupil performing work tasks satisfactorily?		
(3) Is the pupil showing good patterns of		
(a) attendance?		
(b) punctuality?		
(4) Is the pupil showing interest in the work?		
(5) Is the pupil enjoying him/herself?		

Staff comment on pupil's progress

Staff comment on the firm (e.g. is the youngster being given proper instruction and supervision?)

Any problems to be brought to the work-experience co-ordinator's attention?

NAME OF PUPIL _____

FIRM _____

DATE OF VISIT _____

Signature of member of staff

Source: Adapted from Hanson School, Bradford.

---

experience. The work provides material for the students' language folders, for oral assessment and for literature. In addition, the assignments offer work on practical skills, e.g. being interviewed. The module is designed to take up about fourteen lessons, and can of course be adapted by teachers to suit their own needs. Assessed activities in the module include: research into particular jobs and an oral presentation of the findings; language assignments on topics like 'the job of my dreams', and 'a day in the life of ...'; the writing of a script of a job interview; reading the poem 'Work' by D.H. Lawrence and extracts from Carol Adams' work *Ordinary Lives* about working-class life one hundred years ago; interview role-plays; a timed essay on 'first day in a new job'; research on a work-related topic, e.g. the role of unions, or successful people in non-traditional jobs; and the work-experience diary. Work experience is thus used as a vehicle for generating material to assess English language skills. The assessment issues raised are all related to English rather than to work experience *per se*.

Box 13.10   Assessment objectives for the Work Experience Module in the Oxfordshire Modular Citizenship course

Preparation

Planning:
  identifying an area of employment for involvement; identifying a specific placement location; identifying own role and contribution within the work placement; setting personal targets within the context of the chosen work placement and devising strategies for achieving these; making necessary practical arrangements (such as transport, clothing, equipment).

Investigation:
  identifying and developing knowledge related to and necessary for the chosen work placement (gathering information about this kind of employment in general; gathering information about the particular placement; acquiring the specific knowledge needed to carry out the work placement).

Skill development:
  identifying and where appropriate developing the skills necessary to carry out the work placement (e.g. practical skills, personal and social skills).

Application

Implementation:
  carrying out the work placement; taking an active role within the placement; adapting plans and strategies as necessary.

Using acquired knowledge:
  using the information gathered using the preparation to carry out the work placement.

Using skills:
  using and developing skills to carry out the work placement.

Evaluation

Communicating experiences, making and justifying comments and drawing conclusions on:

— the effectiveness of the plans made for carrying out the work placement, the strategies devised for achieving targets, the contribution made within the work placement, and the learning that took place during the placement.

— the effectiveness of the knowledge accumulated during preparation and applied at the work placement.

— the effectiveness of both the identification and development of necessary skills and the use of those skills during the work placement.

Source: Oxfordshire LEA.

In other areas of the curriculum, assessment is potentially more complex because the assessment criteria and related judgments are not wholly derived from the internal logic and data of the subject itself. Instead, they are related at least in part to the nature of the work experience. This is also the case if the curricular frame is world-of-work learning or a vocational course. The difficulties this gives rise to become clear if one examines the assessment objectives of the Work Experience Module in the Oxfordshire Modular Citizenship course (see Box 13.10).

First, there is the problem that not all work-experience placements present students with the same degree of difficulty in achieving the objectives. The investigation objectives in Box 13.10, for example, might be much more difficult to achieve in some work-places than others. If the 'degree of difficulty' is known about in advance and can be accurately assessed, the problem can be overcome using a 'diving-board tariff' technique whereby placements are given a degree-of-difficulty quotient and student results are weighted accordingly (a 'difficult' placement being given a high tariff, as in high-board diving). The problem is that few schools have sufficient knowledge of their placements to make such assessments.

The second set of difficulties also concerns knowledge. If assessment is carried out within a 'world-of-work learning' curricular frame, one has to ask whether most teachers have enough knowledge to assess the work. In the Oxford module, this might apply particularly to judgments made under the 'Application' heading. We can isolate two problems here. In the first place, the 'world of work' does not constitute a traditional subject of study for teachers, nor is it a core part of teacher training (Bloomer and Scott, 1987; Scott and Bloomer, 1988). As a 'subject' it might have been acquired to some extent on in-service training, perhaps as part of a 'teachers into industry' scheme. The Open University has produced a number of modules to help teachers understand the world of work in the context of work experience (Open University, 1989). But the level of penetration of 'teachers into industry' schemes and associated work is as yet modest.

There is also a more general problem which relates to a wider variety of curricular frames. It could be the case that the assessment criteria relate not to knowledge and understanding of the world of work in general, but to specific understanding of the work-place that has provided the placement. It is clear that few if any teachers have detailed knowledge of every work-place used on their work-experience scheme. By contrast, employers are likely to possess detailed knowledge of their own work-place, but they will have no special claim, *qua* employers, to understand the world of work as an object of disinterested study.

The third assessment problem relates to assessment criteria linked to performance within the work-place. One of the distinctive features of the world of work is that the problems with which it confronts workers and students on placement alike are not related to any specific school 'subject'; nor are they, in general, amenable to 'right' and 'wrong' answers. Rather the answers to particular problems have to work in a way that satisfies management at a particular time and in a particular context. This of course is not always the case for routine jobs where there are set procedures and standards of performance, nor do all school subjects find the work-place model wholly alien. But there is a sufficient contrast between practice in this respect in the work-place and in school to produce difficulties in reconciling the two assessment models.

Recording Work

The next problem of work-experience assessment faces all teachers who have to assess work for public examinations where there is a moderation procedure. This is the case for most public examinations where work experience is likely to feature, e.g. GCSE, CPVE and BTEC. The general problem is: what student work should be retained by the school or college for assessment and moderation purposes? One can immediately see that work experience faces some special difficulties here. Many assessments of students are made on the basis of their performance on a job at the work-place. It is difficult to record and retain a record of that performance. Services, for example, will have been 'consumed' in the normal course of trading. Certainly the employer might have made an assessment at the time, but the all-important performance on which that assessment was based is by its nature ephemeral. Other school subjects have a similar problem — for example, subjects concerned with the expressive and performing arts — but in these cases the 'performance' takes place inside the boundary of education and is assessed and moderated simultaneously. This could in principle be done in relation to work-experience debriefing, where much of the learning is captured and internalized (see Chapter 12). Usually, however, assessment is reduced to recording those elements of work experience that can be committed to paper in some way. Effectively this means employer assessments, work-based diaries and logs, and any written work that is based on the experience.

Reporting Assessments

The final question that needs to be addressed is how to report the assessment. If work experience is integrated into a course like GCSE or CPVE or BTEC, it does not have to be separately reported, but merely contributes to the overall assessment of the course. However, it is increasingly common for work experience to result in separate certification. This is largely a function of the introduction of records of achievement. The national report on such records (DES, 1988d) concluded that the summary document should 'include a statement by the pupil and the school of any out-of-school activities, community service, school trips and work experience. Where such activities have resulted in the award of certificates or other reports of achievements these should be recorded' (p. 39).

Work-experience certificates are now commonplace. They can be issued by employers, by LEAs, by organizations like Project Trident, or by the schools themselves. Some are little more than certificates of attendance, but others try to record the nature of the tasks undertaken on work experience. The most detailed certificates analyze the performance of the student on the placement. An example of the latter is reproduced in Box 13.11.

Box 13.11   Project Trident Record of Achievement

Project Trident Record of Achievement

Julia Barry

of   Robert Powell High School

The above Student has successfully completed
three weeks Work Experience

WITH   J P Enterprises

Skills demonstrated

INITIATIVE

Selected suitable methods from several possibilities, supervisor thought
she showed excellent initiative.

CO-OPERATION

All expected duties carried out effectively and efficiently.

SELF CONFIDENCE

Handled herself satisfactorily. Supervisor said that her manual dexterity
was excellent.

MOTIVATION

Eager to please. Style of work reflected her expected occupation.

RESPONSIBILITY

After being shown what to do, she got on with it well and accepted
criticism of mistakes. Punctual and reliable.

COMMUNICATION

Quickly picked up jargon of the job.

TEAMWORK

Worked well with others when the situation arose.

Chairman Trident Trust

Date

One notable feature of the Trident Record of Achievement reproduced in Box 13.11 is that all the statements are positive. This tends to be a general feature of student records of achievement, and also of open references from either school or employment. There is some evidence from the national study on records of achievement that employers are not entirely happy with the principle that only positive achievement can be recorded, and that this is why employers tend also to require confidential references on students (DES, 1988d).

This raises the important question of for whom credentials are being produced: to whom is the assessment being reported? The formal answer is of course 'the student': they own the record of achievement or the examination certificates. Whether they value them or not, however, may depend largely on the value of the documents to *other* people, and crucially to further and higher education and to employers. There is little evidence to suggest that further and higher education as yet take much notice of student records of achievement in general, or certificates of work experience in particular (Fuller, 1987). Their potential exchange value to employers is probably more positive because employers tend to be more interested in the value of relevant *experience*. It is interesting in this respect to note that — as reported earlier (p. 140) — around half the employers in Fuller's study of TVEI work experience kept some sort of record of work-experience placements in their firms. Most of these organizations did this in case the students subsequently applied to them for employment.

Conclusion

One of the worries about assessment techniques applied to work experience is that many teachers believe that they lack the validity and reliability of the traditional methods used to validate more conventional school learning. We have three comments to make about these widespread concerns. First, many of the claims to validity and reliability made by the traditional methods do not stand up to scrutiny (Burgess and Adams, 1980). Second, many educationalists seem to require a certainty and finality about the assessment of student performance on work experience which is quite unreasonable, given the nature of the experience. It is instructive to compare the dilemmas that industrialists have in making judgments about employees' performance in work situations — in, for example, the context of individual performance appraisal. A review of this literature shows that the problems and solutions adopted by the industrial world are remarkably similar to the ones we have described in this chapter (for a review, see Robertson and Cooper, 1983, ch. 6). The difference lies in the pragmatic acceptance by the industrial community of the nature of the problem, and of practical solutions that offer *reasonable* levels of validity and reliability in a complex situation. Industry characteristically looks to a justification through pragmatism and the market, whilst education turns to an appeal to ultimate standards and bureaucratic rules. To some extent this is understandable: educational assessments are expected to be more universalistic in their application. But educationalists have now realized that insisting on such standards and rules unduly limits the range of educational experiences that can be assessed.

Thirdly, we return to the crucial question of the purpose of assessment. It is clear is that there is no one purpose that is served by the assessment of students on a work-experience programme. Assessment looks different in different work-experience schemes because the schemes themselves, and the place of assessment within them, can have quite different objectives. Assessment can thus contribute to the process of career choice; it can help extend subject knowledge; it can act as an employment credential; it can assist in the process of testing out vocational skills. In addition to this variation in purpose, assessment has to serve at least three constituencies: employers, who tend to be concerned with assessment criteria relating to employee performance, perhaps with an eye to future recruitment; teachers, who might operate with a similar frame of reference but are more likely to adopt a curricular framework; and finally, the students themselves, whose frame of reference may or may not overlap with either of the other two.

All of these difficulties are compounded by the large-scale changes which are occurring both in the education system and in the industrial infrastructure. We have only just reached the point where records of achievement are commonplace for all school-leavers, and it is as yet unclear exactly how employers and higher education are using these records (if indeed they are using them at all). They could become important credentials for entry into the labour market and into further and higher education; or the summative record could wither through lack of use and leave us just with formative profiles back in schools.

Employers' needs are also changing. As the service sector of the economy has grown (see pp. 64–5), it has produced large numbers of jobs which require students to possess social and interpersonal skills to deal with the public. Such jobs are often given to students on work experience, and student assessment often concentrates on just such a set of employee skills and related attitudes. On the other hand, there are signs that the economy is increasingly requiring employees with sophisticated technical skills. Insofar as work experience might be thought to encourage young people into the labour market at an early stage, and insofar as it inducts them into an old-style model of 'employee' in jobs with little skill content, work experience might be thought not to fit the real needs of either employers or young people. Indeed, this is one argument for using work experience to increase young people's understanding of the world of work and to focus the assessment here rather than on current employee skills.

In many ways, assessment practices are the touchstone by which we can judge what is happening in work experience. If assessment is entirely absent from both school and work-place, we might reasonably conclude that work experience has an insecure hold in both institutions. If assessment procedures are in place, the criteria being used will tell us a good deal about the aims of a particular work-experience scheme. If the assessment is successfully converted into credentials and used for entry to further and higher education or to local employment, this will be a clear indication that the experience has entered local currency and has acquired exchange value.

Note

1   It should be noted that even such simple questions as these can turn out to be relatively complex. For example, how are part-time employees to be counted? What about work sub-contracted to homeworkers? What if there are large seasonal variations and the organization takes on numbers of casual workers? Again, how are unions to be counted? Does the count only cover those which are recognized and have negotiating rights?

Chapter 14

Evaluation

Ian Jamieson

If assessment is focused narrowly on the student, then educational evaluation is concerned with assessing a much wider range of phenomena. Evaluation is traditionally interested not only in the effects of work experience on students, but also in the effects it has on teachers, schools and employers. In addition, it is interested in unintended consequences as well as intended ones, and in the costs of work experience as well as the benefits.

In this chapter we will try to bring together the existing evidence on the evaluation of work experience. For such a ubiquitous activity, both in this country and abroad (see Chapter 3), it is surprising how little evidence there is. Of course, a great deal turns on the question of what constitutes evidence. There is a good deal on student and teacher perceptions of the effects of work experience, and rather less on employer perceptions. A growing collection of anecdotal evidence exists about what individual students have managed to achieve through work experience: indeed, most involved teachers appear to have their own special stories. What we lack, particularly in Britain, are studies employing a rigorous methodology that systematically examines what happens to students as a result of work experience, whether or not this might have happened without work experience, and whether there are not equally effective and possibly more economic ways of producing the same effects (Macleay, 1973; Watts, 1983a).

There is one particular methodological dilemma that we need to note. When we undertake evaluation of work experience, what is it that we are evaluating? Are we evaluating the experience itself, or the effect of the experience plus the preparation, briefing, and subsequent debriefing and follow-up work? The fact that some schools quite reasonably see the work-experience scheme as an integrated whole makes this a particular difficulty. A related problem is the hybrid nature of many work–experience schemes, which consciously or unconsciously fuse together a number of curricular frameworks and their associated aims (see Chapter 9). Such models of work experience are difficult to evaluate because of their potential for a multiplicity of cross-cutting outcomes (see also p. 29). Of course, there is no particular reason for evaluation to be concerned only with outcomes, and evaluation models which focus on processes as well as outcomes are better equipped to cope with hybrid models.

Work experience as it stands is a great act of faith, with the forces of reason (or at least reasonableness) marshalled more or less equally on both sides. Those who proclaim its merits argue that contact with the 'real world', with its new people, its new tasks and responsibilities and a fresh environment, are exactly the conditions necessary for growth and development in young people. They also point to the generalization that the great majority of young people enjoy work experience, and to numerous specific instances where career choice has been influenced. Finally, and tellingly, they enquire whether experienced teachers involved in work experience are likely to be systematically deceived in their professional judgments about effectiveness. The sceptics' case rests partly on methodological grounds — that there are no proper studies of the effects of work experience — and partly on the generalized nature of the claims for work experience. Critics point to the enormous variation in the duration and type of placements as well as to student variability (by experience, ability, maturity, etc.), and ask how such a variety of combinations can possibly have the generalized effects claimed for it (Hamilton and Crouter, 1980). Other critics focus on the work-place itself and point out that we know from a wide range of industrial studies that different jobs affect people in quite different ways (Steinberg, 1984). Also, when the nature of the great mass of student work-experience placements is examined, revealing the prevalence of low-skill and relatively routine jobs, the critics ask how such jobs can possibly develop young people in the ways claimed (Shilling, 1989; Steinberg, 1982; Watkins, 1987, 1988).

One of the most common models of evaluation is the 'countenance' model advanced by Stake (1967). This model takes the aims or intentions of work experience and uses these as the criteria by which to judge the activity (see pp. 274–5). It is useful here to map the aims on to our curricular frames as we have done in the work-experience triangle (see Chapter 2). This allows us to consider the evaluation evidence for a group of related aims in a way which fits the available data. It is also consistent with an important research finding which we have already noted in Chapter 3 (p. 51). Steinberg (1984), in reviewing the evaluations of ten different community-service programmes with one another and with different types of experiential-learning programmes, and taking note of the most extensive evaluation of experiential-learning programmes in the USA (see Conrad and Hedin, 1982), concluded as follows:

> Taken together, the findings of the Conrad and Hedin study and the various evaluations of career education programs suggest that an adolescent's participation in school-based work activities is likely to have a positive impact on his or her development *only when such participation is well integrated into the adolescent's school program and*

accompanied by structured classroom instruction (Steinberg, 1984, p. 16, our emphasis).

There is then very strong, positive evidence in favour of embedding work experience in a curriculum framework and making sure that the activity is adequately prepared, briefed, debriefed and followed up. There is also some modest British evidence to suggest that if work experience is assessed by schools and therefore part of the school programme, students value it more (Fuller, 1987).

We will accordingly examine the available research evidence in relation to each of the five curricular frames we identified in Chapter 2. After summarizing the evidence, we will then explore how teachers might engage in self-evaluation as a regular part of their work.

Careers Education

It seems appropriate to start with the curricular frame of careers education, and the associated expansive, sampling and anticipatory aims, because these seem the most common, at least in Britain. We have also included the placing aim here because of its close association with some aspects of careers work in schools. The TVEI evaluation studies have consistently shown the careers-education framework to be central to work experience. The national evaluation of work experience conducted by the University of Leeds group concluded that teachers involved in the study generally saw work experience primarily as a resource for informing students about the world of work and as a way of looking at employment possibilities (Leeds National Evaluation Team, 1987). Such aims are also widely held by students. Fuller (1987) showed for her sample of post-16-year-old students that career sampling was the dominant personal goal for them on work experience.

What evidence is there to suggest that these aims are fulfilled? Kirton (1976) found that, in general, boys who had undertaken work experience (including part-time jobs) in a broad job interest area had higher-than-average levels of job knowledge in that area. The results were not consistent, however, and there were no controls for other possible causal factors. A more satisfactory single-school study by Pumfrey and Schofield (1982) found that students who had been on work-experience schemes scored significantly higher on three out of six measures of 'career maturity' (attitudes towards work and career decision-making, self appraisal, and occupational knowledge) than did those who had not. A survey of 771 pupils by the Schools Council Industry Project (Jamieson and Lightfoot, 1982) found that some 23 per cent of students reported that work experience had helped in their career choice, even though the project was more concerned with the investigative aim. A survey of Lanark pupils quoted by Hogg (1976) found that 60 per cent said that their experience had helped them in job choice; and a survey of young people by Millward (1977) found that 40 per cent said their experience had had a definite effect on their career choice. Higher figures have been reported by TVEI evaluations. Saunders (1987) in his study of twelve projects found the following percentages checking positive answers to questions about the value of work experience:

Discovering more about jobs	76 per cent
Choosing a job	69 per cent
Getting a job	52 per cent

The figures are even higher for post-16 students (Fuller, 1987). It is likely that these variations are a function of the curriculum frame within which work experience is placed.

There are other career-related effects claimed by work experience. Watts (1983a) quotes evidence of 'expansive' goals being met, with students broadening the range of occupations they were prepared to consider:

It has provided me with a broader outlook towards different kinds of jobs.

A girl may think office work is a bore, she says that because she hears it from other people but when she tries it herself she might not find it as dull as other people claim (p. 92).

In some cases the evidence can be quite striking. Stronach and Weir (1980) found that in one school there appeared to be a very high proportion of girls interested in nursery nursing: they had all got the idea from work-experience placements. On the other hand, Agnew's (1985) study cited on pp. 204–5 showed that expanding job horizons, particularly in the area of gender stereotyping, can be an uphill task. Black's (1976) survey of the parents of student who had been on work experience found that 28 per cent believed that their children's ideas about careers had been changed by the experience.

Many students use work experience to sample occupations in which they are already interested. In some cases this confirms them in their choices:

It made up my mind as to what I wanted to do when I left school.

I have found the job very interesting and I have learned a lot from the experience and I would like a job like this when I leave school (quoted in Watts, 1983a, p. 92).

But not all sampling exercises have this confirmatory effect. Stronach and Weir (1980) found that 74 per cent of their sample said that work experience had influenced their vocational decision-making in terms of indicating the sort of job that they did *not* want, as opposed to 48 per cent saying they had been influenced in terms of the sort of job they *did* want. Ryrie and Weir (1978) illustrated how negative work identities and even alienation can follow work placements, and the Institute of Careers Officers (1974) reported how a number of girls came to reject a career in management after experiencing a monotonous labour process. Shilling's (1989) small-scale study of two groups of students on work experience produced similar results. Such studies raise questions about the adequacy of the sampling of occupations that takes place in work experience.

Watts (1983a) argues convincingly that although these short experiences can offer a misleading basis on which to make occupational-choice decisions, because the experience could be untypical of the occupation, nevertheless they are often trusted more than less direct or less active forms of information. If we turn to the question of the *effectiveness* of the decision, Steinberg (1982) notes that the positive impact of career education on work-related knowledge, attitudes and habits is reported equally often in evaluations of school-based programmes and in evaluations of experience-based programmes. Steinberg points to the fact that we know very little about the independent effect of the experience *per se* in career choice, because it is usually combined with other school-based work. Finally, he quotes Owens (1982) approvingly as arguing that there is no evidence that experience-based career-education programmes produce wiser career decision-making. To be even-handed, one could observe that equally there is no evidence that they do not.

Finally, several studies show that work experience had a 'placing' effect, i.e. students acquiring jobs through work experience, although few schemes have this as a direct aim. Employers tend to be interested in acquiring youth labour via work experience, particularly when there is a shortage of young people on the labour market (see Chapter 8). Conversely, young people tend to take this goal more seriously when jobs are in short supply. This may be especially true for low achievers in terms of examination qualifications. Law and Watts (1977), for example, found in one school that the non-examination group valued their work-experience course because of the advantage it gave them over students from other schools and over CSE streams from their own school. Schools tend to be uneasy about this, not least because it means that students may relax when they get back to school. Nonetheless, the survey by Millward (1977) found that twelve of his sample of 103 young people were offered permanent jobs, that seven were offered Saturday or holiday employment, that six were told that they would be at a distinct advantage if a vacancy were to occur, and that twenty-three were invited to contact the firm at a later date.

Personal and Social Education

Personal and social education provides an important curricular frame for work experience, particularly for those students still in compulsory schooling.

It is widely claimed that, during work experience, students 'grow up' and become more mature. Employers certainly make this claim (McIntyre and Coombes, 1988) although they are not in a very good position from which to judge. Teachers are in a better position, but though there is a good deal of anecdotal evidence provided by teachers to suggest that such personal and social development occurs, no systematic data exist on teachers' judgments on the matter.

Asking questions of students themselves about their own perceptions of changes in their personal and social development clearly presents some problems. The safest strategy for large surveys is to ask students open-ended questions about their experiences and then to classify the responses. Using just such a strategy, Jamieson and Lightfoot (1982) found that some 10 per cent of students from a large sample (771) believed that work experience had resulted in the development of their social and life skills. Much higher figures have been reported for answers to more specific closed questions. Thus Sims (1987) in a national survey of TVEI students who had undertaken work experience found that 89 per cent of students broadly agreed with the view that they had 'learned how to work with other people', and 84 per cent felt that they had 'gained self confidence'. Another study of TVEI work experience in twelve LEAs produced very similar results, 87 per cent of students stating that work experience had helped them to get on with adults (Saunders, 1987).

These survey data are strongly supported by case-study material. Watts (1983a) quotes the following student statements as illustrations of the development of social skills:

> I found myself communicating with more and more people as the week passed. I now found it easier.

> I have got used to working with older people and feel a more confident person.

Some students mentioned other, more specific skills:

> You get used to being punctual.

> It has made me feel more confident when going for a job (*ibid*, p. 90).

The Leeds TVEI study (Barnes, Johnson and Jordan, 1989) documents examples where 16–18-year-old students had accomplished complex responsible tasks on work experience and consequently felt that they had grown in maturity. Such evidence would surely please employers concerned about the attitudes of young people to the world of work (see pp. 74–5).

Employers seem tacitly to believe that 'hands-on' experience in the work-place 'will induct students into the habits of discipline, regulation, punctual-ity and compliance envisioned in the idealized work-place' (Watkins, 1988, p. 89). It is not clear, however, whether the available evidence supports the employers' hypothesis.

One difficulty here is that growing maturity and responsibility may not necessarily produce ideal employees. If we define development, following Hamilton and Crouter (1980), as 'the growing capacity of a person to understand and act upon the environment' (p. 324), then it is clear that not all developing individuals will conform to the demands of employers. Indeed, in one famous formulation, Argyris (1964) argued that employers typically demand the traditional qualities of children, rather than adults, from their employees.

Such reservations about the potential effects of work experience on students are reinforced when one examines the results of the comprehensive review of the impact of work experience on young people by Hamilton and Crouter (1980). They conclude that it can have *negative* effects in relation to the sorts of qualities that employers seek. In particular, they argue that 'working in uninteresting jobs may ... simply hasten the arrival of the worker alienation that plagues business and industry in the United States' (p. 329).

We have already noted (p. 261) that Steinberg in the USA, Watkins in Australia and Shilling in the UK all wonder how, given the typical nature of work-experience jobs — which they generally characterize as 'highly routi-nized, repetitive work with few opportunities for decision-making or learn-ing' (Steinberg, 1984, p. 13) — such experiences can genuinely develop the individual. There is no reason to believe that the nature of work-experience jobs is significantly different in the UK than in the other two countries. The national TVEI survey suggests that 'jobs have typically been allocated from within a restricted range of rather routine shopfloor or office occupations. Such jobs offer students limited opportunities to exercise discretion or to develop work-related skills' (McIntyre and Coombes, 1988, p. 104).

Although it is difficult to see how personal and social development occurs under such conditions, the literature does offer several clues. In the first place, not all jobs are as limiting as those we have described, and it is possible that the more responsible and interesting jobs are the source of the strongest anecdotal evidence on student development (there are some striking examples of this in Barnes *et al.*, 1989). A second factor is that it is still possible to find out about *oneself* even in the situation provided by monoto-nous jobs. Hamilton and Crouter (1980) advance the hypothesis that such learning is most likely to occur when the work experience is discontinuous with the young person's everyday life experiences, and there may be no necessary connection between this discontinuity and the nature of the job in any particular case. Furthermore, we have to take into account not only the nature of the tasks which students perform on work experience, but also the personal attributes which they bring to the experience. As Hamilton and Crouter argue, 'the contribution of routine work experience to adolescent development is sure to vary depending on each adolescent's past and future' (*ibid*, p. 328). Finally, although work tasks are a fundamental feature of work experience and are relatively easy to characterize as routine etc., it is more difficult to determine the quality of the interpersonal experiences that students have on their placements. As Barnes, Johnson and Jordan (1989) argue, what students subsequently remember is 'the quality of the interpersonal relationships that they experienced' (p. 87). It seems likely that these relationships are particularly important in relation to the maturational effects of work experience. There may be an important trade-off here between the obviously valued camaraderie of many work-places, and curriculum-related goals that could lead to a 'Cook's tour' model which would lack such interpersonal satisfactions.

Vocational Courses

The vocational-course curricular frame for work experience and its associated preparatory aim are not significant for students of compulsory school age: only beyond the age of 16 do they have any real role in work-experience programmes. Even for the 16–19 age-range, there is not a great deal of evidence to suggest that the preparatory aim, whereby students use work experience to acquire skills and knowledge relevant to a particular occupational area, is very significant for most schools or colleges. Hodge's (1987) study of employers offering work-experience placements did not record this aim as significant for the 16–19 age-group. Such a finding would be congruent with the view that employers are more concerned with 'trainability' than with specific job training: even CPVE schemes which include an integral work-experience element rarely embrace the preparatory aim for particular occupational areas. Furthermore, a preparatory aim might well be premature in view of the fact that many students in 16–19 education will go on to further study rather than directly into employment.

The relatively short periods of work experience offered, even in post-16 education, certainly inhibit the development of the preparatory aim. There are clearly limits to the occupational skills which can be gained on even a three-week placement. The only detailed example which appears in the literature is provided by Barnes, Johnson and Jordan (1989) in their study of TVEI 16–18 through case-studies. They describe a college of further education in the south of England which ran a BTEC course in engineering. The course involved extended work-experience placements (two periods of four weeks each), and had been especially adapted to meet the requirements of the Engineering Industries Training Board (EITB) as well as BTEC. The authors concede that this was an unusual example of a vocational work-experience scheme which (a) involved very close cooperation between the college and one company, (b) was professionally and academically validated, and (c) was assessed. There seems little doubt that this combination of factors produced learning gains, but equally there is no doubt that the example is rare in the British context, although the development of TVEI as a four-year programme may have increased the incidence of such examples in both schools and colleges. There is little evidence available on the effectiveness of work experience as a vehicle for occupational learning because it is rarely used overtly to achieve such an end. But it may be that not all students see it like this. Jamieson (1983) argued that one of the dangers of work experience is that some students may believe that they have acquired occupational skills.

Academic Subjects

To what extent does work experience enhance academic subjects? In the British context, it has not in the past been common to use work experience for this purpose. McIntyre and Coombes (1988), in summarizing the various TVEI evaluations, both national and local, concluded that although curriculum enrichment was often evident as an aim, 'there was little to support that this was being achieved to any significant extent' (p. 106). Such a view is echoed in the most recent HMI survey of work experience (HMI, 1990). As Saunders (1987) pointed out after reviewing the practices of twelve TVEI work-experience schemes, 'work experience is predominantly "placement" rather than "curriculum" led' (p. 163).

So unusual has the academic-subjects frame been that much research and evaluation has been anxious to point out that work experience does not appear to *harm* academic work. Most work-experience schemes pursue other curricular frames, and teachers of the academic curriculum become worried about the opportunity costs (see pp. 98–100). This is particularly evident at A-level: Barnes, Johnson and Jordan (1989) reported that one school 'refused to give curriculum time to work experience for fear of doing so at the expense of A-level students' (p. 5). There appears to be no systematic evidence about the academic opportunity costs of work experience, which probably indicates that if such costs exist at all they are not high. Jamieson and Lightfoot (1982) charted teachers' concerns about this, but found no evidence in their study to support the claim that work experience detracted from academic work.

Indeed, some evaluation studies suggest that work experience has a motivational effect on school work. In certain cases, this took a rather fatalistic form:

> It made me realise all the time I wasted at school. I regret not working harder at school (quoted in Watts, 1983a, p. 88).

In others, however, work experience seemed likely to have a positive effect on study behaviour. In most instances, this was related to the general recognition it induced of the importance of examination qualifications if occupational aspirations were to be achieved:

> Work experience has shown me I've got to get more qualifications. I never thought much about what I was going to do until I went out to work. Then I thought, well time's catching up on me. I've got to do something.

> When we went back to school I was more conscious of the fact that if I didn't do well in my exams I just wouldn't get anywhere when I went into the working field. Even to have any kind of job some qualifications are always needed so instead of just messing about in class just about everybody got stuck down to doing their work for a change (quoted in Watts, 1983a, p. 89).

Fitzgerald and Bodiley (1984) in their single-school case-study report that a considerable number of students felt dissatisfied with their examination subject choices after they had done work experience.

In the USA, work experience is often part of a programme which has the objective of improving basic academic skills, primarily numeracy and literacy. Steinberg (1982) reports that such programmes appeared to have little or no impact on the acquisition of these skills, a view supported by Hamilton and Crouter (1980). At the same time, as noted in Chapter 3 (p. 51), the general effects on students' academic performance tend to be neutral or even marginally positive, despite the period of time for which students are out of the classroom.

A further significant finding emerges from the American work of Steinberg outlined in Chapters 2 (pp. 34–5) and 3 (p. 51). He argues, in effect, that work experience has its greatest impact when the young person maintains the *student* role whilst on work experience. In other words, if 'learning' is seen as a key part of the role, then it is likely that learning will take place (Steinberg, 1984). Whether one has to follow Steinberg's view that the student role has to be exhibited at the work-place is less clear (cf. p. 16). It may be the case that such a role could be reserved for out-of-work reflection on the events of the working day.

Returning to this side of the Atlantic, there is plenty of evidence to suggest that work experience *can* enrich academic subjects very effectively even if the practice has not hitherto been widespread. This is conceded by Barnes, Johnson and Jordan (1989). HMI comment:

> Students presented good, and, quite frequently, excellent, quality work in projects and assignments which they produced after they

had returned to school or to college because it was based on their first-hand experiences. They effectively drew upon direct observations made, ideas developed, and materials and information collated whilst at work on employer's premises. Assignments in GCSE English prepared in this way were invariably of a high standard and for the majority of students gained the highest marks for an individual piece of work in their portfolio (HMI, 1990, p. 9).

World-of-work Learning

There are few schools which do not argue that one of the aims of work experience is or should be concerned with understanding the world of work. They face two major problems. In the first place, the subjects of the traditional school curriculum do not easily lend themselves to such a study. Watkins (1988) quotes with approval a number of writers who argue that the 'traditional academic curriculum would seem to have little discernible relationship to either the work performed by most members of society or the actual organization and operation of society' (p. 91). There is a plea here, most clearly articulated by Bates (1984), for 'the incorporation of the "world of work" within education' which would make it the 'subject' of critical study rather than the 'object' of education. The second difficulty in the present context is that in order to embrace the investigative aim, students have usually been required to carry out investigative projects during the course of their work placements. An example of this approach is detailed by Fortune, Jamieson and Street (1983). As noted on p. 220, such a strategy is often resented by students because of the additional burdens it imposes. A great deal seems to turn on how this is handled. In some examples, work-based projects (see pp. 28–9) have been successfully used to achieve investigative aims; other possible strategies for overcoming the problem are outlined on p. 220.

It would appear that few schools have a strong curriculum frame for work experience that fully embraces world-of-work learning. This is partly a function of the fact that few mainstream subjects traditionally deal with the world of work. Instead learning about the world of work is something which many teachers hope/believe will happen as a result of work experience without curriculum support. There is some evidence to suggest that these hopes are not wholly in vain. In the Schools Council Industry Project survey, some 45 per cent of students said that the experience had given them 'insight into working and work skills' (Jamieson and Lightfoot, 1982). In the national survey of TVEI students who had been on work experience, 78 per cent agreed that they had 'discovered how companies work' (Sims, 1987). Again, Saunders (1987) reported in his study of twelve TVEI LEAs that there was evidence that young people had developed a critical perspective on some aspects of work: that is, they were prepared to be critical of aspects of the work tasks and work environment they had experienced.

In general, the American studies, which use more objective tests of knowledge and understanding compared with the British studies (which have tended to gather their data by the use of open-ended questions), are less sanguine about the effects of work experience in relation to this aim. Steinberg (1984), in summarizing the US material, concludes that although work experience probably does result in increased learning about the world of work, these learning gains are modest and weaken over time. Furthermore, he argued in an earlier survey that 'there is no conclusive evidence that information about the world of work cannot be as effectively transmitted through classroom interaction as through work experience' (Steinberg, 1982, p. 199). However, because work experience should not and often does not stand alone from classroom experience, this is something of a false dichotomy.

Very few studies have asked whether work experience has added to the pre-existing knowledge young people have of the world of work (see pp. 31–5). This is an important question in view of the amount of part-time work which students undertake outside school (see p. 71), and the fact that the typical tasks undertaken on work experience are often very similar to those in part-time employment (Steinberg, 1984). The answers to this question are not clear, partly one suspects because schools usually do not enquire what it is that students already know about the world of work before they go on work experience (see p. 176).

Another question which has interested evaluators on both sides of the Atlantic is the sort of picture or perspective on the world of work which students have formed as a result of work experience. In some ways this question is naive, in that the answers must depend on their pre-existing knowledge, the nature of their placement, and the cognitive framework or theoretical perspective which they brought to the experience. The question is usually set against the view that the dominant ideology which surrounds work experience is that students should learn to *adapt* to the demands of the work-place (see Shilling, 1989; Watkins, 1987).

What evidence we have shows that a significant number of students resist such adaptation on the basis of their experience of work. Jamieson and Lightfoot (1982) argue from their survey data that if anything students who had been on work experience tended to have a more negative view of industry and a less negative view of trade unions following their placements. Many students clearly recognized that the work-place was a 'contested terrain', where workers could and often did resist the managerial view of the world. Shilling (1989) argues that the criticisms that students had of the work-place 'were not confined to examples of personal authoritarianism and/or mistreatment they experienced, but were generalized to include features of the structural organization of the work-place into which they had been placed' (p. 163). The need to utilize this potential is strongly developed in the Australian literature on work experience (see pp. 49–50). There seem, however, to be few examples in Britain of teachers deliberately constructing a critical framework in which to view the work-place in work experience. SCIP and EcATT have stimulated some attention to such issues, and the growing attention to equal-opportunities (gender) issues in work experience (see pp. 202–5) is providing opportunities for more critical approaches to existing practices at work. But these remain exceptions rather than the rule.

Reflections on the Research Evidence

Most evaluations of work experience emphasize how *enjoyable* the experience was, and indeed there are few if any studies which do not confirm this overall view. A Project Trident survey of 252 young people found that 85 per cent thought that they had had a good experience (Black, 1976). In the School Council Industry Project survey, 83 per cent of the students had positive views on their experience (Jamieson and Lightfoot, 1982). In an evaluation of Scottish TVEI schemes, work experience emerged as the single most popular activity, although there was significant variation across the different projects (Bell *et al.*, 1988). Another interesting finding in the Scottish study was that girls tended to rate the experience more highly than boys, a finding supported by Jamieson and Lightfoot (1982). The English TVEI studies have confirmed the picture of high satisfaction ratings: Saunders (1987), for example, reported that over 90 per cent of students enjoyed the experience. The American evidence is also broadly consistent with these findings.

Although the evidence on satisfaction with work experience seems clear and uniform, it needs to be interpreted with some caution. It must be borne in mind that, for sound psychological reasons (Festinger, 1962), people tend in general to be predisposed to evaluate their experiences positively, as a way of justifying the time they have invested in them. Moreover, as Stronach and Weir (1980) point out, 'the same pupil-based evaluative criteria would never be applied, say, to the issue of longer school holidays' (p. 48). We have to face the possibility that students might well evaluate *any* time out of school more favourably than time in school. When one places this possibility against the reality of most work-experience tasks, it is difficult not to agree with Steinberg (1982) that 'it is a sad commentary on the state of secondary education (or on the values and tastes of adolescents) that dishwashing has become more appealing to some youngsters than school attendance' (pp. 189–90).

An evaluation that merely looks at student satisfaction/enjoyment of work experience would seem to be unduly simplistic. We need a model which systematically looks at the relationship between students, placements and the curriculum frame. Although we lack any studies of this sophistication, it is possible to begin to piece together what the findings of such a study might look like. It may be the case, following Kolb (1984), that some students possess cognitive structures which are less well suited to learning from experience.

Just how much students learn from work experience depends not only on their own capacities but also on the structure and organization of the work-place and the curricular frame within which they apprehend it. In general, Saunders (1987) argues that the characteristics of a 'good' work-experience placement contain the following features:

- Friendly, helpful colleagues who accept the student as 'one of us'.
- Work which is varied, containing many different aspects.
- Opportunities to 'cope' with other people, particularly adults, in a working environment.
- Opportunities to learn new 'skills' related to the work the student is required to do.

By contrast, Saunders argues that the 'single most important characteristic of a poor "work experience" was where the student was not involved in the routine work practice and was left to either make his/her own work or simply sit around doing nothing' (p. 162).

There are, however, exceptions to this view. Some students engaged in work-based projects, away from routine work, may also be satisfied with their experience. Shilling (1989) also argues that if students feel that they have learned something from the experience, imperfections in the placement itself can often be forgiven.

A further evaluation equation is the curriculum frame placed round the experience. This frame, and especially its organization, provides the key to a successful work experience for HMI. They argue that the key elements are:

- a policy for all work-related activity in which work experience is part of a progression of linked experiences;
- a scheme where the experiences are shared by all concerned through good community links and effective student briefing and staff preparation;
- a strategy for debriefing and follow-up which enables the experience to be extended to its full potential and through understanding become an integral part of a student's school and college experience (HMI, 1990, p. 19).

We have seen that the careers-education frame is the most common in the UK, and that there is some evidence to suggest that its expansive, sampling and anticipatory aims are achieved for some students. The evidence for the personal and social education frame is more difficult to assess: given the nature of many work-experience placements, the claims that they will develop personal competence seem on the face of it unlikely, although these claims may be rescued by the discontinuity thesis which argues that people have the potential to grow and develop when faced with an unfamiliar environment. The world-of-work frame makes strong claims, but the over-all evidence of fulfilment does not look strong unless the placement experi-ence is strongly backed up by classroom work. The academic-subjects frame is supported by school work by definition: although there is not much evidence to suggest that this framing is common, it is growing, and what evidence we have suggests good learning gains. Finally, we have concluded that the preparatory aim of work experience has only been adopted in the post-16 curriculum in the context of vocational courses.

Self-evaluation

The preceding sections on the evaluation of work experience have been based on the work of the evaluation research community. It is traditional to contrast these types of studies with the judgments of practising teachers, and with the evaluations carried out by teachers themselves. In fact, these two groups are not so far apart and arguably are moving ever closer together. In the first place, as we have seen, an important part of the research data on work experience is drawn from teachers' perceptions of its effects. Secondly, teachers themselves are increasingly being encouraged to make evaluation an integral part of their portfolio of professional skills. An important incentive has come from TVEI, which has insisted on evaluation of its programmes. More recently, the advent of the National Curriculum has forced all schools to review the effectiveness of their curriculum, and the Education Reform Act of 1988 has placed upon schools certain requirements to report both on what they are doing and on how effectively they are doing it. There was a time when much of this evaluation would have been left to professional evaluators working out of higher education, but the sheer scale and expense of this model has tended increasingly to rule it out. Furthermore, the com-munity of evaluators has itself become keener to champion self-evaluation models: this is particularly true of those evaluators who are wedded to the illuminative paradigm of educational evaluation, and those who are associ-ated with action-research models or with the teacher–researcher movement (e.g. Elliott, 1985; Hustler, Cassidy and Giff, 1986; Kemmis, 1985; McNiff, 1988).

A traditional model of evaluation compares the *intentions* of the work-experience programme with its *outcomes*. This is based on Stake's (1967) 'countenance' model of evaluation, which is shown diagrammatically in Box 14.1. Evaluation based on the model begins by attempting to tease out the logical relationships between the key features or stages of work experience. *Inputs* refer to the preparation and briefing, the training and allocation of teachers to set up the work experience, and any curricular frame that might

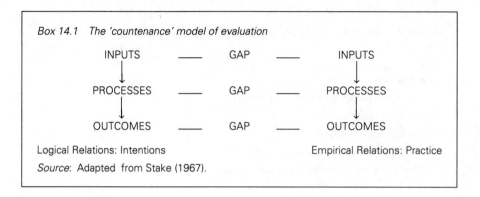

Box 14.1 The 'countenance' model of evaluation

INPUTS	——	GAP	——	INPUTS
PROCESSES	——	GAP	——	PROCESSES
OUTCOMES	——	GAP	——	OUTCOMES

Logical Relations: Intentions   Empirical Relations: Practice

Source: Adapted from Stake (1967).

be used. The *process* refers to what is transacted between the student and the task environment at the work-place. Finally, the *outcomes* focus on the learning gains or other effects of the scheme. This raises again the dilemma noted earlier (p. 260): whether to look for outcomes just from the placement or from the total scheme including preparation, briefing, debriefing and follow-up. Essentially the first part of the evaluation examines the line of reasoning embedded in the scheme, which might be written like this: 'why should these inputs lead to those processes on the placement, and why should those processes produce these outcomes?'. The final part of the evaluation is to study what happened in the work-experience programme, and in particular to see if there was any *gap*, as there almost always is, between intention and practice. The gaps can be examined at all three stages — input, process and outcome. The biggest practical difficulty with this model is that it assumes that the intentions of those who organize work experience are clear and explicit, whereas — as we have seen — this is often far from the case. Teachers frequently load up work experience with a great variety of different aims which make systematic evaluation difficult, or they unwittingly subscribe to the 'miracle' model of work experience (Jamieson, 1983) whereby the experience itself is supposed to have magical effects on the student's knowledge, skills and attitudes. Where such a model is *de facto* in place, the only appropriate evaluation methodology would appear to be a goal-free one (Scriven, 1977) which examines outcomes without any pre-specified view of what to look for.

Recently it has become fashionable to construct performance indicators in education as an aid to measuring activities, and these have begun to make their appearance in the evaluation of work experience. The idea behind performance indicators is very straightforward and is certainly not new in evaluation. In the first place, performance indicators are about *performance*, i.e. observable features of the work-experience process. Secondly, it is important to stress that they are *indicators*: that is, they tell us something of what is going on but by no means the whole story. Following CIPFA (1984), we might usefully see them as *markers*, giving us a view of where we are at the

Ian Jamieson

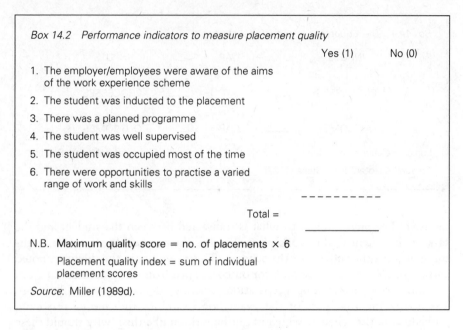

Box 14.2   Performance indicators to measure placement quality

	Yes (1)	No (0)
1. The employer/employees were aware of the aims of the work experience scheme		
2. The student was inducted to the placement		
3. There was a planned programme		
4. The student was well supervised		
5. The student was occupied most of the time		
6. There were opportunities to practise a varied range of work and skills		

Total =

N.B. Maximum quality score = no. of placements × 6

Placement quality index = sum of individual placement scores

Source: Miller (1989d).

moment, and as *signposts* to further questions about what still needs to be achieved.

An interesting example of the potential use of performance indicators in evaluating work experience is shown in Box 14.2 (the list provided the basis for the teacher visit report form shown earlier in Box 12.7 on p. 223). These indicators concentrate on processes at the work-place, with teacher evaluators being invited to score certain features of the placement. The example is of particular interest because it is an example of process indicators, whereas most performance indicators concentrate on the outcomes of the experience. Process indicators — that is, indicators which show whether the appropriate processes have been transacted at various stages — are particularly valuable in activities like work experience, where immediate outcomes are difficult to observe and evaluate.

Most teachers' evaluations of work experience have not embraced the use of performance indicators: their work is understandably much more basic. Many teachers begin evaluation by using some version of the 5WH check-list:

- WHY do I wish to evaluate work experience?
- WHO should I involve in the evaluation?
- WHAT precisely should I be evaluating?
- WHERE should I carry out the evaluation?
- WHEN should I do the evaluation?
- HOW should I do the evaluation?

The *why* questions relate both to the purposes of work experience and to the audience for the evaluation. Evaluators are often faced with a dilemma as to whether they are undertaking the evaluation for accountability purposes (justifying the activity to sponsors or those who control it), or in order to improve the experience. In practice, it is often difficult to sew these two rationales together.

The *who* question has two sides to it. Firstly, it involves deciding who to involve in the collection of information. Teachers are the most obvious evaluators, but several schemes use students to collect some of the information. The other side of the question is who to collect information from. The most likely groups are students, teachers, employers and parents.

The *what* question is the pivotal part of any evaluation exercise. Teachers as evaluators need to be clear about what it is they are looking at. Much of this should be derived from the stated aims and objectives of the work-experience programme, and/or it might focus on those features of the work experience which appear to be problematic. Most school-based evaluations look at the student's experience whilst at work and attempt to gauge the student's estimation of this experience. This is often extended to cover the employers' perspective.

The question of *where* the evaluation should be carried out can be an important issue for work experience and is closely related to the *when* question. The key issues here are whether to build an evaluation element into the work experience itself — for example, as part of the student logbook or diary, or as part of the employer's student assessment — or whether to mount a separate exercise at the end of the placement, perhaps as part of the debriefing cycle. Because the work-experience cycle takes place both in school (preparation, briefing, debriefing and follow-up) as well as in the work-place, teachers also have to decide whether to conduct the evaluation there or back in the classroom, or in both locations.

Finally, there is the *how* question of choosing between the methods of evaluation open to potential evaluators. These methods tend to mirror the ordinary research methods of educational research, although some are more commonly used than others. A list of methods commonly used is reproduced in Box 14.3.

Of course, it is not always necessary to collect information separately for evaluation purposes. A great deal of relevant material is often already available to evaluators. This can include student diaries/reports/logs, staff visit reports, employers' reports, and relevant student classroom work. This material is most commonly supplemented by questionnaires to the various participants (most commonly students and employers), and by group discussions with students as part of the general debriefing procedure.

Another model of evaluation is becoming increasingly popular in schools as a result of developments in the teacher-as-researcher movement. This model is that of action research and draws heavily on the work of Lewin

Box 14.3 Strategies and techniques of data gathering			
Technique	Advantage(s)	Disadvantage(s)	Use(s)
Field Notes	simple; ongoing; personal; aide memoire	subjective; needs practice	• specific issue • case study • general impression
Audio Tape Recording	versatile; accurate; provides ample data	transcription difficult; time consuming; often inhibiting	• detailed evidence • diagnostic
Pupil Diaries	provides pupil perspective	subjective	• diagnostic • triangulation
Interviews and Discussions	can be teacher–pupil, observer–pupil, pupil–pupil	time consuming	• specific in-depth information
Video Tape Recorder	visual and comprehensive	awkward and expensive; can be distracting	• visual material • diagnostic
Questionnaires	highly specific; easy to administer; comparative	time consuming to analyse; problem of 'right' answers	• specific information and feedback
Sociometry	easy to administer; provides guide to action	can threaten isolated pupils	• analyses social relationships
Documentary Evidence	illuminative	difficult to obtain; time consuming	• provides context and information
Slide/Tape Photography	illuminative; promotes discussion	difficult to obtain; superficial	• illustrates critical incidents
Case Study	accurate; representative; uses range of techniques	time consuming	• comprehensive overview of an issue • publishable format

Source: McNiff (1988).

(1951). Action research begins with a question or a problem facing the teacher and proceeds to test out various hypotheses about solutions to the problem by a series of action–research cycles (see Boxes 14.4 and 14.5).

Concluding Comments

Although it is often the case that traditional educational research has had little to offer practising teachers, we do not believe that this is the case with work experience. As we have already pointed out, there is remarkably little

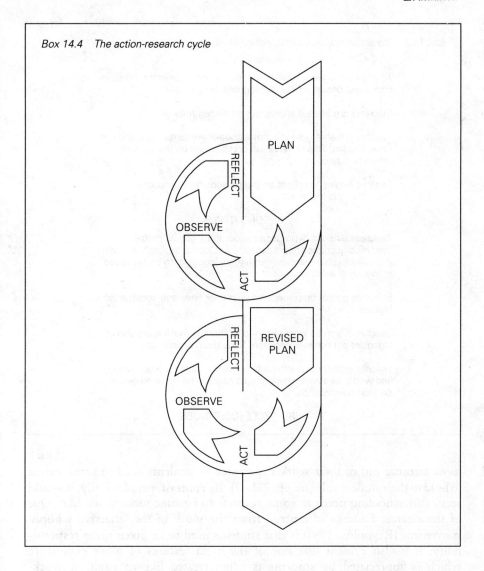

Box 14.4   The action-research cycle

research on work experience which operates with anything like an adequate research design, and there is far too much questionnaire research which goes little beyond eliciting the general satisfaction or otherwise of students with their placements.

Despite these failings, we believe that there is enough evidence, both from researchers and from teachers as researchers, to support the contention that work experience can be a potent source of learning in a number of different areas. It is not, however, a magical remedy for some of the ills of the modern school curriculum. It will only deliver if it is carefully prepared for and followed up. In this respect, we have already noted that — to get the

---

Box 14.5   *The action-research cycle applied to work experience*

FIRST CYCLE

Teacher plans work experience with a world-of-work curriculum frame and designs a student logbook accordingly.

↓

Students are briefed and go out on placements.

↓

Teacher observes on visit that logbooks are rarely used and not often filled in. This observation is confirmed on the students' return to school.

↓

Teacher begins to reflect on the reasons for the apparent 'failure' of the logbooks.

↓

SECOND CYCLE

Teacher develops hypotheses about the logbook 'problem'. Two modifications are proposed: (a) students to construct own logbooks to give them ownership; (b) logbooks to be assessed in follow-up lessons.

↓

Students go out on placement with their new 'self-constructed logbooks'.

↓

Teacher observes logbooks in use. There is much more use of logbooks but not every student finds them appropriate.

↓

Teacher reflects that although self-construction is a good idea and works for some, there should perhaps be more guidance on their construction.

↓

THIRD CYCLE (CONTINUES)

---

most learning out of their work experience — students need to some extent to hold to their student role (see pp. 261–2). By contrast, paradoxically, it would seem that schooling needs in some respects to become more work-like. One of the clearest findings to emerge from the work of the 'effective schools' movement (Reynolds, 1985) is that students need to be given more responsibility; it is also evident that one of the main features of work experience which is appreciated by students is being treated like an adult. If work-experience schemes can help schools to change in such ways, their educational potential will have been richly fulfilled.

Bibliography

AGNEW, D. (1985) *Breaking the Mould: Equal Opportunity Initiatives and Careers Education*, Manchester, Equal Opportunities Commission.

ALDEN, J. (1981) 'Holding Two Jobs: An Examination of "Moonlighting"', in HENRY, S. (Ed.) *Can I Have It in Cash?: A Study of Informal Institutions and Unorthodox Ways of Doing Things*, London, Astragal.

ALLEN, J.A. (1988) 'Work-Related Experience as a Focus for Curriculum Development', *SCIP News*, 22, Winter.

ALLEN, J. (1989) *Industry Month at Ifield*, West Sussex, Ifield Community College, mimeo.

ARGYRIS, C. (1964) *Integrating the Individual and the Organization*, New York, Wiley.

ASHTON, D.N. (1986) *Unemployment under Capitalism: The Sociology of British and American Labour Markets*, Brighton, Wheatsheaf.

ASHTON, D.N. and MAGUIRE, M.J. (1986) *Young Adults in the Labour Market*, Department of Employment Research Paper No. 55, London, HMSO.

ASHTON, D.N., MAGUIRE, M.J. and SPILSBURY, M. (1987) 'Labour Market Segmentation and the Structure of the Youth Labour Market', in BROWN, P. and ASHTON, D.N. (Eds) *Education, Unemployment and Labour Markets*, London, Falmer Press.

ASSISTANT MASTERS AND MISTRESSES ASSOCIATION (1988) *Making the Most of Work Experience*, London, AMMA.

BABBAGE, C. (1971) *On the Economy of Machinery and Manufactures*, Fairfield, NJ, Kelley (first published 1835).

BALL, B. and GORDON, A. (1985) *Employer Liaison with Schools*, IMS Report No. 108, Falmer, Sussex, Institute of Manpower Studies, University of Sussex.

BARNES, D., JOHNSON, G. and JORDAN, S. (1988) *Work Experience in TVEI: 14–16*, Sheffield, Training Agency.

BARNES, D., JOHNSON, G. and JORDAN, S. (1989) *Work Experience in TVEI: 16–18*, Sheffield, Training Agency.

BARNES, D., JOHNSON, G., JORDAN, S., LAYTON, D., MEDWAY, P. and YEO-

MANS, D. (1987) *The TVEI Curriculum 14–16*. Leeds, School of Education, University of Leeds.

BARNES, D., JOHNSON, G., JORDAN, S., LAYTON, D., MEDWAY P. and YEO-MANS, D. (1988) *A Second Report on the TVEI Curriculum: Courses for 14–16 Year-Olds in Twenty-Six Schools*, Sheffield, Training Agency.

BARRETT, M. and MACINTOSH, M. (1980) 'The Family Wage: Some Problems for Socialists and Feminists', *Capital and Class*, 11.

BARRY, M. (1985–86) 'Taskweek, July 1985', *View*, 26, Winter.

BATES, I. (1984) 'From Vocational Guidance to Life Skills: Historical Perspectives on Careers Education', in BATES, I., *et al.* (Eds) *Schooling for the Dole?: The New Vocationalism*, London, Macmillan.

BATES, I., CLARKE, J., COHEN, P., FINN, D., MOORE, R. and WILLIS, P. (1984) *Schooling for the Dole?: The New Vocationalism*, London, Macmillan.

BATES, R.C. (1989) 'The Management of Work Experience', MSc dissertation, University of Reading.

BAXTER, A. (1988) '"Their Fault or Ours?": The Contraction of Work and the "Radicalization" of Young People', *British Journal of Education and Work*, 2, 1.

BELL, C., HOWIESON, C., KING, K. and RAFFE, D. (1988) *Liaisons Dangereuses? Education-Industry Relationships in the First Scottish TVEI Pilot Projects*, Edinburgh, Centre for Educational Sociology, University of Edinburgh.

BENNET, J. (1983) 'Work Visits', in WATTS, A.G. (Ed.) *Work Experience and Schools*, London, Heinemann.

BERKELEY, J. (1988) 'A Better Pay-Off from Work Experience', *Personnel Management*, April.

BERKELEY, J., BRAHAM, J. and MILLER, A.D. (1990) *Towards Quality Work Experience*, Coventry, School Curriculum Industry Partnership.

BERNSTEIN, B. (1975) 'On the Classification and Framing of Educational Knowledge', in BERNSTEIN, B. (Ed.) *Class, Codes and Control*, Volume 1, London, Routledge & Kegan Paul.

BLACK, D. (1976) 'Work Experience: A Systematic Approach', *British Journal of Guidance and Counselling*, 4, 1.

BLOOMER, R.G. and SCOTT, W.H. (1987) 'Linking Industry and Teacher Education: How Do Student Teachers Benefit?', *British Journal of Education and Work*, 1, 2.

BLUM, L. (1985) 'Fidel's Other Revolution', *Times Educational Supplement*, 22 November.

BLYTH, A., COOPER, K., DERRICOTT, R., ELLIOTT, G., SUMNER, H. and WAPLINGTON, A. (1976) *Place, Time and Society 8–13: Curriculum Planning in History, Geography and Social Science*, London, Schools Council.

BOLTON COMMITTEE (1971) *Small Firms*, London, HMSO.

BOSANQUET, N. and BOERINGER, P.B. (1973) 'Is There a Dual Labour Market in Great Britain?', *Economic Journal*, 83.

BOUD, D., KEOGH, R. and WALKER, D. (1985) (Eds) *Reflection: Turning Experience into Learning*, London, Kogan Page.

BOYDELL, T. (1976) *Experiential Learning*, Manchester Monographs, 5, Manchester Department of Adult and Higher Education, University of Manchester.

BRANDES, D. and GINNIS, P. (1986) *A Guide to Student Centred Learning*, Oxford, Blackwell.

BRAVERMAN, H. (1974) *Labor and Monopoly Capital*, New York, Monthly Review Press.

BREAKWELL, G. and WEINBERGER, B. (1987) *Young Women in Gender Atypical Jobs*, Department of Employment Research Paper, 49, London, HMSO.

BROADFOOT, P. (1982) 'Alternatives to Public Examinations', *Educational Analysis*, 4, 2.

BRONFENBRENNER, U. (1979) *The Ecology of Human Development*, Cambridge, Mass., Harvard University Press.

BROWN, R.K. (1984) 'Work', in ABRAMS, P. and BROWN, R. (Eds) *UK Society: Work, Urbanism and Inequality*, London, Weidenfeld and Nicolson.

BURGESS, T. and ADAMS, E. (1980) (Eds) *Outcomes of Education*, London, Macmillan.

CARNEY, M. and TURNER, D. (1987) *Education for Enterprise*, Mirfield, West Yorkshire, Osmosis.

CASTLES, S. and WÜSTENBERG, W. (1979) *The Education of the Future*, London, Pluto.

CATTELL, D. (1989) 'Work Experience and Humanities', *SCIP News*, 24, Summer.

CENTRAL ADVISORY COUNCIL FOR EDUCATION (1963) *Half Our Future* (Newsom Report), London, HMSO.

CENTRAL STATISTICAL OFFICE (1983) *Annual Abstract of Statistics*, London, HMSO.

CENTRAL STATISTICAL OFFICE (1989) *Social Trends 19*, London, HMSO.

CHAMBERS, J.D. (1968) *The Workshop of the World*, Oxford, Oxford University Press.

CHAMBERS, J. (1987) 'Equal Opportunities in TVEI Theory and Practice', in *TVEI Developments 2: Equal Opportunities*, London, Manpower Services Commission.

CHARTERED INSTITUTE OF PUBLIC FINANCE AND ACCOUNTANCY (1984) *Performance Indicators in the Education Service*, London, CIPFA.

CLARKE, E. (1985) *The Renfrew Experience Based Learning Project 1983–1985: Pupils at Work in the Community*, Glasgow, Vocational Initiatives Unit, University of Glasgow (mimeo).

CLOSS, S.J. (1986) 'Current and Future Development of the JIIG-CAL System', *British Journal of Guidance and Counselling*, 14, 1, January.

COCKBURN, C. (1986) *Training for Her Job and for His*, Manchester, Equal Opportunities Commission.

COLE, P. (1979) *Work Experience: An Australian Perspective*, Melbourne, Victoria Education Department.

COLE, P. (1983) 'Work-Experience Schemes in Schools: Some Suggestions for Program Reorientation', *Discourse*, **3**, 2, April.

COLE, P. (1987) *Revealing Work: Some Program Possibilities*, Canberra, Curriculum Development Centre.

COLEMAN, J.S. (1972) 'How Do The Young Become Adults?', *Review of Educational Research,* **42**, 4, Fall.

COMMUNITY SERVICE VOLUNTEERS (1987) *Learning in the Community: A Teachers' Handbook*, London, CSV.

CONFEDERATION OF BRITISH INDUSTRY (1988) *Building a Stronger Partnership between Business and Secondary Education*, London, CBI.

CONRAD, D. and HEDIN, D. (1981) 'The Impact of Experiential Education on Adolescent Development', *Child and Youth Services Journal*, **4**, 3/4.

COPE, S.G. (1983) 'Work Experience: A Local Authority Approach', in WATTS, A.G. (Ed.) *Work Experience in Schools*, London, Heinemann.

COURTENAY, G. (1988) *England and Wales Youth Cohort Study: Report on Cohort 1 Sweep 1*, Sheffield, Manpower Services Commission.

CREIGH, S., ROBERTS, C., GORMAN, A. and SAWYER, P. (1986) 'Self Employment in Britain: Results from the Labour Force Survey 1981–4', *Employment Gazette*, **94**, June.

CROWE, M.R. and ADAMS, K.A. (1979) *The Current Status of Assessing Experiential Programs*, Columbus, Ohio, National Center for Research in Vocational Education.

CUMMING, J. (1988) 'Curriculum Costs: Vocational Subjects', in LAUGLO, J. and LILLIS, K. (Eds) *Vocational Education: An International Perspective*, Oxford, Pergamon.

CURRAN, J. (1986) *Bolton Fifteen Years On: A Review and Analysis of Small Business Research in Britain 1971–1986*, London, Small Business Research Trust.

CURRAN, J., BURROWS, R. and EVANDROU, M. (1987) *Small Business Owners and the Self Employed in Britain*, London, Small Business Research Trust.

CURRAN, J. and STANWORTH, J. (1982) 'The Small Firm in Britain: Past, Present and Future' *International Small Business Journal*, **1**, 1.

CURTHOYS, A. (1987) *Women and Work*, Canberra, Curriculum Development Centre.

DALE, R. (1985) 'The Background and Inception of the Technical and Vocational Education Initiative', in DALE, R. (Ed.) *Education, Training and Employment: Towards a New Vocationalism?*, Oxford, Pergamon.

D'AMICO, R. (1984) 'Does Employment during High School Impair Academic Progress?', *Sociology of Education*, **57**, 3.

DAVIES, E. (1972) 'Work Out of School', *Education*, **140**, 19, 10 November.

DE MULDER, J. (n.d.) 'Narrowing the Gap between School and Society: Work Experience Learning, a Method in the Making', Amsterdam, Stichting

Centrum voor Onderwijsonderzoek, University of Amsterdam (mimeo).

DEPARTMENT OF EDUCATION AND SCIENCE (1974) *Work Experience*, Circular 7/74, London, DES.

DEPARTMENT OF EDUCATION AND SCIENCE (1979a) *Local Authority Arrangements for the School Curriculum*, London, HMSO.

DEPARTMENT OF EDUCATION AND SCIENCE (1979b) *Aspects of Secondary Education in England*, London, HMSO.

DEPARTMENT OF EDUCATION AND SCIENCE (1984) *Records of Achievement: A Statement of Policy*, London, DES.

DEPARTMENT OF EDUCATION AND SCIENCE (1985) *Better Schools*, London, HMSO.

DEPARTMENT OF EDUCATION AND SCIENCE (1987) *Survey of School/Industry Links in Industry Year 1986*, Statistical Bulletin 12/87, London, DES.

DEPARTMENT OF EDUCATION AND SCIENCE (1988a) *Education at Work: A Guide for Schools*, London, HMSO.

DEPARTMENT OF EDUCATION AND SCIENCE (1988b) *Education at Work: A Guide for Employers*, London, DES.

DEPARTMENT OF EDUCATION AND SCIENCE (1988c) *Task Group on Assessment and Testing: Report*, London, DES.

DEPARTMENT OF EDUCATION AND SCIENCE (1988d) *Report on Developments in Records of Achievement 1986–1988*, London, DES.

DEPARTMENT OF EDUCATION AND SCIENCE (1989) *The Work-Related Curriculum: A Paper for Discussion*, Report of Working Group on Work-Related Activities in Design and Technology, London, DES (mimeo).

DEPARTMENT OF EDUCATION AND SCIENCE (1990a) *Technology in the National Curriculum*, London, HMSO.

DEPARTMENT OF EDUCATION AND SCIENCE (1990b) *Survey of School Industry Links*, Statistical Bulletin 10/90, London, DES.

DEPARTMENT OF EMPLOYMENT (1988) *Employment for the 1990s*, London, HMSO.

DEPARTMENT OF TRADE AND INDUSTRY (1988) *The Enterprise Initiative*, London, HMSO.

DEWEY, J. (1963) *Experience and Education*, New York, Collier.

DEX, S. (1985) *The Sexual Division of Work*, Brighton, Wheatsheaf.

DEX, S. (1988) 'Gender and the Labour Market', in GALLIE, D. (Ed.) *Employment in Britain*, Oxford, Blackwell.

DOERINGER, P.B. and PIORE, M.J. (1971) *Internal Labor Market and Manpower Analysis*, Lexington, Mass., Heath.

DORE, R. (1976) *The Diploma Disease*, London, Allen & Unwin.

EGGLESTON, J., DUNN, D. and ANJALI, M. (1986) *Education for Some*, Stoke-on-Trent, Trentham.

ELLIOTT, J. (1985) 'Educational Action Research', in NISBET, J., MEGARRY, J. and NISBET, S. (Eds) *World Yearbook of Education 1985: Research, Policy and Practice*, London, Kogan Page.

ELSOM, D. (1987) 'The Development of Schools/Industry Links in the Cambridge Education Area Set in its LEA and National Context', MPhil thesis, Department of Social Policy, Cranfield Institute of Technology.

ENGINEERING INDUSTRY TRAINING BOARD (1981) *Work Experience Guide*, Watford, EITB.

EQUAL OPPORTUNITIES COMMISSION (1983) *Women and Trade Unions: A Survey*, Manchester, EOC.

EQUAL OPPORTUNITIES COMMISSION (1984) *Annual Report 1983*, Manchester, EOC.

EUROPEAN WORK EXPERIENCE PROJECT (1989) *European Work Experience Resource Pack*, Sheffield, Training Agency.

EVANS, K., BROWN, A. and BATES, T. (1987) *Developing Work-Based Learning: An Evaluation Review of the YTS Core Skills Project*, MSC Research and Development Series No. 39, Sheffield, MSC.

FESTINGER, L. (1962) *A Theory of Cognitive Dissonance*, Stanford, CA., Stanford University Press.

FIEHN, J. (1989) 'The Place of Personal and Social Education in the Curriculum', in *Whole Person: Whole School — Bridging the Academic/Pastoral Divide*, York, Longman for the School Curriculum Development Committee.

FIEHN, J. and MILLER, A.D. (1989) *Gainful Employment: Confidence Building Activities for Work-Experience Preparation*, London, SCIP.

FINEGOLD, D., KEEP, E., MILIBAND, D., RAFFE, D., SPOURS, K. and YOUNG, M. (1990) *A British Baccalauréat*, Education and Training Paper No. 1, London, Institute for Public Policy Research.

FINN, D. (1984) 'Leaving School and Growing Up: Work Experience in the Juvenile Labour Market', in BATES, I., CLARKE, J., COHEN, P., FINN, D., MOORE, R. and WILLIS, P. *Schooling for the Dole?: The New Vocationalism*, London, Macmillan.

FITZGERALD, K. and BODILEY, J. (1984) *Work Experience: A Study of a School-Operated Scheme*, York, Longman for the Schools Council.

FLOCKHART, A. (1988) 'East Side Story', *Employment Initiatives*, **5**, 3, June.

FORTUNE, J., JAMIESON, I.M. and STREET, H. (1983) 'Relating Work Experience to the Curriculum', in WATTS, A.G. (Ed.) *Work Experience and Schools*, London, Heinemann.

FOX, A. (1974) *Beyond Contract: Work, Power and Trust Relations*, London, Faber.

FULLER, A. (1987) *Post-16 Work Experience in TVEI*, Lancaster, Institute for Research and Development in Post-Compulsory Education, University of Lancaster (mimeo).

FURTHER EDUCATION UNIT (1985) *CPVE in Action*, London, FEU.

GERSHUNY, J.I. (1978) *After Industrial Society*, London, Macmillan.

GERSHUNY, J.I. (1986) 'Time Use, Technology and the Future of Work', *Journal of the Market Research Society*, **28**, 4, October.

GERSHUNY, J.I. (1987) 'The Leisure Principle', *New Society*, 1259, 13 February.

GERSHUNY, J.I. and JONES, S. (1987) 'The Changing Work/Leisure Balance in Britain 1961–84', *Sociological Review Monograph*, **33**, January.

GERSHUNY, J.I. and PAHL, R.E. (1979/80) 'Work Outside Employment: Some Preliminary Speculations', *New Universities Quarterly*, **34**, 1, Winter.

GERSHUNY, J.I. and PAHL, R.E. (1980) 'Britain in the Decade of the Three Economies', *New Society*, 900, 3 January.

GIBB, A.A. (1987) 'Enterprise Culture — its Meaning and Implications for Education and Training', *Journal of European Industrial Training*, **11**, 2.

GIDDENS, A. (1981) *A Critique of Historical Materialism*, London, Macmillan.

GOODNOW, J.J. (1988) 'Children's Household Work: Its Nature and Functions', *Psychological Bulletin*, **103**, 1, January.

GRANT, N. (1982) 'Work Experience in Soviet and East European Schools', in EGGLESTON, J. (Ed.) *Work Experience in Secondary Schools*, London, Routledge & Kegan Paul.

GREGORY, D. and REES, T.L. (1980) *The Work Experience Programme: A Case-Study Evaluation from South Wales*, London, Manpower Services Commission.

GRUBB INSTITUTE (1986) *Learning from Working*, London, Grubb Institute.

HAKIM, C. (1984) 'Homework and Outwork: National Estimates from Two Surveys', *Employment Gazette*, **92**, 1.

HAMILTON, S.F. and CROUTER, A.C. (1980) 'Work and Growth: A Review of Research on the Impact of Work Experience on Adolescent Development', *Journal of Youth and Adolescence*, **9**, 4.

HANDY, C. (1984) *The Future of Work*, London, Blackwell.

HANDY, C. (1989) *The Age of Unreason*, London, Business Books.

HARGREAVES, A., BAGLIN E., HENDERSON, P., LEESON, P. and TOSSELL, L.T. (1988) *Personal and Social Education: Choices and Challenges*, Oxford, Blackwell.

HARTLEY, C.K. (1982) 'British Industrialization before 1841: Evidence of Slower Growth during the Industrial Revolution', *Journal of Economic History*, **42**, 2.

HARTMANN, H. (1976) 'Capitalism, Patriarchy, and Job Segregation by Sex', in BLAXALL, M. (Ed.) *Women in the Workplace*, Chicago, University of Chicago Press.

HER MAJESTY'S INSPECTORATE (1983) *A Survey of Work Experience for Year V Pupils*, Cardiff, Welsh Office.

HER MAJESTY'S INSPECTORATE (1983) *A Survey of the Lower Attaining Pupils' Programme — the First Two Years*, London, Department of Education and Science.

HER MAJESTY'S INSPECTORATE (1988a) *Careers Education and Guidance from 5 to 16*, Curriculum Matters 10, London, HMSO.

HER MAJESTY'S INSPECTORATE (1988b) *Secondary Schools: An Appraisal by HMI*, London, HMSO.

HER MAJESTY'S INSPECTORATE (1989a) *The Curriculum from 5 to 16* (2nd edition), Curriculum Matters 2, London, HMSO.

HER MAJESTY'S INSPECTORATE (1989b) *Work-Based Learning in Colleges of Further Education: A Survey of Learning in College Restaurants, Kitchens, Hairdressing Salons, Training Offices and Farms*, London, Department of Education and Science.

HER MAJESTY'S INSPECTORATE (1990) *Work Experience and Work Shadowing for 14–19 Students: Some Aspects of Good Practice 1988/1989*, London, Department of Education and Science.

HERZBERG, F. (1966) *Work and the Nature of Men*, New York, World Publishing.

HODGE, S. (1987) 'Work Experience — Employer's Viewpoints', Unpublished paper, Department of Education, University of Warwick (mimeo).

HOGG, G.C. (1976) 'Work Experience', in *Guidelines*, Institute of Careers Officers (Scottish Branch).

HOLBECKE, L. (1989) 'Work Experience in France, 1987–88', Certificate in Industry and Curriculum Change Case-study, Roehampton Institutue of Higher Education, London, SCIP (mimeo).

HOLMES, S., JAMIESON, I. and PERRY, J. (1983) *Work Experience in the School Curriculum*, London, Schools Council/Trident Trust.

HOLT, M. (1987) (Ed.) *Skill and Vocationalism: The Easy Answer*, Milton Keynes, Open University Press.

HOPE HIGH SCHOOL (1989) *Case Study Submission for Rover Quality in Work Experience Award 1990*, Salford, Hope High School (mimeo).

HOPKINS, D. (1990) (Ed.) *TVEI at the Change of Life*, Clevedon, Multilingual Matters.

HOYT, K., EVANS, R., MANGUM, G., BOWEN, E. and GALE, D. (1977) *Career Education in the High School*, Salt Lake City, Utah, Olympus.

HUMPHRIES, J. (1977) 'The Working Class Family, Women's Liberation and Class Struggle: The Case of Nineteenth Century British History', *Review of Radical Political Economics*, **9**.

HURT, J. (1981) (Ed.) *Children, Youth and Education in the Late Nineteenth Century*, Leicester, History of Education Society.

HUSTLER, D., CASSIDY, T. and GIFF, T. (1986) (Eds) *Action Research in Classrooms and Schools*, Oxford, Oxford University Press.

IFAPLAN (1986) *The World of Work as a Learning Resource*, Brussels, IFAPLAN.

IFAPLAN (1987) *Guidance and the School*, Brussels, IFAPLAN.

IFAPLAN (1988) *The Leading Edge: A Review of the Growth of School-Industry Partnership in the European Community*, Brussels, IFAPLAN.

INCOMES DATA SERVICES (1990) *Industry Links with Schools*, IDS Study No. 456, London, IDS.

Inglehart, R. (1977) *The Silent Revolution*, Princeton, Princeton University Press.

INSTITUTE OF CAREERS OFFICERS (1974) *Work Experience in British Secondary Schools* (2nd edition), Stourbridge, ICO.

INSTITUTE OF PERSONNEL MANAGEMENT (1988) *Improving Work Experience: A Statement of Principles*, London, IPM.

JAMIESON, I.M. (1983) 'Miracles and Mirages? Some Elements of Pupil Work Experience', *British Journal of Guidance and Counselling*, **11**, 2.

JAMIESON, I.M. (1985) 'Corporate Hegemony or Pedagogic Liberation?: The Schools-Industry Movement in England and Wales', in DALE, R. (Ed.) *Education, Training and Employment: Towards a New Vocationalism?*, Oxford, Open University/Pergamon.

JAMIESON, I.M. and LIGHTFOOT, M. (1982) *Schools and Industry*, London, Methuen.

JAMIESON, I.M. and TASKER, M. (1988) 'Schooling and New Technology: Rhetoric and Reality', in *World Yearbook of Education*, London, Kogan Page.

JAMIESON, I.M., MILLER, A.D. and WATTS, A.G. (1988) *Mirrors of Work: Work Simulations in Schools*, London, Falmer Press.

JAMIESON, I.M., NEWMAN, B. and PEFFERS, J. (1986) *Work Experience Workbooks: A Critical Review*, York, Longman for the School Curriculum Development Committee.

JOHNS, A. (1987) *Work Experience 'Within the Spirit of the Law'* (draft), Published privately.

JOINT BOARD FOR PRE-VOCATIONAL EDUCATION (1985) *The Certificate of Pre-Vocational Education Handbook*, London, JBPVE.

JONES, B. (1982) *Sleepers Awake! Technology and the Future of Work*, Melbourne, Oxford University Press.

JONES, B. and SCOTT, P. (1987) 'FMS in Britain and the USA', *New Technology and Work Environment*, **2**, 1.

JONES, K. (1988) *Interactive Learning Events: A Guide for Facilitators*, London, Kogan Page.

KAESTLE, C.F. (1976) 'Between the Scylla of Brutal Ignorance and the Charybdis of a Literary Education: Elite Attitudes towards Mass Schooling in Early Industrial England and America', in STONE, L. (Ed.) *Schooling and Society: Studies in the History of Education*, Baltimore, Johns Hopkins University Press.

KEMMIS, S. (1985) 'Action Research', in HUSEN, T. and POSTLETHWAITE, T. *(Eds) International Encyclopedia of Education*, Volume 1, Oxford, Pergamon.

KEMMIS, S., COLE, P. and SUGGETT, D. (1983) *Orientation to Curriculum and Transition: Towards the Socially-Critical School*, Melbourne, Victorian Institute of Secondary Education.

KERRY, J. (1983) 'Work Experience: The Project Trident Approach', in WATTS, A.G. (Ed.) *Work Experience in Schools*, London, Heinemann.

KIM, L. (1979) 'Widened Admission to Higher Education in Sweden (the 25/5 Scheme)', *European Journal of Education*, **14**, 2.

KIRTON, M. (1976) *Career Knowledge of Sixth Form Boys*, Sheffield, COIC.

KOLB, D.A. (1984) *Experiential Learning*, Englewood Cliffs, NJ Prentice-Hall.

LANDES, D. (1983) *Revolution in Time: Clocks and the Making of the Modern World*, Cambridge, Mass., Harvard University Press.

LAQUEUR, T.W. (1976) 'Working Class Demand and the Growth of English Elementary Education 1750–1850', in STONE, L. (Ed.) *Schooling and Society: Studies in the History of Education*, Baltimore, Johns Hopkins University Press.

LAW, B. (1986) *The Pre-Vocational Franchise*, London, Harper & Row.

LAW, B. and WATTS, A.G. (1977) *Schools, Careers and Community*, London, Church Information Office.

LAWLOR, S. and McKAY, F. (1989) *Compacts: An Approach through Key Questions*, York: Longman.

LAZERSON, M. and GRUBB, N. (1974) *American Education and Vocationalism*, New York, Teachers College Press.

LEEDS NATIONAL EVALUATION TEAM (1987) *Work Experience TVEI 14–16*, Leeds, School of Education, University of Leeds.

LEINER, M. (1975) 'Cuba: Combining Formal Schooling with Practical Experience', in AHMED, M. and COOMBS, P.H. (Eds) *Education for Rural Development: Case Studies for Planners*, New York, Praeger.

LEVY, M. (1987) *Core Skills Project and Work Based Learning*, Blagdon, Further Education Staff College.

LEWIN, K. (1951) *Field Theory in Social Sciences*, New York, Harper & Row.

LISHMAN, J. (1984) (Ed.) *Evaluation* (2nd edition), London, Jessica Kingsley.

LLOYD, J. (1986) 'Trade Union Policy: Consumerism over Politics?', *Manpower Policy and Practice*, **1**, 4, Summer.

LLOYD-THOMAS, D.A. (1977) 'Competitive Equality of Opportunity', *Mind*, **86**.

LONDON BOROUGH OF EALING (1989) *School-Based Enterprises: Guidelines for Teachers*, London, London Borough of Ealing.

LUPSON, P. (1989) 'Languages Post-16: Preparing for 1992', *SCIP News*, 23, Spring.

LUXTON, R. (1987) 'In Their Own Interest', in *TVEI Developments 2: Equal Opportunities*, London, Manpower Services Commission.

McINTYRE, T. and COOMBES, H. (1988) 'Work Experience: An Evaluation', in *Education, Enterprise and Industry*, Sheffield, Training Agency.

MACLEAY, D.M. (1973) *Work Experience*, Working Paper 7, Ormskirk, National Association of Careers Teachers.

MACLENNAN, E., FITZ, J. and SULLIVAN, J. (1985) *Working Children*, London, Low Pay Unit.

McNIFF, J. (1988) *Action Research: Principles and Practice*, London, Macmillan.

MANPOWER SERVICES COMMISSION (1984) *TVEI Annual Review*, Sheffield, MSC.

MANPOWER SERVICES COMMISSION (1985) *Work-Based Projects in YTS*, Sheffield, MSC.

MARSDEN, C. (1983) *What Industry Really Wants: Implications for Education and the Community*, London, British Petroleum (mimeo).

MARSDEN, C. (1989a) 'Why Business Should Work with Education', *British Journal of Education and Work*, **2**, 3.

MARSDEN, C. (1989b) 'Understanding and Developing the Interaction', in BLANDFORD, P.D. and JAMIESON, I.M. (Eds) *Building Partnerships with Education*, Cambridge, CRAC.

MARSDEN, C. and PRIESTLAND, A. (1989) *Working with Education: A Framework of Business Objectives and Activities*, London, British Petroleum.

MARTIN, J. and ROBERTS, C. (1984) *Women and Employment*, London, HMSO.

MARTON, F. and SÄLJÖ, R. (1976) 'On Qualitative Differences in Learning: 1. Outcomes and Processes', *British Journal of Educational Psychology*, **46**.

MARX, K. (1887) *Capital*, London, Swan, Sonnenschein and Lowrey.

MEDICK, H. (1976) 'The Proto-Industrial Family Economy: The Structural Function of Household and Family during the Transition from Peasant Society to Industrial Capitalism', *Social History*, **1**, 3.

MILLER, A.D. (1988) *On Debriefing*, SCIP Views No. 4, London, SCIP/ School Curriculum Development Committee.

MILLER, A.D. (1989a) *Case Study: Work Experience in Coventry*, Coventry, SCIP/University of Warwick (mimeo).

MILLER, A.D. (1989b) *Case Study: Work Experience in Doncaster*, Coventry, SCIP/University of Warwick (mimeo).

MILLER, A.D. (1989c) *Case Study: Work Experience in Newham*, Coventry, SCIP/University of Warwick (mimeo).

MILLER, A.D. (1989d) 'Placement Quality', in MILLER, A.D. (Ed.) *Work Experience INSET: Professional Development Activities*, Warwick, SCIP.

MILLER, A.D. (1990) 'Towards the Work-Related Curriculum', *SCIP News*, 25.

MILLER, A.D., JAMIESON, I.M. and WATTS, A.G. (1989) *Reviewing Work Experience: A National Perspective*, SCIP Views 6, London, SCIP/ National Curriculum Council.

MILLMAN, V. and WEINER, G. (1987) 'Engendering Equal Opportunities: The Case of TVEI', in GLEESON, D. (Ed.) *TVEI and Secondary Education: A Critical Appraisal*, Milton Keynes, Open University Press.

MILLWARD, S. (1977) 'The Youngster's Point of View', in WALTON, P. (Ed.) *A Survey of Work Experience in British Secondary Schools*, Icon Series No. 6, Stourbridge, Institute of Careers Officers.

MOORMAN, P. (1976) 'School for Life is Cornerstone of the Permanent Revolution', *Times Educational Supplement*, 5 March.

MUMFORD, L. (1973) *Interpretations and Forecasts*, New York, Harcourt, Brace Jovanovitch.

MURRAY, F. (1983) 'The Decentralization of Production — the Decline of the Mass-Collective Worker?', *Capital and Class*, **19**, Spring.

NASH, K. (1980) 'Work Experience in Australian Schools', *Curriculum and Research Bulletin*, **15**, 4, October.

NATIONAL CURRICULUM COUNCIL (1990a) *Curriculum Guidance 3: The Whole Curriculum*, York, National Curriculum Council.

NATIONAL CURRICULUM COUNCIL (1990b) *Curriculum Guidance 4: Education for Economic and Industrial Understanding*, York, NCC.

NATIONAL CURRICULUM COUNCIL (1990c) *Curriculum Guidance 6: Careers Education and Guidance*, York: NCC.

NATIONAL CURRICULUM COUNCIL (1990d) *Core Skills 16–19*, York, NCC.

NATIONAL ECONOMIC DEVELOPMENT OFFICE (1988) *Young People and the Labour Market: A Challenge for the 1990s*, London, NEDO.

NATIONAL SWEDISH BOARD OF EDUCATION (1974) 'Study and Vocational Orientation (SYO) in the Swedish School System', Stockholm, NSBE (mimeo).

NATIONAL SWEDISH BOARD OF EDUCATION (1978) 'Study and Vocational Orientation in Secondary Schools', Stockholm, NSBE (mimeo).

NATIONAL SWEDISH BOARD OF EDUCATION (1984) 'Working Life Orientation in Swedish Schools — a Short Description of Aims, Means and Experience', Stockholm, NSBE (mimeo).

NATIONAL UNION OF TEACHERS (1989) *Towards Equality for Girls and Boys: Guidelines on Countering Sexism in Schools*, London, NUT.

NORA, S. and MINC, A. (1978) *L'Information de la Société Rapport de la Republique*, Paris, La Documentation Francaise.

NORTHCOTT, J. and ROGERS, P. (1985) *Microelectronics in Industry: An International Comparison — Britain, Germany and France*, London, Policy Studies Institute.

OFFICE OF POPULATION CENSUSES AND SURVEYS (1984) *General Household Survey*, London, HMSO.

OPEN UNIVERSITY (1989) *Teachers into Business and Industry*, Course PE 634, Milton Keynes, Open University.

OWENS, T.R. (1982) 'Experience-Based Career Education: Summary and Implications of Research and Evaluation Findings', *Child and Youth Services Journal*, **4**, 3/4.

PAHL, R.E. (1984) *Divisions of Labour*, Oxford, Blackwell.

PAHL, R.E. (1988) (Ed.) *On Work: Historical, Comparative and Theoretical Approaches*, Oxford, Blackwell.

PALMER, A.J. (1979) 'Concepts and Trends in Work-Experience Education in the Soviet Union and the United States', PhD thesis, Northwestern University.

PARNELL, K.G. and ROBERTS, B. (1988) *Work Appreciation: A Description and Evaluation of Current Practice*, Clwyd, Deeside High School (mimeo).

PILCHER, J. and WILLIAMSON, H. (1988) *A Guide to Young People's Experience in a Changing Labour Market: An Uphill Struggle*, London, Youthaid.

PLANT, P. (1988) 'Educational and Vocational Guidance Services for the 14–25 Age-Group in Denmark', in WATTS, A.G., DARTOIS, C. and PLANT, P. (Eds) *Educational and Vocational Guidance Services for the 14–25 Age-Group: Denmark, Federal Republic of Germany and the Netherlands*,

Luxembourg, Office for Official Publications of the European Communities.

POLLARD, A., PURVIS, J. and WALFORD, G. (1988) (Eds) *Education, Training and the New Vocationalism*, Milton Keynes, Open University Press.

POLLARD, S. (1963) 'Factory Discipline in the Industrial Revolution', *Economic History Review*, **16**, 2.

PRAIS, S. (1982) 'Strike Frequencies and Plant Size: A Comment on Swedish and UK Experiences', *British Journal of Industrial Relations*, **20**, 1.

PRICE, R. and BAIN, G.S. (1983) 'Union Growth in Britain: Retrospect and Prospect', *British Journal of Industrial Relations*, **21**, 1.

PUMFREY, P.D. and SCHOFIELD, A. (1982) 'Work Experience and Career Maturity of Fifth-Form Pupils', *British Journal of Guidance and Counselling*, **10**, 2, July.

PURCELL, K. (1988) 'Gender and the Experience of Employment', in GALLIE, D. (Ed.) *Employment in Britain*, Oxford, Blackwell.

RAJAN, A. (1985) *Recruitment and Training Effects of Technical Change*, Aldershot, Gower.

RAJAN, A. (1987) 'Technology in the Workplace: Assessing the Impact', *Manpower Policy and Practice*, **2**, 4.

RAJAN, A. and PEARSON, R. (1986) *UK Occupation and Employment Trends to 1990*, Guildford, Butterworths.

RAVEN, J. (1980) 'Bringing Education Back into Schools', in BURGESS, T. and ADAMS, E. (Eds) *Outcomes of Education*, London, Macmillan.

REED, B. and BAZALGETTE, J. (1983) 'TWL Network and Schools', in WATTS, A.G. (Ed.) *Work Experience and Schools*, London, Heinemann.

REES, T. (1988) 'Education for Enterprise: The State and Alternative Employment for Young People', *Journal of Education Policy*, **3**, 1.

REUBENS, B.G. (1977) *Bridges to Work: International Comparisons of Transition Services*, Montclair, NJ, Allanheld Osmun.

REVANS, R. (1971) *Developing Effective Management*, London, Longman.

REYNOLDS, D. (1985) (Ed.) *Studying School Effectiveness*, London, Falmer Press.

RICHMOND, M. (1983) 'Preparation for the Transition from School to Work in Socialist Cuba', in WATSON, K. (Ed.) *Youth, Education and Employment — International Perspectives*, Beckenham, Croom Helm.

ROBERTS, K. (1967) 'The Incidence and Effects of Spare-Time Employment amongst School-Children', *Vocational Aspect of Education*, **19**, 43, Summer.

ROBERTS, K., DENCH, S. and RICHARDSON, D. (1987) *The Changing Structure of Youth Labour Markets*, Research Paper No. 59, London, Department of Employment.

ROBERTS, K., DUGGAN, J. and NOBLE, M. (1983) 'Young, Black and Out of Work', in TROYNA, B. and SMITH, D.I. (Eds) *Racism, School and the Labour Market*, Leicester, National Youth Bureau.

ROBERTSON, I.T. and COOPER, C.L. (1983) *Human Behaviour in Organizations*, Plymouth, MacDonald & Evans.

ROSE, M. (1985) *Re-Working the Work Ethic: Economic Values and Socio-Cultural Politics*, London, Batsford.

ROSE, M. (1988) 'Attachment to Work and Social Values', in GALLIE, D. (Ed.) *Employment in Britain*, Oxford, Blackwell.

RUSSELL, R. (1982) (Ed.) *Studies in Vocational Education and Training in the Federal Republic of Germany, No. 7: Learning About the World of Work in the Federal Republic of Germany*, Blagdon, Bristol, Further Education Staff College.

RYRIE, A.C. and WEIR, A.D. (1978) *Getting a Trade*, London, Hodder & Stoughton.

SANDFORD, F. (1989) *A Survey of Work Experience in Hertfordshire*, Hertford, Hertfordshire County Council.

SAUER, F. (1988) 'Educational and Vocational Guidance Services for the 14–25 Age-Group in the Grand Duchy of Luxembourg', in WATTS, A.G., DARTOIS, C. and PLANT, P. (Eds) *Educational and Vocational Guidance Services for the 14–25 Age-Group: Belgium, France and the Grand Duchy of Luxembourg*, Luxembourg, Office for Official Publications of the European Community.

SAUNDERS, M. (1987) 'At Work in TVEI: Students' Perceptions of their Work Experience', in GLEESON, D. (Ed.) *TVEI and Secondary Education: A Critical Appraisal*, Milton Keynes, Open University Press.

SCHON, D.A. (1983) *The Reflective Practitioner*, London, Temple Smith.

SCHOOL CURRICULUM DEVELOPMENT COMMITTEE (1988) *Curriculum Issues No. 2: Curriculum Continuity*, London, SCDC.

SCHOOL CURRICULUM INDUSTRY PARTNERSHIP (1988) *Rethinking Work Experience: Local Employers' Workshop*, London, SCIP (mimeo).

SCOTT, W.H. and BLOOMER, R.G. (1988) 'Industry Related Activities in Initial Teacher Education', Bath, University of Bath (mimeo).

SCRIVEN, M. (1977) 'Goal Free Evaluation', in HAMILTON, D., *et al.* (Eds) *Beyond the Numbers Game*, Basingstoke, Macmillan.

SHARP, R. (1982) 'Response to Wexler', *Interchange*, **13**, 3.

SHATKIN, L., WEBER, A. and CHAPMAN, W. (1980) *Career Information Resources and Delivery Systems in Secondary Schools: Review of the Literature*, Princeton, NJ, Educational Testing Service (mimeo).

SHERMAN, B. and JENKINS, C. (1979) *The Collapse of Work*, London, Eyre Methuen.

SHILLING, C. (1987) 'Work-Experience as a Contradictory Practice', *British Journal of Sociology of Education*, **8**, 4.

SHILLING, C. (1989) *Schooling for Work in Capitalist Britain*, London, Falmer Press.

SILVER, H. (1977) 'Ideology and the Factory Child: Attitudes to Half-Time Education', in McCANN, P. (Ed.) *Popular Education and Socialisation in the Nineteenth Century*, London, Methuen.

SIMON, R.I. (1983) 'But Who Will Let You Do It? Counter-Hegemonic Possibilities for Work Education', *Journal of Education*, **165**, 3, Summer.

SIMON, R.I. and DIPPO, D. (1987) 'What Schools Can Do: Designing Programs for Work Experience that Challenge the Wisdom of Experience', *Journal of Education*, **169**, 3.

SIMS, D. (1987) 'Work Experience in TVEI: Student Views and Reactions — a Preliminary Study', in HINCKLEY, S.M., POLE, C.J., SIMS, D. and STONEY, S.M. (Eds) *The TVEI Experience: Views from Teachers and Students*, Sheffield, Manpower Services Commission.

SLOANE, P.J. (1987) *Male-Female Earnings Differences Revisited: A Disaggregated Analysis of the New Earnings Survey Data Tapes*, Discussion Paper 87–03, Aberdeen, Department of Economics, University of Aberdeen.

SMITH, D. (1983) 'Going Dutch ...', *SCIP News*, 8, Autumn.

SMITH, D. (1988) *Industry in the Primary School Curriculum*, London, Falmer Press.

SMITH, D. and STOREY, J. (1988) 'Is It Working?: The Wider Concepts of Work Project', in SMITH, D. (Ed.) *Partners in Change: Education-Industry Collaboration*, York, Longman for the School Curriculum Development Committee.

SMITH, D. and WOOTTON, R. (1988) *Understanding Trade Unions: Curriculum Principles and Practice*, York, Longman for the School Curriculum Development Committee.

SORGE, A., HARTMANN, G., WARNER, M. and NICHOLS, I. (1983) *Microelectronics and Manpower in Manufacturing*, Aldershot, Gower.

SPITTLE, B.M. (1989) 'Managing Pupils' Work Experience — Reasserting the Management Control of a Local Education Authority', MSc in Public Service Management dissertation, South Bank Polytechnic.

STAKE, R. (1967) 'The Countenance of Educational Evaluation', *Teachers College Record*, **68**, 7, April.

STEELE, J. (1977) *Socialism with a German Face*, London, Cape.

STEINBERG, L.D. (1982) 'Jumping Off the Work Experience Bandwagon', *Journal of Youth and Adolescence*, **11**, 3.

STEINBERG, L.D. (1984) 'The Varieties and Effects of Work During Adolescence', in LAMB, M.E., BROWN, A.L. and ROGOFF, B. (Eds) *Advances in Developmental Psychology*, Volume 3, Hillsdale, NJ, Erlbaum.

STEINBERG, L.D., GREENBERGER, E., GARDUQUE, L., RUGGIERO, M. and VAUX, A. (1982) 'Effects of Working on Adolescent Development', *Developmental Psychology*, **18**, 3.

STEINBERG, L.D., GREENBERGER, E., JACOBI, M. and GARDUQUE, L. (1981) 'Early Work Experience: A Partial Antidote for Adolescent Egocentrism', *Journal of Youth and Adolescence*, **10**, 2.

STERN, D., SMITH, S. and DOOLITTLE, F. (1975) 'How Children Used to Work', *Law and Contemporary Problems*, **39**, 3.

STERNBERG, R.J. and WAGNER, R.K. (1986) (Eds) *Practical Intelligence*, Cambridge, Cambridge University Press.

STOREY, D. and JOHNSON, S. (1986) 'Job Generation in Britain: A Review of Recent Studies', *International Small Business Journal*, **4**, 4.

STRONACH, I. (1984) 'Work Experience: The Sacred Anvil', in VARLAAM, C. (Ed.) *Rethinking Transition: Educational Innovation and the Transition to Adult Life*, London, Falmer Press.

STRONACH, I. and WEIR, A.D. (1980) *Experiences of Work: In, Out, and Round About*, Second Evaluation Report on the Clydebank EEC Project, Glasgow, Jordanhill College of Education.

SUTTON, M. (1989) *Work Experience: A Teacher's Handbook*, York, Longman.

SWEDISH INSTITUTE (1979) *Higher Education in Sweden*, Stockholm, Swedish Institute.

THOMPSON, E.P. (1967) 'Time, Work-Discipline and Industrial Capitalism', *Past and Present*, **38**.

TRADES UNION CONGRESS (1973) *Report of 105th Annual Trades Union Congress*, London, TUC.

TRADES UNION CONGRESS (1974) 'Work Experience for Schoolchildren', Circular No. 10, London, TUC (mimeo).

TRADES UNION CONGRESS (n.d.) *Work Experience Guidelines*, London, TUC.

UNESCO (1981) 'Interaction Between Education and Productive Work', Paper prepared for the International Conference on Education, Geneva, 10–19 November (mimeo).

VAN DEN BOSCH, L. (1983) 'The Netherlands', in CHISNALL, H. (Ed.) *Learning from Work and Community Experience: Six International Models*, Windsor, NFER-Nelson.

VAN MENTS, M. (1983) *The Effective Use of Role-Play: A Handbook for Teachers and Trainers*, London, Kogan Page.

VARLAAM, C. (1983) 'Making Use of Part-Time Job Experience', in WATTS, A.G. (Ed.) *Work Experience and Schools*, London, Heinemann.

VICARY, E. (1987) 'Linking School and Work: Work Experience', in *About Writing*, SCDC National Writing Project Newsletter No. 5, London, SCDC Publications.

VICARY, E. (1988) 'GCSE and the World of Work — English and Across the Curriculum', in *Writing and the World of Work*, SCDC National Writing Project Newsletter No. 2, London, SCDC Publications.

VICARY, E. (1989) 'Work Experience across the Curriculum', in WARWICK, D. (Ed.) *Linking Schools and Industry*, Oxford, Blackwell.

WALKER, A. (1982) *Unqualified and Underemployed*, London, Macmillan.

WALTON, P. (1977) *A Survey of Work Experience in British Secondary Schools*, Stourbridge, Institute of Careers Officers.

WATKINS, P. (1980) 'Curriculum Change and the School-Work Interface: A Critical Analysis of Work Experience', *Australian and New Zealand Journal of Sociology*, **16**, 2, July.

WATKINS, P. (1985) 'Work-Experience and the Legitimation and Motivation Crises', *New Education*, **7**, 1/2.

WATKINS, P. (1987) *An Analysis of the History of Work*, Canberra, Curriculum Development Centre.

WATKINS, P. (1987) 'Student Participation-Observation in the Contested

Workplace: The Policy Dilemmas of In-School Work Experience', *Journal of Education Policy*, **2**, 1.

WATKINS, P. (1988) 'Reassessing the Work-Experience Bandwagon: Confronting Students with Employers' Hopes and the Reality of the Workplace'. *Discourse*, **9**, 1, October.

WATTS, A.G. (1981) 'Careers Guidance in Sweden: A British Perspective', *International Journal for the Advancement of Counselling*, **4**, 3.

WATTS, A.G. (1983a) *Work Experience and Schools*, London, Heinemann.

WATTS, A.G. (1983b) *Education, Unemployment and the Future of Work*, Milton Keynes, Open University Press.

WATTS, A.G. (1985) 'The Japanese "Lifetime Employment System" and its Implications for Careers Guidance', *International Journal for the Advancement of Counselling*, **8**, 2.

WATTS, A.G. (1986) *Work Shadowing*, York, Longman for the School Curriculum Development Committee.

WATTS, A.G. (1988) *Executive Shadows*, York, Longman for the School Curriculum Development Committee.

WATTS, A.G. and KANT, L. (1986) *A Working Start: Guidance Strategies for Girls and Young Women*, York, Longman for the School Curriculum Development Committee.

WATTS, A.G. and MORAN, P. (1984) (Eds) *Education for Enterprise*, Cambridge, CRAC.

WEBSTER, F. and ROBINS, K. (1986) *Information Technology: A Luddite Analysis*, Norwood, NJ, Ablex.

WHARTON, A.S. and BARON, J. (1987) 'So Happy Together?: The Impact of Gender Segregation on Men at Work', *American Sociological Review*, **52**, October.

WIENER, M.J. (1981) *English Culture and the Decline of the Industrial Spirit 1850–1980*, Cambridge, Cambridge University Press.

WILLIAMS, V. (1984) 'Employment Implications of New Technology', *Employment Gazette*, **95**, 2, May.

WOOD, S. and KELLY, J. (1982) 'Taylorism, Responsible Autonomy and Management Strategy', in WOOD, S. (Ed.) *The Degradation of Work*, London, Hutchinson.

YOUNG, M.F.D. (1971) 'An Approach to the Study of Curricula as Socially Organised Knowledge', in YOUNG, M.F.D. (Ed.) *Knowledge and Control*, London, Collier-Macmillan.

YOUNG, M. and WILLMOTT, P. (1983) *The Symmetrical Family*, London, Routledge & Kegan Paul.

ZELIZER, V.A. (1985) *Pricing the Priceless Child*, New York, Basic Books.

Index

Index

experience-based career education
  (EBCE), 50–1

factory system, 58
feminism, 76–7
follow-up, 210, 230, 232
Fordism, 60, 79
France, 43

gender stereotyping, 61–3, 72–3, 75–6,
  79–80, 204–5
  see also discrimination
General Certificate of Secondary
  Education (GCSE), 8–9, 100, 156, 220,
  270
government
  establishments insurance scheme, 133
  training, 6

health and safety, 128–30, 215
Health and Safety at Work Act (1974),
  128
Her Majesty's Inspectorate (HMI), 7,
  174, 202
homeworking, 66
household
  economy, 55, 77
  work, 32, 56

industrial management, 57–9, 60
industry
  history of, 56–8
  needs of, 139
  student perceptions of, 80
Industry Year (1986), 7
INSET, 169
  Coventry, 117
  needs, 172, 234
  Newham, 115–16
  organisation, 106–7
  school-based, 97–8
insurance, 130–4
integration, 151–72
  cross-curricular, 103, 167–71
  experiential, 151–4
  personal, 152–4
  subject, 97, 153–4

Japan, 52
jobs, 26, 72
  see also work

Khruschev
  educational reforms, 44–5, 46

labour
  child, 61–3
  gender and, 58, 61–3, 75–6
  market
    sectors, 71
    segmentation, 80
    youth and, 71–5
  organized, 60–1
  relations, 19
learning
  agreements, 177
  culture at work, 221
  difficulties, 205–7
  experiential, 12–13, 22–3, 230
  objectives, 211–12
  progression, 173–85
legal issues
  children, protection of, 135–6
  costs, 134–5
  discrimination, 127–8
  health and safety, 128–30
  insurance, 130–4
  permissibility, 125–6
liability, 124–5, 132–3
licensed premises, 126
local education authorities (LEAs)
  equal opportunities policy, 202
  organization of work experience
    case studies, 110–18
    models, 105–8, 120–2
    policy, 108
    resources, 108–9
    roles, 109
Local Management of Schools (LMS),
  11, 12, 89, 103, 107
Lower Attaining Pupils' Programme
  (LAPP), 8
Luxembourg, 43

Manpower Services Commission, 6
Marxism, 43, 46–7, 63

Author Index